Antique

®

STONEWARE
and Blue & White Pottery

PRICE GUIDE

Edited by

Kyle Husfloen

Contributing Editors

Bruce and Vicki Waasdorp, Gail Peck, Steve Stone

©2005 KP Books

Published by

kp books

An Imprint of F+W Publications

700 East State Street • Iola, WI 54990-0001
715-445-2214 • 888-457-2873

Our toll-free number to place an order or obtain
a free catalog is (800) 258-0929.

Library of Congress Catalog Number: 2004113666
ISBN: 0-89689-135-6

Designed by Wendy Wendt
Edited by Kyle Husfloen

Printed in Canada

TABLE OF CONTENTS

A Word to the Reader

Ever since the early days of collecting in this country, all types of ceramic wares have been eagerly sought. Even in the early 20th century many pioneering collectors who appreciated the "primitive charm" of Early American antiques kept an eye out for unusual examples of handcrafted pottery.

Various types of pottery have been made in this country since the earliest days of settlement, and by the late 18th century a wide range of wares were available, with dozens of large and small potters operating up and down the Eastern Seaboard. Although the most common wares were made with the abundant redware clay, slightly better pottery could be crafted using a yellowish colored clay (for yellowware) and buff-colored clays. The most durable pottery was produced using a dense gray clay that was not as widely available. It was this dense clay that, when fired at high temperatures, produced fine stoneware pottery.

Unlike the other types of pottery, which had to be glazed inside and out to make them impermeable, a fired piece of stoneware could actually be left unglazed and would still hold liquids. However, over its centuries of production in Europe, most stoneware pottery was glazed, often by throwing raw rock salt into the kiln during the firing. This, of course, produced the shiny saltglazed stoneware that became the standard for the best quality utilitarian pottery. Following this tradition, individual potters and, later, major stoneware potteries of the 19th century around the United States continued turning out these wares.

I am very pleased to present here a brand new guide to American stoneware. Since there are other country-style pottery wares that are also widely collected today, it was decided to broaden the scope of this guide. Thus, in addition to true "stoneware" pottery, we also include some non-stoneware pottery lines, specifically those decorated with blue on white or gray glazed grounds. This only makes sense, since the choicest examples of early American stoneware were also decorated with brushed-on or slip-decorated cobalt blue designs. Although not made with stoneware clay, today brightly decorated Spongeware pottery and the molded and blue-decorated wares commonly called Blue & White Pottery have a huge following. Now, in one volume, you will find a comprehensive, up-to-date guide to all these types of charming and utilitarian wares.

This book, of course, would not have been possible without the expert assistance of several knowledgeable experts who generously shared their time and expertise in compiling all this data.

For the best coverage of classic American Stoneware pottery I couldn't have found any contributor more knowledgeable than Bruce Waasdorp, who, along with his wife, Vicki, operate American Pottery Auction sales, which set the standard in this field. Each September and March in Clarence, New York, the Waasdorps present a huge auction of American stoneware. Hundreds of lots of the best examples are offered with sales prices ranging from under $200 to well over $10,000 for especially unique examples. My sincere thanks to Bruce and Vicki for their invaluable guidance.

Although the Waasdorps' main focus is American stoneware produced from all over the East Coast, by the late 19th century quite a number of important stoneware manufacturers had opened potteries in the Midwest. One of the most famous was the Red Wing Stoneware Union Stoneware Company of Red Wing, Minnesota. For help with pictures and listings of Red Wing wares I was very pleased to garner the input of a leading expert in this field, Gail Peck. Gail has been studying and collecting Red Wing and other Midwestern stoneware pottery for decades and has written numerous features on the topic as well as a book, *Red Wing Stoneware and Red Wing Collectibles* (Collector Books). Today Gail operates Country Crock Antiques in Fremont, Nebraska, and I am truly indebted to her for providing the in-depth coverage of not only Red Wing pottery wares but the similar stoneware products of well known Western Stoneware Pottery of Monmouth, Illinois. Gail, my sincerest thanks.

Finally, I am extremely happy to include here an extensive listing of the very popular Blue & White Pottery wares. This style of pottery includes a wide variety of patterns and decorations and is the special love of collector/researcher/writer Steve Stone of Lakewood, Colorado. For several years Steve has been providing me with detailed listings and wonderful color photos of every design in Blue & White Pottery collectors seek. Here we have brought together an extensive and colorful array of these wares provided by Steve. In addition, he has written in-depth histories of the most popular patterns to be found in Blue & White, much of this information not available in other references. As always, Steve, your enthusiasm and expertise are an inspiration to me.

Although the vast majority of the material included in *Antique Trader Stoneware and Blue & White Pottery Price Guide* was prepared by the above contributors, I also must thank the following auction houses for allowing us to draw listings and illustrations from some of their sales: Charlton Hall Galleries, Columbia, South Carolina; Garth's Auctions, Delaware, Ohio;

Jackson's International Auctioneers, Cedar Falls, Iowa; and Skinner, Inc., Bolton, Massachusetts.

My staff and I hope you will find our new guide an invaluable reference, both informative and educational. With some 1,500 individual listings and nearly 1,100 color illustrations you're sure to find it useful. As always, we remind you that this book should be used only as a guide to this collecting field since many factors, including condition and local market demand, can influence what a specific piece may sell for. Although we have worked diligently to present the most accurate descriptions possible, neither the compilers, editors nor publisher can assume responsibility for any losses that might be incurred as a result of consulting this guide, or of errors, typographical or otherwise.

Have a wonderful time reviewing this unique guide. I'll be happy to hear your comments or suggestions. Happy Hunting!

Kyle Husfloen, Editor

Contact Information

Vicki and Bruce Waasdorp
P.O. Box 434
Clarence, NY 14031
(716) 759-2361
Web: www.antiques-stoneware.com

Gail Peck
Country Crock Antiques
2121 Pearl St.
Fremont, NE 68025
(420) 721-5721

Steve Stone
12795 W. Alameda Pkwy.
Lakewood, CO 80225
e-mail: Sylvanlvr@aol.com

Introduction to Stoneware Collecting

by Bruce and Vicki Waasdorp

Stoneware is described in Webster's dictionary as "an opaque pottery that is fired at a high temperature, non porous, that may be glazed and that is commonly made from a single clay." Stoneware was produced primarily in the 18th and 19th centuries in this country as a utilitarian household necessity. We like to define it as 19th century "Tupperware." Stoneware containers were used to store dried corn and grains, cooking fats and oils, and salts and seasonings. They were also used for preserving foods in pickling mixtures and brines. Smaller stoneware pieces such as pitchers, milk pans and mugs were used for serving food and drink. In any case, you could find stoneware in abundance in any 19th century American household.

History of American stoneware

Around 1750, we saw the first stoneware production in the United States. It began in the larger settled coastal areas of New York City and Boston. The European Old World influence can be seen in these first potteries. This stoneware is identified by classic ovoid shapes, open applied handles and an overall crude appearance compared to later American pottery. Some of the first factories were those of Crolius, Remmey, and Morgan in New York and Fenton and Carpenter in Boston. The decoration was primarily fine line incised designs of stylized flowers and birds. Pieces were usually further enhanced or accented with a blue cobalt wash before firing. Little has survived from these early potteries. Today a collector should expect to pay premium prices of $1,000 and up for good signed examples of this early decorated stoneware.

As we approached the middle of the 19th century, there was tremendous growth in this cottage industry. The development of the U.S. river and canal

Today, interest in decorated stoneware as Americana is very high. This crock features a crudely drawn house with "No 4" on the door to indicate the crock's 4-gallon capacity. Impressed with the mark of C.W. Braun of Buffalo, New York, it dates to ca. 1870 and is valued at $7,425.

Photo courtesy Waasdorp, Inc.

The paddletail bird design is associated with Whites' Utica, New York, factory. This ca. 1870 4-gallon crock comes with the impressed mark "N.A. White & Son – Utica, NY – 4" and is valued at $798.

Photo courtesy Waasdorp, Inc.

systems made for easy transportation of raw material and finished goods throughout the Northeast. Literally hundreds of these wood fired pottery kilns began production to service the demand of the burgeoning population. They varied in size from one- and two-man operations to large factories with as many as 50 employees.

This was when decorated stoneware really became Americanized. Straight-sided crocks and jugs were the standard shape in the industry. Since product lines were now so similar, decoration became an important selling point in a very competitive industry. The type of

decorating technique also changed at this time. The painstaking detailed incised lines and cobalt wash decoration gave way to the less time-consuming method of applying cobalt blue. (Cobalt blue was used as it could withstand the high firing temperature of a stoneware kiln.) Salt was thrown in during the firing and, vaporizing at this high temperature, created a shiny glaze. Hence, the name of this collecting field: *blue decorated salt-glazed stoneware.*

Stoneware became a medium for unsophisticated folk design. The unfired clay crocks and jugs provided a large "canvas" for the new itinerant

The reclining deer design has long been associated with the Norton factory in Bennington, Vermont. This 2-gallon cake crock is impressed with the mark of J. & E. Norton and dates to 1855. It's valued at $18,700.

Photo courtesy Waasdorp, Inc.

Space constraints might make a collector look to miniatures. This ca. 1900 jug features blue stenciled advertising for "Phill. G. Kelly – R – Straight Whiskey – Richmond, VA." Standing only 4 1/2" high, it's valued at $110.

Photo courtesy Waasdorp, Inc.

imaginative artists. Now the design was an integral part of the marketing of stoneware. Some factories could be recognized by their trademark designs.

The paddletail and running birds are associated with the Whites' Utica, New York, factory. The peacock on a stump and reclining deer designs have long been associated with the Norton factory in Bennington, Vermont. Norton's distinctive bird and stylized floral dotted spray are also signatures of this large Vermont pottery. The long-running pottery in Fort Edward, New York, was known for its robin-style bird on a plume design and bull's-eye stylized floral motifs. Designs on pottery from the highly prized Rochester, New York, factories include artfully executed flowers, birds and animals. The factory names to look for are Burger, Harrington, Stetzenmeyer and Clark. In Pennsylvania and Maryland, the rolling flower and vine designs are prevalent from the Remmey and Bell factories. In the Midwest later factories in Red Wing, Minnesota, and Monmouth, Illinois, provided pieces with stylized gallon designations and leaf designs that are highly prized today.

Unfortunately for this industry as a whole, refrigeration and the use of glass and tin containers brought about

Prices can approach $100,000 for rare pieces decorated with patriotic motifs. This late 19th century cylindrical crock boasts a spread-winged eagle with shield surrounded by the marking "T.F. Reppert – Eagle Pottery – Greensboro, PA," decorative scrolls and "10" at the bottom to indicate gallon capacity. It's valued at $2,875.

Photo courtesy Skinner Inc.

its demise. Most factories had closed by the turn of the century due to lack of demand. A few exceptions like the Whites' Utica Pottery and Robinson Clay factory in Ohio continued in business. They began making molded souvenir stoneware to compete with the Flemish ware from Europe. These factories finally succumbed in the early 20th century.

Today, interest in decorated stoneware as Americana is very high. Today's collector has found its decorative and display appeal works in any setting from country to modern. When you consider the many forms, factories and designs involved in stoneware collecting, the possibilities for focusing a collection on a particular theme are endless.

Methods of decoration

There are basically four methods that were used to decorate stoneware. Incised and then blue accented lines were the first method. Impressed into the wet clay were vines, florals and stylized bird designs. Occasionally more elaborate fish, serpents and sailing ships were executed. The more ambitious the design, obviously, the more expensive the piece. One-of-a-kind, dated, special order or commemorative designs that are highly detailed can go for well into the tens of thousands of dollars today.

This time-consuming deliberate decorating gave way to the faster applied methods. The first is brush application. A small paint brush was dipped into the cobalt blue and then painted designs were applied to the clay "canvas." Generally, these designs consist primarily of stylized flowers, vines and gallon number capacity. Most are repetitive and hastily done, but complex figures of people, animals and houses have been done using this method. This was the most common decorating tool in the mid-19th-century heyday of the industry.

A slower but more precise method was the slip trail method. Much like squeeze cake decorating, deliberate lines were applied to the clay to create the designs. This is probably the most sought after artwork, as the designs are imaginative and distinct in many forms. Unsophisticated, self-taught artists created repetitive signature trademark designs and large freehand folk painting on clay. Prices run the gamut. Common wreaths, flowers and birds are priced in the hundreds to the low thousands of dollars. On the other end of the scale are one-of-a-kind special orders, animals, figures, patriotic

This crock is decorated with a slip-quilled floral design enclosing the numeral "3" to indicate gallon capacity and the impressed mark "Burger & Co. – Rochester, NY." Dating to ca. 1869, it's valued at $248.

Photo courtesy Waasdorp, Inc.

This unsigned ca. 1860 jug features rare applied grape cluster and leaf designs and a dark brown alkaline glaze. It's valued at $440.

Photo courtesy Waasdorp, Inc.

motifs and presentation pieces. Today, prices approach $100,000 for these rare American folk art masterpieces.

Focusing a collection

Stoneware was produced throughout the United States, and many collectors choose to concentrate on a specific region. Signed examples and signature-attributed designs from a specific locale are categories collected by many people. Other collectors seek obscure one- or two-year marks of early factories. The Norton Factory in Bennington, Vermont, Cowden & Wilcox in Harrisburg, Pennsylvania, and John Burger in Rochester, New York, produced some of the most dynamic and imaginative art work. These "Cadillacs" of the industry are synonymous with stoneware and the focus of many great collections today.

Form and size are other considerations. For example, collectors may choose pitchers as a theme and line an open cupboard with many varied examples. Larger open crocks can accent a wall in a family room. Small jars and mugs can hold kitchen utensils or desk accessories. Large pieces are used in entrances for umbrellas and boots. Space constraints might make you look to miniatures or small sizes as an alternative. Some other common forms to complete your collection are spittoons, inkwells, footwarmers, batter pails, and bottles.

Early vendors, grocers and liquor dealers saw the potential in stoneware for advertising their businesses. They commissioned potters to imprint or script their names and wares across the fronts of the jugs and crocks. Today's collector looks for these as a way to expand their regional interests.

Condition

Remember, stoneware pieces were not originally intended as elegant expensive objects created for beauty and display. They were utilitarian goods meant to be used as well as admired. Therefore, minor flaws like rim chips, hairlines and stains have to be accepted or your selection will be limited. Cosmetic restoration may be necessary if the damage is too distracting or severe. The extent of this damage helps determine price on each individual piece.

Always buy from reputable dealers and auctions that stand behind their sales. Rely on knowledgeable sellers that guarantee authenticity, age and condition. Buy what you like and the best you can afford.

We have been selling decorated stoneware for more than 25 years. Feel free to contact us at Box 434, Clarence, NY 14031 or e-mail waasdorp@antiques-stoneware.com. We would be happy to hear from you.

PART I: EASTERN STONEWARE

Rare Early Stoneware Anchovy Jar

Anchovy jar, wide cylindrical body w/angled shoulder to a wide molded mouth, blue-trimmed impressed swimming fish & balloon design all around the shoulder, attributed to Old Bridge, New Jersey potter, in-the-making dark clay color, rare, ca. 1810, 1 qt., 6 1/2" h. (ILLUS.) **$743**

Unusual Glazed Stoneware Frog Bank

Bank, figural, seated frog w/open mouth for coin opening, the back w/applied dark green alkaline Bristol glaze, bottom in tan, probably from Ohio, early 20th c., minor surface chips at lower lip of mouth, 2 1/2" h. (ILLUS.) **121**

Bank, figural, model of a round cylindrical clock dial w/molded clock hands & Roman numerals trimmed in cobalt blue, Bristol glaze, on a three-foot base, coin slot in top, ca. 1880, 2" deep, 4" h. (minor glaze spiders at coin slot, some chips on rim of dial) **550**

Bank, figural, reclining cat w/head raised & back leg lifted & scratching its side, realistic molded fur & details, overall mottled brown Rockingham glaze, probably 20th c., 6" h. **44**

Blue-trimmed Bulbous Batter Jug

Batter jug, wide ovoid body w/a short wide cylindrical shoulder spout & wide molded mouth, wire bail handle w/wooden grip, cobalt blue brushed blue accent bands around the base of the spout & shoulder handle brackets, impressed mark "N. White & Co. - Binghamton - 4," minor surface chip under spout, ca. 1860, 4 qt., 8 1/2" h. (ILLUS.) **413**

Cowden & Wilcox Early Batter Jug

Batter jug, wide ovoid body tapering to a short, wide cylindrical neck, short angled shoulder spout, shoulder loops for holding the wire bail handle w/turned wood grip, cobalt blue brushed drooping flower below the impressed mark of Cowden & Wilcox, Harrisburg, Pennsylvania, on the back, brushed plume accents at spout & shoulder loops, design fry on blue, large, long stack mark in the back design, surface wear at base & bail handle, use staining, ca. 1850, 1 gal., 9" h. (ILLUS., bottom previous page) **880**

Binghamton, New York Batter Jug

Batter jug, wide ovoid body w/a short wide cylindrical shoulder spout & wide molded mouth, wire bail handle w/wooden grip, cobalt blue brushed blue accent bands around the base of the spout & shoulder handle brackets, impressed mark on back "W. Roberts - Binghamton, NY - 6," some use staining & stack marks at base, ca. 1860, 6 qt., 9 1/2" h. (ILLUS.) **303**

Batter jug, cov., ovoid shape w/bale handle & old tin lid, angled straight spout w/tin collar, 11" h. **468**

Batter pail, wide bulbous ovoid body tapering to a short cylindrical neck flanked by small loops holding the wire bail handle w/turned wood grip, short cylindrical spout on the shoulder, bold cobalt blue brushed design of a very large horizontal flower on the back below the blue-tinted impressed mark of Cowden & Wilcox, Harrisburg, Pennsylvania, a brushed plume below the spout, blue accents on handle loops, minor surface chip at rim above name, very minor bubbling in the blue, ca. 1870, 1 gal., 8" h. (ILLUS. right with two unsigned pitchers, bottom of page) **2,530**

Blue-trimmed Batter Pail

Batter pail, bulbous ovoid body tapering to a thin molded rim flanked by small loops missing bail handle, lug handle on the back & angled tapering cylindrical spout at front, large cobalt blue brushed accents at spout, loops, lug handle & impressed mark of W. Roberts, Binghamton, New York, cinnamon clay color, ca. 1860, 4 qt. (1 gal.), 8 1/2" h. (ILLUS.) **413**

Rare Cowden & Wilcox Batter Pail with Two Unsigned Pitchers

Signed Decorated Batter Pail & Unsigned Milk Pan

Batter pail, wide ovoid body tapering to a wide flat mouth flanked by molded small loops to attach the wire bail handle w/wooden grip, short angled cylindrical shoulder spout, cobalt blue brushed round blossom on a double-leaf stem below the spout, unsigned, ca. 1870, 1 gal., 9" h. (interior rim chipping, stone ping on shoulder) **413**

Nice Bird-decorated Batter Pail

Batter pail, wide ovoid body tapering to a ringed cylindrical mouth, tapering angled shoulder spout, side loop brackets for the wire bail handle w/wooden grip, cobalt blue slip-quilled bird perched on twig below the spout, unsigned but associated w/Whites factory, Utica, New York, professional restoration to freeze line all around the base, repaired chip at spout & at rim, ca. 1875, 1 gal., 10" h. (ILLUS.)..... **1,018**

Batter pail, cov., wide ovoid body tapering to a flat rim flanked by small molded loops for the wire bail handle w/wooden grip, short angled cylindrical shoulder spout, lug handle at the back shoulder, cobalt blue brushed rings around the base of the spout & the handle loops, impressed mark of W. Roberts, Binghamton, New York, fitted w/a handled tin cover, ca. 1857-82, 4 qts. (1 gal.), 10 3/8" h. (minor chips) **353**

Batter pail, bulbous ovoid body w/an eared handle at the back base, a narrow molded mouth flanked by small loop ears holding the end of the wire bail handle w/wooden grip, short cylindrical shoulder spout, cobalt blue brushed large drooping tulip on the back below the blue-trimmed impressed mark of Evan R. Jones, Pittston, Pennsylvania, & the impressed size number, professional restoration to a freeze line around the base, surface chips on spout, ca. 1870, 6 qt. (1 1/2 gal.), 10" h. (ILLUS. right with unsigned milk pan, top of page)...................... **385**

Bean pot, cov., footed squatty spherical salt-glazed body w/C-scroll handle & fitted flattened cover w/knob finial, the body molded in relief & trimmed in cobalt blue on one side w/"Boston Baked Beans" & on the other w/a scene of children eating beans, faint hairline coming up from base, tight hairline in handle, ca. 1900, 6 1/2" h. (ILLUS. far left with two humidors & other bean pot, top of next page) **154**

Two Stoneware Bean Pots & Two Stoneware Humidors

Bean pot, cov., footed squatty spherical salt-glazed body w/C-scroll handle & fitted flattened cover w/knob finial, the body molded in relief & trimmed in cobalt blue on one side w/"Boston Baked Beans" & on the other w/a scene of children eating beans, minor clay separation in the making, ca. 1900, 6 1/2" h. (ILLUS. far right with two humidors & other bean pot, top of page) **220**

spigot hole w/brass spigot, England, late 19th c., 12 1/2" h. (ILLUS.) **316**

Bottle, figural, model of a recumbent pig, decorated w/cobalt blue spots & accents on the face, unsigned, two flakes, wear on ears & snout, late 19th - early 20th c., 6 1/8" l. **978**

Fancy English Stoneware Beverage Dispenser

Beverage dispenser, cov., tall ovoid body tapering to a flared rim & inset cover w/disk finial, ornately molded on the sides w/raised figures of knights on horseback, recumbent lions, floral swags & ribbons, a royal coat-of-arms above the

Tan-colored Stoneware Bottle

Bottle, cylindrical w/paneled sides & a/tapering neck w/bulbous small mouth, tan glaze, impressed badge on base reads "Patent Pressed W. Smith NY," some surface chipping along base, small size, late 19th c., 6 1/2" h. (ILLUS.)........................ **99**

Bottle, cylindrical w/rounded shoulder tapering to a blob top, the shoulder & top covered in blue above tan lower body, unmarked, 19th c., 6 1/2" h. (very tight hairline down from top) **143**

Two Small & a Larger Stoneware Bottle

Bottle, cylindrical body w/conical shoulder
& molded top, shoulder impressed "J. &
P. Chester," some use staining, 7" h.
(ILLUS. left with two other stoneware bot-
tles, top of page) **77**
Bottle, cylindrical body w/conical shoulder
& molded top, shoulder impressed "J.
Chester," stack marks on side & back,
7" h. (ILLUS. center with two other bot-
tles, top of page) **110**
Bottle, slightly swelled cylindrical body w/ta-
pering neck w/a thick molded rim, impressed mark "Mead," dark brown lower
body & light tan mottled neck, stack
marks on side, late 19th c., 8" h. (ILLUS.,
to the right) **165**

Stoneware Bottle Signed "Mead"

Row of Six Stoneware Bottles

Bottle, tapering cylindrical body w/conical shoulder w/a molded top, blue accents, shoulder impressed "White Root Beer," bubbling to cobalt blue trim, short clay separation line in base, 9" h. (ILLUS. far left with five other stoneware bottles, above) **132**

Bottle, cylindrical w/conical neck w/a thick blob top, impressed & blue-tinted name of J. Francis on shoulder, 19th c., 9 1/4" h. (surface wear, some staining, surface chip at base) **66**

cellent condition, second half 19th c., 9 1/2" h. (ILLUS.) **165**

Bottle, cylindrical body w/conical shoulder & molded blue-trimmed top, shoulder impressed "LEMON BEER," also impressed on the back "J. Chester," minor glaze spider crack at base, 9 1/2" h. (ILLUS. right with two smaller stoneware bottles, top previous page) **88**

Marked Grey Stoneware Bottle

Bottle, cylindrical body w/a tapering neck & molded mouth, grey w/blue-trimmed impressed shoulder mark "M.C. Heald," ex-

Bottle with Blue-washed Marked Shoulder

Bottle, crude cylindrical body w/a tapering neck & molded mouth, grey glaze w/the blue-washed shoulder impressed "Hiram V. Heaton - 1875," excellent condition, ca. 1875, 10" h. (ILLUS.) **440**

Marked Tan Stoneware Bottle

Bottle, cylindrical body w/a tapering neck & molded mouth, tan glaze w/impressed shoulder mark "R. Holloway," minor discoloration from kiln burn on back, second half 19th c., 10" h. (ILLUS.) 99

Bottle, cylindrical body w/conical shoulder w/a molded top, blue accents, shoulder impressed "J.P. Plummer - 1852," minor staining & surface chipping at back of the top, 10" h. (ILLUS. third from right with five other stoneware bottles, top previous page) 248

Bottle, cylindrical w/conical neck w/a thick blob top, impressed & blue-tinted name of M.E. Scott & a five-point star, 19th c., 10" h. (mottled clay color from firing, very minor surface chip at back base) 143

Bottle, cylindrical w/conical neck w/a thick blob top, impressed name of John Howell on shoulder, shoulder covered in an ochre glaze, 19th c., 10" h. (chips at top, use staining) 77

Bottle, paneled cylindrical body w/conical shoulder w/a molded top, shoulder impressed in a starred circle "DL Ormsby 1849," also impressed in a badge frame on the bottom "Patent Pressed W. Smith," uncommon form, tight hairline up from base, 10" h. (ILLUS. far right with other stoneware bottles, top previous page) 187

Bottle, cylindrical w/conical neck w/a thick blob top, impressed & blue-tinted mark of Kelly on the shoulder, 19th c., 10 1/4" h. (bottom half stained from use, large surface chip on bottom of back) 22

Bottle, cylindrical body w/conical shoulder & molded top trimmed in cobalt blue, shoulder impressed "E-Ferris," some staining from use, couple of short spider cracks at base, interior chipping on mouth, 10 1/2" h. (ILLUS. second from left with five other stoneware bottles, top previous page) 110

Bottle, cylindrical body w/conical shoulder & molded top trimmed in cobalt blue,

shoulder impressed in large letters "J. DEVINE," underglaze blue spot on front base, stone ping & clay separation line at base, 10 1/2" h. (ILLUS. second from right with five other stoneware bottles, top previous page) 110

Bottle, cylindrical body w/conical shoulder w/a molded top trimmed in cobalt blue, shoulder impressed "Boston Root Beer - F. Gleason," long spider cracks on side & below mark, stone ping on the front, 10 1/2" h. (ILLUS. third from left with five other stoneware bottles, top previous page) 22

Bottle, cylindrical w/conical neck w/a thick blob top, large cobalt blue slip-quilled dotted initials "J.C." on the shoulder, 19th c., 10 3/4" h. (somewhat overglazed in firing, some staining & surface chipping at front base) 132

Bottle, cylindrical w/conical neck w/a thick blob top, large cobalt blue slip-quilled dotted initials "J.C." on the shoulder, impressed on the back shoulder w/name J. Cunningham, 19th c., 11" h. (some staining around base, surface chip at base front) 187

Bough pot, tall bulbous baluster-form body tapering to a slightly flaring cylindrical neck, decorated overall w/cobalt blue brushed stylized tulip buds & flowers on stalks w/tiny foliage between, unsigned but attributed to Peter Bell, Muskingham County, Ohio, late 19th c., small area of flaking on one leaf, 18" h. 11,500

Rare Early Brandy Keg

Brandy keg, barrel-shaped, four pairs of hand-incised bands trimmed in cobalt blue, large incised & blue-trimmed word "BRANDY" in upper band & a finely incised design of a wooden rowboat & oars in a middle band, twice stamped w/the mark of potter Tyler & Dillon, Albany, New York, chip on left top edge w/radiating hairline across top & down the side, rare short-lived maker, ca. 1825, 2 gal., 13 1/2" h. (ILLUS.) 5,500

Early Table-top Churn & Two Signed Connecticut Pieces

Butter churn, table-top size, simple ovoid body w/a flaring flat rim, light blue slip-quilled size number at front rim, unsigned, uncommon form, ca. 1870, 1 1/2 gal., 10" h. (couple of base chips, a spider crack at right side).................................. **110**

Butter churn, table-top model, tall slender tapering cylindrical style w/flat rim & large eared handles, cobalt blue large brushed tulip design on the front, unsigned but possibly from the Ingalls factory, Taunton, Massachusetts, some use staining, couple of surface flakes at base & rim, ca. 1830, 2 gal., 11 3/4" h. (ILLUS. left with Hartford, Connecticut-made crock & jug, top of page) **1,073**

Butter churn, swelled cylindrical body tapering to a thick molded mouth flanked by eared handles, cobalt blue slip-quilled large three-leaf clover design below the blue-tinted impressed mark of S. L. Pewtress & Co., Fairhaven, Connecticut & a size number, design fry, uncommon small size, ca. 1880, 2 gal., 12" h. (ILLUS., next column) **358**

Small Churn with Clover Decoration

Butter churn, table-top model, tapering cylindrical body w/a thick molded rim & eared handles, cobalt blue slip-quilled bird on sprig above three other sprigs & a size number, unsigned, very tight small rim hairline, small clay separation line at base on back, minor interior wear, ca. 1870, 2 gal., 12" h. (ILLUS. left with Edmands crock & unsigned jug, bottom of page).. **1,705**

Rare Small Churn with a Crock & Unsigned Jug

Three Rare Whites, Utica Pieces with Paddletail Bird Designs

Butter churn, swelled tapering cylindrical shape w/molded rim & eared handles, very large & unusual cobalt blue slip-quilled paddletail bird perched on a tall flowering leafy stem, impressed mark of N.A. White & Son, Utica, New York, chip at front & right handle professionally restored, tight short hairline from back rim, minor glaze flake on right handle, ca. 1870, 3 gal., 15" h. (ILLUS. left with other Whites paddletail bird & crock pieces, above) **9,900**

Butter churn, tall swelled cylindrical body w/a narrow molded mouth & eared handles, cobalt blue slip-quilled delicate design of a cluster of three ruffled round blossoms surrounded by short feathery leaves, unmarked, probably New York state origin, ca. 1870, 3 gal., 15" h. (some minor surface chipping on rim & some use staining) **248**

Butter churn, swelled tapering cylindrical shape w/molded rim & eared handles, very large & unusual cobalt blue slip-quilled paddletail bird perched on a tall leafy stem w/a single blossom, impressed mark of N.A. White & Son, Utica, New York, restored chip on left handle, ca. 1870, 3 gal., 16" h. (ILLUS. right with other Whites, Utica churn & crock with paddletailed birds, above) **2,420**

Butter churn, swelled tall cylindrical form tapering slightly to a flattened flaring mouth, thick eared handles, unusual cobalt blue slip-quilled decoration of looping leafy scrolls w/dots above a small tornado design & flanked by size numbers, blue-trimmed impressed mark of A.O. Whittemore, Havana, New York, professional restoration to a long hairline up from bottom & a few flakes on back & a small front rim chip, ca. 1870, 4 gal., 16" h. (ILLUS. center with Whittemore crock & jug, bottom of page) **495**

Butter churn, tall swelled cylindrical form w/a narrow molded rim & eared handles, large cobalt-blue slip-quilled dotted bird perched on a long fern leaf, impressed round & blue-tinted mark of N. Clark, Jr., Athens, New York, ca. 1850, 4 gal., 16" h. (glaze flake spots overall, surface chips on interior rim, long in-body Y-shaped crack on the front, large stone ping on back & left of design, professionally replaced left handle) **330**

A Churn, Crock & Jug Produced at the A.O. Whittemore Pottery

Three Stoneware Pieces Made in Fort Edward, New York

Butter churn, cov., advertising-type, tall swelled cylindrical body w/a narrow molded mouth & inset cover w/dasher guide hole, eared handles, large & unusual very dark blue slip-quilled design of two bold blossoms with five round petals issuing from a short stem & surrounded by tightly scrolled leaves, impressed & blue-tinted size number & advertising reading "Wm. Peck. - Druggist & Grocer - Glens-Falls, NY - Bennington, VT," lightly impressed w/Bennington, Vermont mark, ca. 1865, 4 gal., 16 1/2" h. (professional restoration to overall hairlines)........ **2,200**

Butter churn, cov., tall slender baluster-shaped body w/molded rim, eared handles & the original inset cover w/cupped dasher guide decorated in cobalt blue, cobalt blue slip-quilled delicate floral wreath on the center front enclosing the date "1866," impressed & blue-tinted mark of Whites, Utica, New York, ca. 1866, 4 gal., 17" h. (professional restoration to a continuous looped crack along the back & up through one handle) **825**

Butter churn, tall ovoid form tapering to a molded rim flanked by eared handles, cobalt blue brushed design of a bull's-eye flower flanked by long leafy scrolls, impressed mark of the New York Stoneware Co., Fort Edward, New York, professional restoration to overall hairlines, some interior rim wear, ca. 1880, 4 gal., 17" h. (ILLUS. right with two other pieces made in Fort Edward, New York, top of page) **303**

Butter churn, tall slightly tapering cylindrical body w/a wide molded rim & eared handles, large cobalt blue slip-quilled

double round blossoms flanking a thin stem & a cluster of three dotted leaves below the impressed & blue-tinted size number & mark of Frank B. Norton, Worcester, Massachusetts, third quarter 19th c., 4 gal., 17" h. (minor interior rim chips) **764**

Plain Miniature Stoneware Churn

Butter churn, miniature, replaced cover & wood dasher, ovoid body tapering to a molded rim, undecorated, excellent condition, ca. 1890, 4 1/4" h. (ILLUS.) **66**

Very Rare Star Face Butter Churn & Two Other Pieces From Lyons, New York

Butter churn, tall gently swelled cylindrical body w/a thick molded rim & eared handles, cobalt blue very large slip-quilled design of an eight-point star centered by a small face below two size numbers & the blue-tinted impressed mark of T. Harrington, Lyons, New York, professional restoration to rim chips & hairlines, ca. 1850, 4 gal., 17" h. (ILLUS. center with a crock & jug made in Lyons, New York, above) **6,875**

Butter churn, tall slightly swelled cylindrical form w/a wide molded rim & a small loop handle at one shoulder, overall fine brown & tan mottled glaze, impressed oval mark in black for W.D. Suggs, Smithville, Mississippi, ca. 1900, 5 gal., 17" h. (very minor interior wear, otherwise excellent) **358**

Butter churn, cov., tall ovoid body w/a molded mouth & inset cover w/cobalt-blue trimmed dasher opening, eared handles, cobalt blue slip-quilled very large, dramatic paddle-tailed bird w/ribbed wings perched on a very tall curving leafy stem w/a tall cluster of flowers, impressed mark of N.A. White & Son, Utica, New York, ca. 1865, 5 gal., 17 1/2" h. (some very minor staining) **13,200**

Butter churn, cov., tall ovoid body w/a molded mouth & inset cover w/cobalt-blue trimmed dasher opening, eared handles, four pairs of cobalt blue-trimmed bands up around the body, impressed mark of Whites, Utica, New York, ca. 1865, 5 gal., 18" h. (some minor design fry, couple of glaze flake spots on back)...... **248**

Butter churn, tall gently swelled ovoid body tapering to a flaring rim flanked by eared handles, dark cobalt blue slip-quilled large thistle-like flower beside a large hex sign-style blossom, both on a stem w/long shaped leaves & below a script size number & the impressed & blue-tinted mark of J. Burger, Jr., Rochester, New York, ca. 1885, 5 gal., 18" h. (professional restoration to rim chips & crack on the front).. **1,485**

Butter churn, tall ovoid shape tapering to a thick molded mouth & eared handles, cobalt blue stenciled design of a spread-winged eagle clutching a banner reading "E Pluribus Unum" below a circle w/the size number, unsigned, western Pennsylvania or Ohio origin, some grease stains, ca. 1800, 6 gal., 17" h. (ILLUS. right with unsigned crocks, bottom of page)... **550**

Eagle-decorated Butter Churn & Two Unsigned Crocks

Rare Early Iowa Stoneware Butter Churn

Butter churn, tall slightly tapering cylindrical body w/a flared molded rim & eared handles, cobalt blue brushed long stylized floral design at the top below the impressed mark "Cedar Falls, Iowa - 6," probably by Martin White, ca. 1865, crack on reverse w/minor losses, 6 gal., 17 1/4" h. (ILLUS., left) **2,875**

Butter churn, cov., tall slightly tapering cylindrical form w/molded rim & eared handles, very large dark cobalt blue slip-quilled large detailed paddle-tailed bird perched on a large plume design, impressed mark of N.A. White & Son, Utica, New York, replaced cover w/dasher hole, minor rust stains from use, long surface chip under back rim, ca. 1870, 6 gal., 18" h. (ILLUS. right with orchid-decorated Whites, Utica churn, below) **2,640**

Butter churn, tall slightly tapering cylindrical form w/molded rim & eared handles, very large dark cobalt blue slip-quilled orchid & leaves design up the front, impressed mark of Whites, Utica, New York, professional restoration to hairlines from rim, ca. 1865, 6 gal., 18" h. (ILLUS. left with other Whites, Utica butter churn, bottom of page)... **688**

Two Fine Whites, Utica Decorated Butter Churns

Butter churn, tall ovoid form tapering to a molded rim flanked by eared handles, cobalt blue slip-quilled design of a large plump bird perched on a long leafy plume, blue-tinted impressed mark of the New York Stoneware Co., Fort Edward, New York, w/a period replacement fitted carved wood churn guide, significant & deep pitting around the base & left side, X-shaped crack on left of design, ca. 1870, 6 gal., 19" h. (ILLUS. left with two other pieces made in Fort Edward, New York, top page 20).. **633**

Miniature Churn with Cover & Dasher

Butter churn, miniature, w/original cover & wooden dasher, ovoid body tapering to a low flared rim, overall dark brown Albany glaze, some rim surface wear, unsigned, ca. 1880, 6 3/4" h. (ILLUS.) **303**

Churn with Paddletail Bird & Flowers

Butter churn, slightly ovoid body w/a molded rim & eared handles, slip-quilled cobalt blue large paddletail bird perched on a long flowering stem, fine shading & detail, impressed mark of N.A. White & Son,

Utica, New York, chip at front & right ear professionally repaired, tight short hairline from rim on back, ca. 1870, 3 gal., 15" h. (ILLUS.) **9,900**

Butter Churn Made in Maine

Butter churn, tall ovoid body tapering to a flared flat rim, eared shoulder handles, original stoneware dasher guide cover, impressed & blue-trimmed swan design below the incised lines & the oval mark of Gardiner Stoneware Manufactory, Gardiner, Maine, professional restoration to rim chips, ca. 1880, 3 gal., 15 1/2" h. (ILLUS.).. **495**

Churn with Less Detailed Bird & Flower

Butter churn, slightly ovoid body w/a molded rim & eared handles, slip-quilled cobalt blue large paddletail bird perched on a long flowering stem, impressed mark of N.A. White & Son, Utica, New York, chip at leaf ear professionally restored, ca. 1870, 3 gal., 16" h. (ILLUS.) **2,420**

Large Churn with Four-leaf Decoration

Butter churn, tall slightly ovoid body w/molded rim & one eared handle, dark cobalt blue slip-quilled design of four large spearpoint leaves, impressed mark of Whites, Utica, New York, fire damage on left side, one handle missing, ca. 1865, 4 gal., 16" h. (ILLUS.)......................... **330**

Rare Early Tall Boston Butter Churn

Butter churn, tall slender cylindrical body w/three tooled bands at the slightly tapering shoulder below the flared mouth, early handles, deeply impressed maker's

mark of a banner, undecorated, attributed to Frederick Carpenter, Boston, Massachusetts, very rare early form, ca. 1805, 2 gal., 17" h. (ILLUS.) **2,530**

Butter Churn with Large Stylized Flower

Butter churn, tall slightly ovoid body w/molded rim & eared handles, cobalt blue large slip-quilled bull's-eye flower design, impressed mark of New York Stoneware Co., Fort Edward, New York, ca. 1880, 5 gal., 17 1/2" h. (ILLUS.) **330**

Churn with Bold, Large Bird Decoration

Butter churn, w/original dasher guide cover, tall slightly ovoid body w/a molded rim & eared handles, very large & bold cobalt blue slip-quilled paddle-tail bird on a long flowering leafy branch up the side, impressed mark "White & Wood - Binghamton, NY - 5," long surface chip on front & about left handle, in-the-making clay separation at applied left handle, minor stone fleck near bottom, ca. 1885, 5 gal., 17 1/2" h. (ILLUS., bottom previous page) **8,800**

Boldly Decorated Stoneware Butter Churn

Butter churn, w/dasher guide cover, tall slender slightly ovoid body w/molded rim & eared handles, large cobalt blue brushed design of a cluster of very tall leaves & triple blossoms up the front below the impressed mark "H.M. Whitman - Havana, N.Y. - 5," long in-body hairline through the flowers, some design fry, ca. 1860, 5 gal., 18" h. (ILLUS.) **2,200**

Butter churn, slightly swelled cylindrical body w/a molded rim & eared handles, advertising-type, cobalt blue slip-quilled very large spread-winged dotted bird w/pointed crest perched atop a tall leafy stalk & w/a banner issuing from its bill reading "Akron - Ohio," a band around the top w/the name of the merchant in cobalt blue "D.S. Alexander" above a script "6," one-of-a-kind display piece, unsigned by maker, two clay separation lines down from the rim on the back, ca. 1870, 6 gal., 18" h. (ILLUS., top next column) **18,150**

Very Rare Advertising Butter Churn

Bold Decorated Bennington Churn

Butter churn, tall slightly ovoid body w/a molded rim & eared handle, original pottery dasher guide cover, very large dark cobalt blue slip-quilled cornucopia overflowing w/large flowers, impressed mark of J. Norton & Co., Bennington, Vermont, very minor staining, short tight hairline on one side, ca. 1861, 6 gal., 19" h. (ILLUS.).. **8,250**

Tall Churn with Large Bird Design

Butter churn, w/stoneware dasher guide cover, tall ovoid body w/a molded rim & eared handles, large bold cobalt blue slip-quilled design of a bird perched on a tall tree stump looking back over its shoulder, impressed mark "West Troy - NY - Pottery - 6," restoration to glaze flaking at bottom half, ca. 1880, 6 gal., 19" h. (ILLUS.).. **1,018**

Tall Churn with Dotted Bird Decoration

Butter churn, tall slightly ovoid body w/a flared wide mouth & eared handles, cobalt blue slip-quilled dotted bird looking over its shoulder & perched on a small tree stump below a "6" & the impressed mark "J. Burger, Jr. - Rochester, NY," professional restoration to hairlines down from rim, significant chipping on left handle, ca. 1885, 6 gal., 20" h. (ILLUS.)... **1,210**

Butter crock, wide low cylindrical form w/molded rim & eared handles, cobalt blue brushed wide repeating bands of flowers & leaves around the sides, unsigned but attributed to Richard Remmey, Philadelphia, Pennsylvania, mottled clay color, professional restoration to tight hairline along the base & up one side through the decoration, ca. 1850, 6" h. (ILLUS. right with unsigned cake crock & milk pan, bottom of page) **468**

Unsigned Butter Crock, Cake Crock & Milk Pan

Full-page Illustration of a Variety of Stoneware Pieces

Butter crocks, cov., each of cylindrical form w/molded sprigs of leaves on the front trimmed in cobalt blue, two w/flat covers & one w/a wire bail handle w/wooden grip, unmarked, late 19th - early 20th c., the group (ILLUS. third row down, second from right & the bottom row, second from right in the full-page picture) **441**

A Stoneware Advertising Cake Crock & Two Bulbous Pitchers

Cake crock, cov., advertising-type, Bristol-glazed cylindrical body w/flattened cover, the front molded in low relief & trimmed in cobalt blue w/a center rectangular panel flanked on one side w/grapevines & the figure of a gnome speaking into a phone, the other side of the panel w/another gnome listening to a phone, the panel stenciled in black "S.S. Pierce Co. - Est. 1831 - 1894 - Inc. - Boston Brookline," the back side & cover molded w/further grapevines, ca. 1894, 1 gal., 6" h. (ILLUS. right with two bulbous pitchers, above) **468**

Cake crock, wide low cylindrical form w/flat molded rim flanked by large eared handles, dark cobalt blue brushed wide band w/a leafy vine below the rim suspending large drooping blossoms, unsigned, ca. 1850, 1 gal., 9" d., 4 1/2" h. (professional restoration to glued cracks emanating from base & to some rim chipping) **468**

Cake crock, wide low cylindrical form w/molded rim & eared handles, dark cobalt blue slip-quilled horizontal plume design, impressed mark of the New York Stoneware Co., Fort Edward, New York, tight hairline at back rim, some use staining, design fry, ca. 1870, 1 1/2 gal., 10" d., 5 1/4" h. (ILLUS. center with two other cake crocks made in Fort Edward, New York, below).. **248**

Three Cake Crocks Made in Fort Edward, New York

A Vermont-made Cake Crock & Cream Pot

Bird-decorated Cake Crock, Crock & Jar

Cake crock, wide cylindrical form w/a molded rim flanked by eared handles, cobalt blue slip-quilled thistle flowers & looped leaves below the blue-tinted impressed mark of J. & E. Norton, Bennington, Vermont, couple of minor rim chips, small tight hairline extending up from base, ca. 1855, 1 1/2 gal., 7" h. (ILLUS. left with Vermont-made cream pot, bottom previous page) **633**

Cake crock, wide low cylindrical form w/molded rim & eared handles, dark cobalt blue slip-quilled dotted simple triple-leaf design, impressed mark of Haxstun, Ottman & Co., Fort Edward, New York, few rim chips, tight glaze spider crack up from base, ca. 1870, 2 gal., 7 1/2" h. (ILLUS. right with two other cake crocks made in Fort Edward, New York, middle previous page) **165**

Cake crock, wide low cylindrical form w/molded rim & eared handles, dark cobalt blue slip-quilled dotted & scrolled plume below the blue-tinted impressed mark of J.A. & C.W. Underwood, Fort Edward, New York, large rim chip at front, interior rim chip at back, two exterior rim chips & a T-shaped long horizontal freeze line at the base back, some design fry, ca. 1865, 2 gal., 7 1/2" h. (ILLUS. left with two other cake crocks made in Fort Edward, New York, middle previous page) **176**

Cake crock, wide low cylindrical form w/molded rim & eared handles, dark cobalt blue slip-quilled plump bird perched on a squiggle branch below the impressed and blue-tinted size number & mark of Bullard & Scott, Cambridgeport, Massachusetts, ca. 1870, 2 gal., 7 3/4" h. (professional restoration to some rim chipping) **633**

Cake crock, wide cylindrical shape w/molded rim & eared handle, Bristol glaze decorated w/a large cobalt blue slip-quilled singing bird on a squiggle twig, unsigned but probably New Jersey origin, uncommon form, ca. 1880, 3 gal., 8 1/2" h. (ILLUS. left with other bird-decorated pieces, top of page) **468**

Cake crock, cov., wide low cylindrical form w/lightly molded rim & eared handles, flat cover w/disk finial, Bristol-glazed w/cobalt blue brushed repeating swag design around body & on the cover, unsigned, interior rim wear & some exterior rim chipping, ca. 1880, 10 1/2" d., 5 1/2" h. (ILLUS. center with unsigned butter crock & milk pan, bottom page 26) **303**

Nice Covered Cake Crock with Flowers

Cake crock, cov., eared handles, large cobalt blue brushed flower & leaves band around the sides, flat cover w/brushed blue leaves, unsigned, couple of rim chips, extensive knob chipping on cover, ca. 1850, 2 gal., 11" d., 7" h. (ILLUS.) **688**

Very Rare Bennington Cake Crock with Stag Decoration

Cake crock, wide cylindrical body w/molded rim & eared handles, exceptional cobalt blue slip-quilled decoration w/a large recumbent dotted stag between fences & fir trees, impressed mark of J. & E. Norton, Bennington, Vermont, two very tight hairlines, ca. 1855, 2 gal., 12" d., 7 1/2" h. (ILLUS., above).......................... **18,700**

Cake crock, wide cylindrical body w/a flat molded rim & eared handles, cobalt blue large slip-quilled fern-like leaf w/petaled flower, probably New York state, some use staining, in-the-making clay separation line at the base, ca. 1870, 4 gal., 9 1/2" h. (ILLUS., next column) **275**

Canister, cylindrical w/indented neck band below the thick squared flat mouth, simple brushed cobalt blue stroked accents around shoulder, unsigned, mottled clay color, couple of minor surface chips at base & rim, ca. 1850, 1/2 gal., 6 1/4" h.

(ILLUS. far left with unsigned jug & preserve jars, bottom of page) **176**

Cake Crock with Leaf & Flower Design

Stoneware Canister & Three Other Unsigned Pieces

Early Indiana-made Canning Jar

Canning jar, slightly tapering cylindrical body w/a wide molded mouth, marked by Geo. Husher, Brazil, Indiana, fairly uncommon maker, overall brown alkaline glaze, minor surface wear, ca. 1860, 1 qt., 7" h. (ILLUS.) **248**

Stoneware Canning Jar with Stripes

Canning jar, slightly tapering cylindrical body w/a slightly flared rim, decorated w/five brushed cobalt blue stripes across the front, unsigned, small hairline & chip on front rim, minor use staining, ca. 1860, 1/2 gal., 8 1/2" h. (ILLUS.) **303**

One-quart Brown Canning Jar

Canning jar, cylindrical w/narrow flattened shoulder, short wide neck & thick molded rim, impressed mark at the base for Adams, Allison & Co. Manufacturers, Middlebury, Summit County, Ohio, light brown mottled glaze, excellent condition, ca. 1890, 1 qt., 8" h. (ILLUS.) **132**

Stencil-marked Canning Jar

Unusual Stoneware Coffeepot & Eagle-molded Pitcher

Canning jar, slightly tapering cylindrical body w/a thick molded rim, decorated around the sides w/five brushed cobalt blue bands flanking the stenciled marking for Hamilton & Jones, Greensboro, Green County, Pennsylvania, some use staining, ca. 1870, 1/2 gal., 9 1/2" h. (ILLUS.) **578**

Stoneware Chicken Feeder & Cooler

Chicken feeder, beehive-shaped w/large indented opening on one side, small neck, overall dark brown & mustard yellow mottled glaze, unsigned, tight spider crack in the bottom, ca. 1870, 1/2 gal., 8 1/2" h. (ILLUS. left with small water cooler) **66**

Coffeepot, cov., tapering cylindrical body w/a sand-colored unglazed exterior & brown Albany slip-glazed interior, tin strap around the body & forming the handle, tin spout, rim band & hinged cover & wire bail top handle, all original, unsigned, rare form, use staining, short crack up from base below spout, tin thumbrest missing, attributed to the Bodine Pottery Co., Zanesville, Ohio, ca. 1880, 9" h. (ILLUS. right with eagle-molded pitcher, top of page) **660**

Cream pot, deep bulbous bowl-form w/thick molded footring & wide flat molded rim, applied strap handle at back, cobalt blue stenciled design of four panels w/snowflakes, unsigned but attributed to F.H. Cowden, Harrisburg, Pennsylvania, ca. 1890, 1 gal., 6" h. (kiln burn & some design fry, minor surface chipping at rim, small very tight hairline on left side) **303**

Stoneware Cream Pot, Crock & Jug

Cream pot, wide bulbous ovoid form w/a wide flat molded mouth flanked by eared handles, cobalt blue slip-quilled tornado & feather design, unsigned by maker, short hairline above left handle, some use staining, ca. 1870, 1 gal., 7 1/2" h. (ILLUS. right with a decorated crock & jug, top of page) 303

Cream pot, wide tapering ovoid form w/a thick molded rim above eared handles, a large simple cobalt blue drooping blossom on a leaf stem across the front, impressed & blue-tinted mark of Evan R. Jones, Pittston, Pennsylvania, ca. 1870, 1 gal., 8" h. (some overall staining, very tight hairline in front of right handle)............. 248

Cream pot, wide bulbous ovoid body w/a wide flat mouth flanked by eared handles, cobalt blue slip-quilled small date "1832" below the impressed & blue-washed mark of E.S. Fox, Athens, New York, blue accents at handles, ca. 1832, 2 gal., 11" h. (minor glaze spider at rim, minor overglazing on right side) 688

Cream pot, wide bulbous ovoid shape w/a wide flat rim flanked by eared handles, cobalt blue slip-quilled rare design of an urn-shaped trophy filled w/flowers, im-

pressed name on rim of N. Clark & Co., Lyons, New York, very tight long hairline in front, minor surface rim chip above the mark, ca. 1850, 2 gal., 12" h. (ILLUS. left with very rare Lyons-made butter churn & jug, top page 21) **1,073**

Cream pot, flat-bottomed wide slightly swelled cylindrical body w/a thick molded rim flanked by eared handles, cobalt blue brushed stylized double tulip & leaves design below the blue-tinted impressed mark of Ballard & Brothers, Burlington, Vermont, minor bubbling on design, some chipping under left handle, minor use staining, ca. 1860, 3 gal., 10 1/2" h. (ILLUS. right with Vermont-made cake crock, bottom page 28) **248**

Cream pot, wide ovoid body tapering to a wide flat molded mouth flanked by eared handles, cobalt blue brushed large double flowers on leafy stems beside a large size numeral below the blue-trimmed impressed mark of T. Harrington, Lyons, New York, excellent condition, ca. 1850, 3 gal., 12" h. (ILLUS. right with rare Lyons, New York, crock & preserve jar, bottom of page)... **2,200**

Three Rare Decorated Pieces Made in Lyons, New York

Large Cream Pot & Two Decorated Crocks

Cream pot, wide bulbous ovoid body tapering to a thick molded rim & eared handles, cobalt blue slip-quilled slender long-necked dotted goony bird on blossom branch, some in-the-making overglazing, tight long hairline up from base on back, ca. 1860, 4 gal., 12" h. (ILLUS. left two decorated crocks, top of page) **468**

Early Cream Pot with Script Name

Cream pot, ovoid body w/a wide cylindrical neck & flat rim flanked by eared handles, double stamped "2" above a cobalt blue script "Butter" on one side & "Dolly" on the other side, probably New York state, ca. 1840, professional restoration to a hairline, 2 gal., 10 1/2" h. (ILLUS.) **798**

Cream pot, wide slightly ovoid body w/a wide flat molded mouth flanked by eared handles, bold cobalt blue brushed wreath enclosing a large "2" below the impressed mark of T. Harrington, Lyons, New York, couple of very minor surface chips at rim, ca. 1850, 2 gal., 10 1/2" h. (ILLUS., next column) **330**

Wreath-decorated Cream Pot

Cream Pot with Large Three-petal Flower

Cream pot, wide slightly ovoid body w/a wide flat rim & eared handles, cobalt blue slip-quilled large three-petal trillium-like blossom on a leafy stem w/a numeral "2" above, impressed mark of F. Stetzenmeyer, Rochester, New York, tight X-shaped in-body hairline, ca. 1860, 2 gal., 11" h. (ILLUS.) **3,300**

Cream Pot with Bold Blue Flowers

Cream pot, ovoid form w/a molded rim & eared handles, slip-quilled large cobalt blue blossoms on leafy stems below the number "3," impressed mark of T. Harrington, Lyons, New York, washed in blue, ca. 1850, 3 gal., 12" h. (ILLUS.) **2,200**

Large Cream Pot with Trumpet Flower

Cream pot, wide ovoid body tapering to a molded rim & eared handles, cobalt blue slip-quilled large trumpet flower on leafy stem w/a script "4" above, impressed mark of Harrington & Burger, Rochester, New York, very tight hairline down from rim through design, second hairline from rim through number, some design bubbling, ca. 1853, 4 gal., 14" h. (ILLUS.) ... **1,540**

Cream Pot with Large Double Flowers

Cream pot, wide ovoid body tapering to a molded rim & eared handles, cobalt blue slip-quilled huge double flower design w/unique blossoms above long leaves below a script "5" & the impressed mark of N. Clark & Co., Rochester, New York, hairline through rim & down through design, couple of other through lines in body, overglazed in the making, ca. 1850, 5 gal., 15 1/2" h. (ILLUS.) **1,100**

Very Rare Pair of Cream Pots Decorated with Reclining Stags

Cream pots, bulbous ovoid body tapering to a flattened molded rim & eared handles, each decorated w/a cobalt blue slip-quilled design of matching recumbent spotted stags above low picket fences flanked by fir trees, impressed mark for Edmands & Co., one w/a stone ping on front & tight hairline on front, another very tight hairline down the back from rim, glaze spider crack on bottom, other piece w/very short hairline & chip, ca. 1870, 2 gal., 10" h., pr. (ILLUS., bottom previous page) **13,200**

1930s Glazed Stoneware Creamer

Small Decorative Tanware Creamer

Creamer, tanware, baluster-form body w/a flaring neck & pinched spout, dark brown wide drape band around the rim, squiggle line around the middle above large flowers & plume-like leaves, attributed to western Pennsylvania, excellent condition, ca. 1870, 5" h. (ILLUS.) **1,760**

Creamer, slender ovoid body tapering to a flat rim w/pinched spout, applied S-scroll strap handle, overall olive green mottled glaze, possibly Midwestern or Southern, surface wear at spout, ca. 1930, 6 1/2" h. (ILLUS., top next column) **22**

Small Crock with Tornado Decoration

Crock, cylindrical w/molded rim & eared handle, dark cobalt blue slip-quilled tornado design below the impressed mark "Geddes, NY - 2," some in-the-making overgrazing, minor stone ping in the design, ca. 1870, 2 gal., 9" h. (ILLUS.) **198**

A Varied Grouping of Stoneware Pieces

Four Various Pieces of Stoneware

Crock, swelled cylindrical body w/a wide molded rim & loop shoulder handles, cobalt blue slip-quilled squiggled swags & band accents, initials "I.M." below one handle, unsigned, possibly American or German, hairlines in one handle, ca. 1850, 1 pt., 5" h. (ILLUS. second from left with vase, shard, flowerpot & jar, bottom previous page) **143**

Unsigned Flower-decorated Small Crock

Crock, flat-bottomed wide ovoid body tapering to a flattened molded wide mouth, light cobalt blue large brushed tulip above leaves design, unsigned but probably Pennsylvania origin, minor glaze burn or cinnamon clay color occurred in the making, minor surface wear & use staining on the back, ca. 1850, 1 pt., 5 1/4" h. (ILLUS.) **688**

Crock, cylindrical w/molded rim & eared handles, small cobalt blue slip-quilled singing bird, unsigned but probably Poughkeepsie, New York, origin, large stain spot on back from a full-length hairline, dime-sized stone ping on back, some use staining, ca. 1870, 1 gal., 7" h. (ILLUS. second from left with flowerpot & various other pieces, top of page) **248**

Crock, cylindrical w/thick molded rim flanked by eared handles, impressed & blue-trimmed design of a flying bird on an arrow, impressed mark of Gardiner Stoneware, Maine, minor glaze burning, some minor glaze flaking, ca. 1880, 1 gal., 7" h. (ILLUS. center with Standish & Wright jug & Edmans & Co. preserve jar, bottom of page).. **66**

Crock, cylindrical w/thin molded rolled rim & eared handles, dark cobalt blue slip-quilled small double flowers on a leafy stem near the top rim, unsigned, probably New York state origin, couple of very minor surface chips, ca. 1870, 1 gal., 7" h.. **248**

A Signed Crock, Jug & Large Preserve Jar

Decorated Stoneware Crock, Jug & Preserve Jar

Crock, cylindrical w/molded rim & eared handles, cobalt blue simple brushed stylized double flower design, impressed mark of Adam Caire, Poughkeepsie, New York, extensive chipping at rim, two glued cracks from back rim, in-the-making clay discoloration, ca. 1850, 1 gal., 7 1/4" h. (ILLUS. center with decorated jug & preserve jar, above).. **99**

Three Decorated Crocks from Whites, Utica

Crock, cylindrical w/molded rim & eared handles, cobalt blue brushed large oak leaf design below the impressed mark of Whites, Utica, New York, chip on rim on back & on one handle, some lime staining, ca. 1865, 1 gal., 7 1/2" h. (ILLUS. center with two other Whites, Utica crocks)............ **303**

A Crock, Jar & Jug Made in Massachusetts or Maine

Three Crocks & a Jug Made in Fort Edward, New York

Crock, cylindrical w/molded rim & eared handles, cobalt blue slip-quilled double bull's-eye design below the blue-tinted impressed mark of Frank B. Norton, Worcester, Massachusetts, one chip at rim above left handle, minor surface chipping on edge of handles, ca. 1870, 1 gal., 7 1/2" h. (ILLUS. center with a decorated jar & jug, bottom previous page) **248**

Crock, cylindrical w/molded rim & eared handles, cobalt blue slip-quilled dotted scroll design, unsigned by maker, orange peel overglazing in-the-making, ca. 1870, 1 gal., 7 1/2" h. (ILLUS. left with cream pot & jug, top of page 33) **275**

Crock, cylindrical w/molded rim & eared handles, cobalt blue slip-quilled stylized dotted plume design w/a long curved tail, impressed mark of the New York Stoneware Co., Fort Edward, New York, minor interior wear to glaze, ca. 1870, 1 gal., 7 1/2" h. (ILLUS. second from right with

three other pieces made in Fort Edward, New York, top of page) **275**

Crock, cylindrical w/molded rim & eared handles, cobalt blue slip-quilled stylized plume design w/a long curved tail below the blue-tinted impressed mark of Satterlee & Mory, Fort Edward, New York, few small interior surface chips at rim, some use staining, ca. 1870, 1 gal., 7 1/2" h. (ILLUS. left with three other pieces made in Fort Edward, New York, top of page) **413**

Crock, bulbous ovoid body tapering to a wide molded flat mouth flanked by large looped side handles, cobalt blue slip-quilled swirl designs around the shoulder w/blue band around rim & base, unsigned but probably early New York City origin, mottled clay color, ca. 1800, 1 gal., 8" h. (ILLUS. right with two other very early decorated crocks, bottom of page) **2,310**

Three Very Early Handled & Decorated Crocks

Ovoid Crocks & Jar from Various New York Potters

Crock, wide ovoid body tapering to a wide, thick molded rim flanked by eared handles, dark cobalt blue slip-quilled stylized double flowers flanking a squiggle, all on a leafy stem, blue-trimmed impressed mark for W. Roberts, Binghamton, New York, some design fry, filled rim chip above right handle, ca. 1860, 1 gal., 8" h. (ILLUS. right with other ovoid crock & jar, above) **578**

Crock, wide ovoid body w/a very wide flat molded mouth, cobalt blue small stylized brushed flower sprig repeated three times around the upper sides, impressed size number in a circle, unsigned, mottled clay color, stack marks & kiln burn, minor use staining, ca. 1850, 1 gal., 8" h. (ILLUS. left with large decorated pitcher, bottom of page) **198**

Unsigned Crock & Large Decorated Pitcher

Crock and Preserve Jars from Cortland, New York

Crock, bulbous ovoid body tapering to a wide flat mouth flanked by eared handles, simple small cobalt blue brushed flower below the blue-washed deeply impressed mark of S. Blair, Cortland, New York, somewhat overglazed in-the-making, overall use stain, ca. 1830, 1 gal., 8 1/2" h. (ILLUS. right with two Cortland preserve jars, top of page) **358**

Crock, wide ovoid body tapering to a wide cylindrical flat mouth flanked by eared handles, brushed cobalt blue long curly design somewhat resembled eyeglasses across the front, unsigned but probably New York state origin, two very tight hairlines down from rim, ca. 1830, 1 gal., 8 1/2" h. (ILLUS. center with two other early crocks, bottom of page) **248**

Crock, wide ovoid body tapering to a wide, flat rim flanked by eared handles, overall brown alkaline glaze w/cobalt blue brushed plume & accents w/blue wash on the impressed mark of W.H. Farrar & Co., Geddes, New York, few very minor wear spots in glaze, ca. 1850, 1 gal., 8 1/2" h. (ILLUS. left with other crock & jar by various New York potters, top of previous page) **413**

Crock, bulbous ovoid body tapering to a wide molded flat mouth flanked by up-turned loop side handles, cobalt blue brushed snowflake design on the front & back w/blue trim on handles, possibly New York City origin, in-the-making glaze run, tight hairline up from base, ca. 1800,

1 gal., 9" h. (ILLUS. left with two other early decorated crocks, bottom of page 39)... **743**

Crock, bulbous ovoid body tapering to a wide molded flat mouth flanked by looped side handles, incised & cobalt blue-trimmed swag band around the shoulder above the large impressed word "COMMERAWS" on one side & "STONEWARE" on the other, extensive professional restoration, both handles replaced, restoration to full-length crack, ca. 1800, 1 gal., 9" h. (ILLUS. center with two other decorated crocks, bottom of page 39) **908**

Crock, wide ovoid body tapering to a wide cylindrical flat mouth flanked by eared handles, advertising-type, brushed cobalt blue leaves on curved stem below impressed advertising "Smith & Brickner - 221 Washington St. - Albany," probably from an Albany, New York, area maker, few interior & exterior surface chips at rim, X-shaped crack under left handle, signs of a burgundy overpaint, ca. 1830, 1 gal., 9" h. (ILLUS. left with two other decorated crocks, bottom of page) **385**

Crock, wide ovoid body tapering to a wide cylindrical flat mouth flanked by eared handles, cobalt blue brushed large stylized fern leaf design on front & back, blue handle trim, unsigned but probably New York state origin, one minor spider crack at base, ca. 1830, 1 gal., 9" h. (ILLUS. right with two other decorated crocks, below) **385**

Three Early Ovoid Crocks with Blue Decoration

Stoneware Crock, Jug & Pitcher with Decoration

Crock, wide ovoid body tapering to a wide flat mouth flanked by eared handles, undecorated, impressed & blue-washed mark of Goodwin & Webster, Hartford, Connecticut, ca. 1840, 1 gal., 9 1/2" h. (minor surface wear at rim) **358**

Crock, wide ovoid body w/a wide flat mouth flanked by eared handles, blue band around the rim & the impressed blue-washed mark of Goodwin & Webster, Hartford, Connecticut, horizontal in-body tight hairline extending from below mark to behind right handle, some surface chipping & use staining, ca. 1830, 1 gal., 9 1/2" h. (ILLUS. right with early table-top churn & other signed Hartford piece, top page 18) **198**

Crock, cylindrical w/molded rim flanked by eared handles, cobalt blue bold slip-quilled plume design, unsigned by probably Fort Edward Pottery, New York, horizontal freeze line extending halfway around base, overall use stain, few minor surface chips at rim, ca. 1870, 6 qt., 8" h. (ILLUS. center with unsigned jug & pitcher, top of page) **66**

Crock, advertising-type, cylindrical w/molded rim & eared handles, cobalt blue slip-quilled plume-style dotted leaf below the impressed & blue-tinted marking "Ayres Bros. - Jobbers Crockery & Glass - Stamford, Conn.," unsigned by maker, short hairlines extending down from rim, ca. 1870, 1 1/2 gal., 8 1/4" h. **187**

Crock, cylindrical w/molded rim & eared handles, unique & very rare cobalt blue brushed design of a standing camel by a palm tree w/a pyramid in the background below the impressed mark of Wm. A. Macquoid & Co., Little West 12th St., New York, small rim chip on front, full-length hairline down the back, ca. 1870, 1 1/2 gal., 10" h. (ILLUS. center with two decorated preserve jars, bottom of page) **12,650**

Crock, wide swelled cylindrical body tapering slightly to a wide, flat molded rim flanked by eared handles, cobalt blue slip-quilled fat, long-tailed bird perched on a small sprig, impressed mark of the New York Stoneware Co., Fort Edward, New York, hairline down from rim to left of mark, another on the back, some overall glaze flaking, scattered brown paint deposits on the interior, ca. 1880, 6 qt. (1 1/2 gal.), 10" h. (ILLUS. far right with three other pieces made in Fort Edward, New York, top page 39) **908**

Extremely Rare Crock with Camel & Two Preserve Jars

Early Flower-decorated Crock Flanked by Two Early Jugs

Crock, wide bulbous ovoid body tapering to a wide flat cylindrical mouth flanked by large eared handles, finely incised five-petaled flower on a leafy stem highlighted in cobalt blue on front & back, unsigned but probably New York City origin, tight hairline extending down from rim, short interior in-the-making clay separation inside one handle, some surface chipping at base, ca. 1830, 1 1/2 gal., 11" h. (ILLUS. center with two early ovoid jugs, above) **1,485**

Flower-decorated Crocks & a Jug

Crock, cylindrical w/thick rounded molded rim flanked by eared handles, cobalt blue large brushed flowers on leafy stems below a size numeral & the impressed mark of Lyons, New York, use staining, ca. 1860, 2 gal., 8 3/4" h. (ILLUS. right with other flower-decorated crock & jug) **303**

Three Decorated Crocks From Rochester, New York

Crock, cylindrical w/a molded rim & eared handles, cobalt blue slip-quilled large three-petal tulip on a leafy stem & the size number below the blue-trimmed impressed oval mark of Burger & Lang, Rochester, New York, glaze spider crack on back, some use staining, ca. 1870, 2 gal., 9" h. (ILLUS. center with two other decorated Rochester-made crocks) **743**

A Crock & Two Jugs Manufactured in New Jersey

Crock, cylindrical w/a molded rim & eared handles, cobalt blue slip-quilled plump singing bird on a small twig, impressed mark of G.W. Fulper & Bros., Flemington, New Jersey, stack marks along base, ca. 1880, 2 gal., 9" h. (ILLUS. center with jugs made in New Jersey, above) **770**

Crock, cylindrical w/flat molded rim & eared handles, fine cobalt blue brushed & dotted four-bloom flower on leafy stem flanked by size numbers below the blue-trimmed impressed mark of N. Clark & Co., Lyons, New York, minor chip on left handle & at rim, minor design fry, ca. 1850, 2 gal., 9" h. (ILLUS. center with two other rare decorated pieces made in Lyons, New York, bottom page 33) **1,595**

Crock, cylindrical w/molded rim & eared handles, cobalt blue slip-quilled stylized flower & squiggle design below the impressed mark of S. Hart & Son, Fulton, New York, professional restoration to full-length hairline on back, minor rim chip on front, ca. 1877, 2 gal., 9" h. (ILLUS. right with two other decorated New York crocks, middle this page) **99**

Crock, cylindrical w/molded rim & eared handles, cobalt blue slip-quilled large petaled flower on a leafy stem below a script size number & the blue-tinted impressed mark of J. Burger, Jr., Rochester, New York, some use staining, ca. 1885, 2 gal., 9" h. (ILLUS. right with two other J. Burger crocks, bottom next page) **220**

Three Decorated Crocks from New York State Factories

A Crock & Three Jugs Made in Lyons, New York

Three Bird-decorated Cylindrical Crocks from Fort Edward, New York

Crock, cylindrical w/molded rim & eared handles, cobalt blue slip-quilled delicate feathered leaf sprig enclosing size number below the impressed mark of J. Fisher & Co., Lyons, New York, lime-stained interior, overall exterior cinnamon clay color, ca. 1880, 2 gal., 9" h. (ILLUS. far right with three Lyons, New York, jugs, bottom of previous page) 303

Crock, cylindrical w/molded rim & eared handles, cobalt blue slip-quilled rare spread-winged eagle design, impressed mark of Whites, Utica, professional restoration to chips at rim & handles, two hairlines on back, ca. 1865, 2 gal., 9" h. (ILLUS. right with two other decorated Whites, Utica crocks, center page 38) 413

Crock, cylindrical w/molded rim & eared handles, cobalt blue slip-quilled small fat bird on a squiggle twig, impressed mark of Ottman Bros., Fort Edward, New York, interior lime staining, minor exterior use staining, round stack mark at front below design, ca. 1870, 2 gal., 9" h. (ILLUS. left with two other bird-decorated crocks from Fort Edward, New York, top of page) 440

Crock, cylindrical w/molded rim & eared handles, cobalt blue slip-quilled large petaled flower on a leafy stem below a size number & the impressed mark of J. Burger, Jr., Rochester, New York, spider crack under the right handle w/staining, minor spider crack & a few stain spots on the back, ca. 1885, 2 gal., 9" h. (ILLUS. left with two other J. Burger crocks, bottom of page) 523

Crock, cylindrical w/molded rim & eared handles, cobalt blue slip-quilled large & elegant paddletailed bird perched on a tall flowering stem, impressed mark of N.A. White & Son, Utica, New York, stone ping on base, some lime staining on interior & a few stain spots on exterior, ca. 1870, 2 gal., 9" h. (ILLUS. center with two Whites, Utica butter churns with paddletailed birds, top page 19)... **2,090**

Crock, cylindrical w/molded rim & eared handles, large dark cobalt blue slip-quilled heart-shaped ribbed & dotted orchid blossom on a leafy stem up the front, impressed mark for White & Wood, Binghamton, New York, ca. 1885, 2 gal., 9" h. (interior rim chip, short tight hairlines at rim near left handle) 275

Crock, cylindrical w/molded rim & eared handles, large dark cobalt blue brushed very large horizontal leafy stem w/a large petaled drooping flower below the impressed & blue-tinted mark of E.W. Farrington & Co., Elmira, New York, ca. 1885, 2 gal., 9" h. (chip at front rim)............. 605

Crock, cylindrical w/molded rim & eared handles, light cobalt blue slip-quilled unusual starburst design w/alternating blue & plain rays below a script size number beside the blue-tinted impressed mark of J. Burger, Rochester, New York, some interior lime staining, long surface chip on back interior rim, ca. 1880, 2 gal., 9" h. (ILLUS. center with two other J. Burger crocks, bottom of page) 660

Three Decorated Crocks Made by J. Burger, Rochester, New York

Long Island Crock with Rare Design & Jug

Crock, cylindrical w/molded rim & eared handles, rare cobalt blue stenciled design of a spread-winged eagle below the impressed mark of maker Brown Brothers, Huntington, Long Island, New York, grease stain spot on hairline from the base on back, minor stone ping on front, ca. 1890, 2 gal., 9" h. (ILLUS. right with Brown & Bros. jug).. **468**

Rare White & Son Heron-decorated Crock & Two Whites Jugs

Crock, wide cylindrical form w/thick molded rim & eared handles, dark cobalt blue slip-quilled rare design of a large walking heron w/its head down & flanked by small trees, impressed mark of N.A. White & Son, Utica, New York, professional restoration to a tight hairline on the left side & minor surface wear around the rim, ca. 1870, 2 gal., 9" h. (ILLUS. left with two jugs from the Whites pottery) **7,700**

A Decorated Advertising Crock & Two Jugs Made in Bennington, Vermont

Crock, Flowerpot & Preserve Jar Made in Fort Edward, New York

Crock, advertising-type, cylindrical w/a thick molded rim & eared handles, cobalt blue slip-quilled large chicken pecking at corn, impressed advertising for Cornells & Mumford, Providence, Rhode Island, unsigned but attributed to Norton of Bennington, Vermont, excellent condition, ca. 1865, 2 gal., 9 1/2" h. (ILLUS. center with two marked Bennington jugs, bottom previous page) **3,300**

Crock, cylindrical w/a thick molded rim flanked by eared handles, cobalt blue slip-quilled tall dotted & swirled leafy plume, blue-tinted impressed mark of the New York Stoneware Co., Fort Edward, New York, one interior rim chip, couple of glaze flakes on the side, ca. 1880, 2 gal., 9 1/2" h. (ILLUS. left with a flowerpot & preserve jar made in Fort Edward, New York, top of page) **495**

Crock, cylindrical w/molded rim & eared handles, cobalt blue brushed & slip-quilled large stylized double blossoms on fanned leaves below the impressed mark of F.J. Elliott & Co., Penn Yan, New York, rare mark, few minor flake spots on base, ca. 1870, 2 gal., 9 1/2" h. (ILLUS. left with two other decorated New York crocks, center page 44) **523**

Crock, cylindrical w/molded rim & eared handles, cobalt blue large slip-quilled singing bird on a log, unsigned, some surface chipping on interior rim, stone ping at base, minor glaze wear along base, ca. 1880, 2 gal., 9 1/2" h. (ILLUS. right with two other bird-decorated pieces, top page 29) **495**

Crock, cylindrical w/molded rim & eared handles, cobalt blue slip-quilled large spade-shaped flowers on ribbed leafy stem, impressed mark of Edmands & Co., Charleston, Massachusetts, some use staining, ca. 1870, 2 gal., 9 1/2" h. (ILLUS. center with scarce bird-decorated table-top butter churn & unsigned jug, bottom page 18) **209**

Crock, cylindrical w/molded rim & eared handles, cobalt blue slip-quilled large plump long-tailed bird on a leafy blossom stem below the impressed mark of Whites, Utica, New York, tight crack from rim in front to left handle, some rim chipping, in-body spider crack touching the design, glaze flaking on back, ca. 1865, 2 gal., 9 1/2" h. (ILLUS. left with two other bird-decorated Whites, Utica crocks, bottom of page) **330**

Three Bird-decorated Crocks from Whites, Utica, New York

Three Early Crocks from New York State

Crock, cylindrical w/molded rim & eared handles, cobalt blue slip-quilled long singing bird perched on a long S-scroll twig below the blue-tinted impressed mark of Haxstun & Co., Fort Edward, New York, few glaze flakes on back, ca. 1870, 2 gal., 9 1/2" h. (ILLUS. right with two other bird-decorated crocks from Fort Edward, New York, top page 45) **495**

Crock, cylindrical w/molded rim & eared handles, cobalt blue slip-quilled large fan-tailed running bird on feathered stem, impressed mark for Whites, Utica, some chipping on left handle, couple interior rim chips, some design fry, small tight clay separation on rim, ca. 1865, 2 gal., 9 1/2" h. (ILLUS. right with two other bird-decorated Whites, Utica crocks, bottom previous page) **688**

Crock, cylindrical w/molded rim & eared handles, dark cobalt blue slip-quilled delicate running bird w/a wide fanned tail perched on a slender stem w/fern-like leaf, impressed mark of Whites, Utica, New York, ca. 1865, 2 gal., 9 1/2" h. (chip at left handle, minor surface chipping at front rim)... **523**

Crock, cylindrical w/thick molded rim & eared handles, dark cobalt blue slip-quilled design of a large plump dotted hen pecking at corn, unsigned but probably New York state origin, ca. 1880, 2 gal., 9 1/2" h. (very tight crack on back, a minor chip on back rim)............................... **523**

Crock, bulbous ovoid body w/a wide slightly flared mouth flanked by eared handles, large brushed cobalt blue tulip design below the impressed mark of C. Hart & Co., Ogdensburg, New York, & impressed number, some glaze spider cracks & crazing on back, ca. 1855, 2 gal., 10" h. (ILLUS. right with two other New York state crocks, top of page)............................ **220**

Crock, wide ovoid body tapering to a wide molded rim & eared handles, cobalt blue slip-quilled long-tailed bird perched on a squiggle branch, impressed mark of J.A. & C.W. Underwood, Fort Edward, New York, ca. 1865, 2 gal., 10 1/4" h. (some rim chips, T-shaped very tight hairline at base, another short one up from base on left, stone ping on bottom right side, apparent filled-in lamp hole at back base) **495**

Very Early Incised Crock & Jug

Three Bird-decorated Pieces Made in Fort Edward, New York

Crock, wide ovoid body tapering to a wide flat incised neck flanked by upturned loop handles, deeply incised & cobalt blue-trimmed intricate pinwheel or snowflake design on the front & back, probably early New York City origin, glued cracks up the front & back into bottom of design, old surface chipping, stained from use, ca. 1800, 2 gal., 11 1/2" h. (ILLUS. left with early Hartford jug, bottom previous page) **880**

Crock, cylindrical w/molded rim & eared handles, fine cobalt blue slip-quilled design of a dotted hen pecking at corn, blue-tinted impressed mark of Haxstun & Co., Fort Edward, New York, some design fry, short clay separation line about right handle, few minor glaze flakes, minor interior glaze wear, ca. 1870, 3 gal., 9 1/2" h. (ILLUS. right with two other bird-decorated pieces from Fort Edward, New York, top of page) **1,760**

Crock, cylindrical w/narrow molded wide mouth flanked by eared handles, dark cobalt blue slip-quilled large shaded triple-petaled flower above a leafy stem w/two spotted buds & flanked by script size numbers below the impressed & blue-tinted mark of T. Harrington, Lyons, New York, ca. 1850, 3 gal., 9 3/4" h. (professional restoration to tight hairline in front through design, few overglazing spots, tight short hairline extending from back rim, interior wear) **248**

Crock, bulbous ovoid body w/a wide slightly flared mouth flanked by eared handles, cobalt blue slip-quilled antler design below a number, impressed mark of John B. Caire & Co., Pokeepsie (sic), New York, very tight hairline behind one handle, X-shaped body spider crack by other, heavy wear to interior brown Albany slip glaze, fairly uncommon maker, ca. 1850, 3 gal., 10" h. (ILLUS. left with two other New York state crocks, top previous page) **220**

Crock, cylindrical w/a molded rim & eared handles, large cobalt blue brushed blos-

som above a leafy stem below the impressed mark of N. Clark, Jr., Athens, New York, & a size number, full-length glued crack on back, couple of interior surface chips at rim, ca. 1850, 3 gal., 10" h. (ILLUS. left with two other flower-decorated pieces, center page 43) **198**

Rare "Wedding Proposal" Portrait Crock

Crock, cylindrical w/a thin molded rim & eared handles, a unique cobalt blue slip-quilled design with a large bust portrait of a young moustached man facing a pretty young woman & proposing marriage, impressed & blue-tinted mark for the Pottery Works, Little West, 12 St., New York, ca. 1870, rim chips, very minor tight hairlines overall, 3 gal., 10" h. (ILLUS.) **10,450**

Crock, cylindrical w/heavy molded rim flanked by eared handles, cobalt blue large slip-quilled fat oblong tornado or beehive design below a script size number & the impressed mark of Burger & Co., Rochester, New York, ca. 1877, 3 gal., 10" h. (grease stain spots on back & left side issuing from very tight in-body cracks) **187**

Extremely Rare Crock with Two Other Pieces Made in New York State

Crock, cylindrical w/molded rim & eared handle, cobalt blue exceptional slip-quilled large fat hen pecking at corn, unsigned but probably made in New York state, some minor use staining, full-length tight crack on back, ca. 1880, 3 gal., 10" h. (ILLUS. center with very rare Brady & Ryan crock & Brady & Ryan jug, top of page) **743**

Crock, cylindrical w/molded rim & eared handle, cobalt blue exceptional slip-quilled large, detailed scene of a two-masted sailing ship, impressed mark of Brady & Ryan, Ellenville, New York, minor use staining, hairline above the right handle, some minor surface flaking on back, ca. 1885, extraordinary piece, 3 gal., 10" h. (ILLUS. left with a Brady & Ryan jug & another New York crock, top of page) **10,725**

Crock, cylindrical w/molded rim & eared handles, cobalt blue slip-quilled long, small paddletailed bird on a long leafy stem near the bottom, impressed mark of White & Wood, Binghamton, New York, two stone pings in the design, some glaze flaking & stone pings on back, some chipping on rim, ca. 1885, 3 gal., 10" h. (ILLUS. center with another crock & jug made in Binghamton, New York, bottom of page) **550**

Crock, cylindrical w/molded rim & eared handles, cobalt blue slip-quilled fan-tailed bird perched on leafy stem near the bottom, impressed mark of White & Wood, Binghamton, New York, couple of chips behind right handle & long glued crack up from the base near this handle, ca. 1885, 3 gal., 10" h. (ILLUS. center with large cream pot & double poppy-decorated crock, top page 34) **578**

Crock, cylindrical w/molded rim & eared handles, dark cobalt blue slip-quilled design of a stem w/a pair of very large pointed leaves & a pair of small leaves w/a large drooping three-petal orchid blossom issuing from the top, impressed mark of N.A. White & Son, Utica, New York, ca. 1870, 3 gal., 10" h. (professional restoration to rim chips & a hairline on the back, restoration & probably replacement of left handle) **198**

Crock, cylindrical w/flared molded rim & eared handles, cobalt blue slip-quilled design of two ribbed oblong leaves above a thick feathered short stem, impressed size number & mark of J.M. Pruden, Elizabeth, New Jersey, ca. 1870, 3 gal., 10 1/2" h. (fairly large surface chip at side of base, stone ping in left handle) **99**

Rare Crocks & a Jug Made in Binghamton, New York

Parrot & Bird-decorated Pieces from Whites, Utica

Crock, cylindrical w/molded rim & eared handles, cobalt blue slip-quilled large plump bird w/wide dropping tail perched on a blossom & fern leaf stem, impressed mark of Whites, Utica, New York, full-length glued crack along bottom & up back, some surface chipping all along rim, short hairline down from rim, ca. 1865, 3 gal., 10 1/2" h. (ILLUS. center with two other bird-decorated Whites, Utica crocks, bottom page 47)........................... **330**

Crock, cylindrical w/molded rim & eared handles, cobalt blue slip-quilled large bird w/droopy tail perched on a blossom & fern leaf branch, impressed mark of Whites, Utica, New York, professional restoration to glaze flaking, ca. 1865, 3 gal., 10 1/2" h. (ILLUS. center with bird and parrot-decorated jugs from Whites, Utica, top of page).. **908**

A Rare Crock & Two Jugs Made in Troy, New York

Crock, cylindrical w/molded rim & eared handles, cobalt blue slip-quilled handsome bird perched on a fenced panel enclosing the date "1871," impressed mark of the West Troy Pottery, Troy, New York, some use staining, ca. 1871, 3 gal., 10 1/2" h. (ILLUS. left with two jugs made in Troy, New York) **2,970**

Rare Crock, Jug & Preserve Jar From Bennington, Vermont

Crock, cylindrical w/molded rim & eared handles, cobalt blue slip-quilled detailed design of a large standing striped stag flanked by a tree stump & fir tree, impressed mark of J. & E. Norton, Bennington, Vermont, professional restoration to full-length lines in the front & back, ca. 1855, 3 gal., 10 1/2" h. (ILLUS. center with fine jug & preserve jar made in Bennington, Vermont, bottom previous page) **5,500**

Crock, cylindrical w/molded rim & eared handles, fine cobalt blue slip-quilled design of a fat bird on a swirled twig, blue-tinted impressed mark & size number for Ottman Bros. & Co., Fort Edward, New York, few interior surface chips, some exterior staining, stack mark at base front, ca. 1870, 3 gal., 10 1/2" h. (ILLUS. left with two other bird-decorated pieces from Fort Edward, New York, top page 49) **550**

Crock, cylindrical w/thick molded rim & eared handles, cobalt blue slip-quilled leafy wreath enclosing a size number below the impressed & blue-washed mark of Burger & Co., Rochester, New York, ca. 1877, 3 gal., 10 1/2" h. (heavy use staining, heavy chipping on right handle) **176**

Crock, cylindrical w/thick molded rim & eared handles, cobalt blue slip-quilled plumb bird w/head raised perched on a squiggle branch, impressed mark of Ottman Bros. & Co., Fort Edward, New York, ca. 1870, 3 gal., 10 1/2" h. (long U-shaped glued crack around right handle)..... **198**

Crock, cylindrical w/thick molded rim & eared handles, cobalt blue slip-quilled large five-petaled daisy flowers on a stem w/large oblong ribbed leaves below a script size number & the oval impressed & blue-tinted mark of Burger & Lang, Rochester, New York, ca. 1870, 3 gal., 10 1/2" h. (couple of minor glaze spider cracks, short tight hairline down from rim to right of design) **468**

Crock, cylindrical w/thick molded rim & eared handles, cobalt blue slip-quilled design of a flying bird chasing a butterfly, unsigned, probably New York state origin, surface chipping on inner & outer rim, two hairlines extending from rim at front & back of left handle, ca. 1880, 3 gal., 10 1/2" h. **495**

Crock, cov., pail-shaped, cylindrical w/wide flat rim, eared handles & a low slightly stepped cover w/disk finial, cobalt blue brushed open-sided oval design w/ribbing along the lower half, impressed & blue-tinted mark of E.S. Fox, Athens, New York, ca. 1840, 3 gal., 11" h. (significant design fry, some use staining & minor surface wear) **303**

Crock, cylindrical w/molded rim & eared handles, cobalt blue slip-quilled plump long-tailed bird on a leafy branch, impressed mark & size number for the New York Stoneware Co., Fort Edward, New York, professional restoration to a full-length crack in back of left handle & one in front of right handle, ca. 1870, 3 gal., 11" h. (ILLUS. center with two other bird-decorated crocks from Fort Edward, New York, top page 45) **413**

Crock, cylindrical w/molded rim & eared handles, large cobalt blue slip-quilled dotted flower design all across the front, impressed mark of Whites, Utica, New York, use staining, few glaze flakes, ca. 1865, 3 gal., 11" h. (ILLUS. left with two other decorated crocks by Whites, Utica, center page 38)... **248**

Crock, wide ovoid body w/a very wide flat mouth flanked by eared handles, cobalt blue large brushed triple flower decoration below the blue-washed impressed mark of Norton & Fenton, East Bennington, Vermont, T-shaped tight hairline touching design at right, lime-stained from use, few surface chips at rim, ca. 1840, 3 gal., 12" h. (ILLUS. center with two Bennington jugs, bottom of page) **165**

A Bennington Crock & Two Jugs

Crock, bulbous ovoid body w/a wide slightly flared mouth flanked by eared handles, cobalt blue large brushed stylized flower & stem below the blue-trimmed impressed mark "Manufactured for and Sold by Chapman & Thorp, Oxford, NY," rare mark, probably Albany area, cinnamon-colored glaze, stack marks, 3 gal., 12 1/2" h. (ILLUS. center with two other New York state crocks, top page 48) **743**

Crock, tall ovoid body w/a wide lopsided rim flanked by upturned loop shoulder handles, blue trim at impressed mark & handles, mark of C. Crolius, Manufacturer, Manhattthen Wells, New York, some chipping from use at base, minor crow's foot & glaze spider at shoulder, ca. 1800, 3 gal., 13" h. **990**

Unusual Covered Miniature Crock

Crock, cov., miniature, wide ovoid body tapering to a rim incised w/fine bands below the high flat-topped cover w/matching bands, eared side handles, brown clay, excellent condition, ca. 1880, 3 1/2" h. (ILLUS.) **143**

Crock, cylindrical w/thick molded rim & eared handles, cobalt blue fancy brushed tightly scrolled large & small clusters on a large scrolling stem below the impressed & blue-washed mark of O.L. & A.K. Ballard, Burlington, Vermont, 19th c., 4 gal. (ILLUS. bottom row, far left, with full page of various stoneware pieces, page 27) **118**

Crock, cylindrical w/thick molded rim & eared handles, cobalt blue slip-quilled long angled leafy branch across the front centered by a large round striped & dotted flower, impressed mark of Frye & Burrill, Orange, Massachusetts, 19th c., 4 gal. (ILLUS. top row, left, with the full-page of various stoneware pieces, page 27)... **118**

Crock, cylindrical w/a thin molded rim & eared handles, dark cobalt blue large slip-quilled decoration of a fancy stylized floral design w/two oblong ribbed buds above a stem w/incurved scrolls & open-ribbed leaves above a pair of horizontal oblong ribbed leaves at the base, design somewhat resembles animal face, impressed & blue-tinted size number & mark of D. Weston, Ellenville, New York, ca. 1870, 4 gal., 10" h. (professional restoration to a full-length crack on right side, large interior stone ping near the bottom)... **440**

Crock, cylindrical w/a molded mouth & eared handles, cobalt blue slip-quilled design of three five-lobed dotted blossoms issuing from a thick feathered stem w/two long ribbed serpentine leaves below, impressed & blue-tinted mark of C. Hart, Sherburne, New York, ca. 1870, 4 gal., 11" h. (full-length very tight hairline on back) **303**

Crock, cylindrical w/a molded rim & eared handles, dark cobalt blue slip-quilled large triple leaf cluster enclosing the size number below the impressed mark of Burger & Co., Rochester, New York, excellent condition, ca. 1877, 4 gal., 11" h. (ILLUS. left with two other decorated Rochester-made crocks, bottom page 43) **468**

Parrot-decorated Crock & Jug by F.B. Norton & Company

Two Jugs & a Crock Produced in Fort Edward, New York

Crock, cylindrical w/molded rim & eared handles, cobalt blue slip-quilled large parrot perched on a plumed leaf below the impressed mark of F.B. Norton & Co., Worcester, Massachusetts, freeze line three-quarters of the way around the base, ca. 1870, 4 gal., 11" h. (ILLUS. left with F.B. Norton jug with parrot design, bottom previous page) 330

Crock, cylindrical w/molded rim & eared handles, cobalt blue slip-quilled plump singing bird w/its head pointed up & perched on a scrolling twig, impressed mark of Ottman & Bros., Fort Edward, New York, minor glaze spiders & use staining, ca. 1870, 4 gal., 11" h. (ILLUS. center with two jugs made in Fort Edward, New York, top of page)...................... 468

Crock, cylindrical w/molded rim & eared handles, cobalt blue slip-quilled large crossed love birds beside a number & squiggle below the impressed mark of S. Hart, Fulton, New York, tight hairline down from back rim & another up from base on back, ca. 1875, 4 gal., 11" h. (ILLUS. center with two other decorated New York crocks, center, page 44) 963

Crock, cylindrical w/thick molded rim & eared handles, cobalt blue brushed design of three large tulip-like flowers above slip-quilled stems & curved leaves below a script size number & the impressed oval & blue-tinted mark of J. Burger, Jr., Rochester, New York, ca. 1885, 4 gal., 11" h. (some design fry, a few use stains) 385

Crock, cylindrical w/thick molded rim & eared handles, cobalt blue slip-quilled large petaled cabbage flower on a stem above long oblong ribbed leaves below the script size number & the impressed oval & blue-tinted mark of Burger Bros., Rochester, New York, ca. 1869, 4 gal., 11" h. (two stone pings & stain spots flanking the design, tight Y-shaped hairlines under each handle) 330

Crock, cylindrical w/thick rounded molded rim & eared handles, cobalt blue slip-quilled design of a large multi-lobed conical & dotted flower on a stem over long leaves, a script size number above, impressed mark of C.W. Braun, Buffalo, New York, ca. 1870, 4 gal., 11" h. (large chip & some glaze flaking at front base, short tight hairline down from rim on front, grease stain spots)..................................... 165

Crock, wide cylindrical form w/a molded rim & eared handles, cobalt blue brushed short large-blossomed flower tree above the date "1893," lightly impressed & blue-tinted mark of Athens Pottery, Athens, New York, ca. 1893, 4 gal., 11" h. (tight in-body crack on base, long surface chip at back rim, few minor use stain spots)....... 385

Crock, cylindrical w/a molded rim & eared handles, cobalt blue slip-quilled large cluster of three pointed leaves on a squiggled stem, impressed & blue-tinted mark of Geddes, New York, ca. 1870, 4 gal., 11 1/2" h. (front rim surface chip, some minor staining, tight crack up from bottom on back, minor glaze burn at bottom front) 143

Crock, cylindrical w/a molded rim & eared handles, dark cobalt blue large brushed flower flanked by tall leaves below the impressed mark of Martin White flanked by impressed size numbers, extremely rare Rochester, New York, potter, two very tight glued cracks on back, ca. 1847, 4 gal., 11 1/2" h. (ILLUS. right with two other decorated Rochester-made crocks, bottom page 43)... 880

Crock, cylindrical w/molded rim & eared handles, cobalt blue slip-quilled large folk art bird w/ruffled breast feathers & a short head comb, perched on a scrolled & dotted branch, unsigned but probably New York state origin, ca. 1880, 4 gal., 11 1/2" h. (few glaze flakes & a drip stain on right of bird, two chips at base).............. 248

Crock, cylindrical w/molded rim & eared handles, large dark cobalt blue slip-quilled dotted & ribbed bird standing on a very long curved fern-like leaf up around the front side, impressed & blue-tinted mark of W. Roberts, Binghamton, New York, ca. 1860, 4 gal., 11 1/2" h. (very tight long spider cracks on side & back, overall tan clay color from the firing) 1,073

Cornucopia-decorated Crock & Two Pieces by A.O. Whittemore

Crock, cylindrical w/thick molded rim & eared handles, wonderfully detailed dark cobalt blue slip-quilled large cornucopia overflowing w/flowers, grapes & fruit above a size number, unsigned but Midwestern, probably from Ohio, glaze drip to left of design, very tight hairline up from base on back, ca. 1860, 4 gal., 11 1/2" h. (ILLUS. left with signed Whittemore pieces, top of page) **1,815**

Crock, wide bulbous ovoid body tapering to a wide molded mouth flanked by eared handles, cobalt blue slip-quilled large double poppy blossoms on a large leafy stem, impressed & blue-trimmed mark of Whites, Binghamton, New York, stack mark at tip of left flower, some interior lime staining, somewhat overglazed in firing, ca. 1860, 4 gal., 11 1/2" h. (ILLUS. right with large cream pot & small bird-decorated crock, top page 34) **633**

Crock, cylindrical w/molded rim & eared handles, cobalt blue slip-quilled long-tailed upright bird perched on a horizontal fern-like leaf, impressed & blue-tinted mark of E. & L.P. Norton, Bennington, Vermont, 4 gal., 11 3/4" h. (chips) **764**

Crock, cov., wide swelled cylindrical body w/a thick molded rim flanked by eared handles, w/original large flat cover marked "John Bell - Waynesboro," Pennsylvania, dark cobalt blue slip-quilled profuse bands of flowering vines around the sides & on the cover, slip-quilled date "1874" below each handle, impressed Bell mark on one side w/hand-inscribed size number, further signed w/a "J" on one side & a "B" on the other, a tightly glued hairline behind the right handle, small pie-shaped reglued piece in back, rare, ca. 1874, 4 gal., 13" h. (ILLUS. center with the unsigned jar & water cooler, bottom of page) **11,550**

Crock, wide swelled cylindrical body w/a thick molded rim & eared handles, cobalt blue large slip-quilled rose blossom among scrolling leafy stems, impressed mark of Haxstun & Co., Fort Edward, New York, stone pings on back & inside, ca. 1870, 4 gal., 13 1/2" h. (ILLUS. center with two other pieces made in Fort Edward, New York, top of page 20) **633**

Rare John Bell Decorated Crock with an Unsigned Jar & Water Cooler

A Vermont-made Crock & Two Jugs

Crock, bulbous ovoid body w/a very wide flat mouth flanked by eared handles, a simple brushed ochre flower design on the front, impressed size number & the mark of L. Norton & Son, Bennington, Vermont, professional restoration to a full-length hairline at left of design, ca. 1830, 4 gal., 14" h. (ILLUS. left with two Vermont-made jugs, top of page)................ **495**

Crock, cylindrical w/thick molded rim & eared handles, cobalt blue slip-quilled large fan-tailed bird in a stepping pose on a leafy branch flanked by size numbers, impressed mark at top of A.O. Whittemore, Havana, New York, professional restoration to significant cracks & chips overall, ca. 1870, 5 gal., 12" h. (ILLUS. right with crock with cornucopia & other signed Whittemore piece, top previous page) **1,925**

Crock, cylindrical w/molded rim & eared handles, very rare cobalt blue slip-quilled large landscape scene w/a reclining stag on a mound w/a tree & rail fence, a two-story house & fir tree in the background, blue-tinted impressed mark of J. & E. Norton, Bennington, Vermont, minor surface chipping on interior rim & handles, very minor glaze wear on interior bottom, very minor hairline at left handle, ca. 1855, 5 gal., 13" h. (ILLUS. right with other rare pieces made in Vermont, bottom of page)... **23,650**

Crock, cylindrical w/molded rim & eared handles, great cobalt blue brushed deco-ration w/a rectangular panel near the rim enclosing "Five" & the date "1864" at the bottom, a center band flanked by pairs of scrolled leaves, unsigned but probably western Pennsylvania origin, fine Civil War era piece, tight hairline extending from rim through the painted panel, very tight lines at bottom flanking the date, very tight & Y-shaped long hairline from bottom on back, some use staining on the lower half, 5 gal., 13 1/2" h. (ILLUS. left with eagle-decorated churn & other unsigned crock, bottom page 21)................ **990**

Crock, cylindrical w/molded rim & eared handles, cobalt blue slip-quilled large dotted & ribbed partridge walking on a mound w/leafy scrolls, a large size number on each side of it, blue-tinted impressed mark of A.O. Whittemore, Havana, New York, professional restoration to hairlines & glaze flakes, ca. 1870, 6 gal., 12 1/2" h. (ILLUS. left with Whittemore churn & jug, bottom page 19) **1,210**

Crock, cylindrical w/a flat flared molded rim & eared handles, dark cobalt blue large slip-quilled decoration of a large hen standing on a rounded mound & pecking at scattered corn, a tall grass sprig at each side of the mound, illegible lightly impressed mark but probably New York state, ca. 1870, 6 gal., 13" h. (surface chip at front rim, overglazing, a few glaze spider cracks overall) **688**

Three Rare Decorated Pieces Made in Vermont

Crock, wide ovoid body tapering to a molded rim fitted w/a wooden cover, early handles, finely done cobalt blue slip-quilled large double poppy blossoms on a long-leaved stem, blue-trimmed impressed size number & mark of Whites, Binghamton, New York, couple of minor surface chips at bottom, short clay separation at rim on back, ca. 1860, 6 gal., 13 1/2" h. (ILLUS. right with a small crock & jug made in Binghamton, New York, bottom page 50) **3,410**

Early Indiana Stoneware Crock

Crock, wide ovoid body tapering to a wide molded mouth flanked by eared handles, overall dark greenish brown glaze, impressed size number & mark for C.M. Dustin, Jeffersonville, Indiana, late 19th c., 6 gal., 15 1/4" h. (ILLUS.) **288**

Stoneware Crock with Profile Portrait

Crock, cylindrical w/molded flat rim & eared handles, cobalt blue slip-quilled bust profile portrait of a Victorian-style lady wearing a blossom-form cap, attributed to Macquoid & Co. Pottery Works, New York City, some minor staining, tight hairline down from rim, few other short in-the-making hairlines at base & rim, ca. 1870, 1 gal., 7" h. (ILLUS.) **4,620**

Large Singing Bird on Unsigned Crock

Crock, cylindrical w/molded rim & eared handles, cobalt blue slip-quilled large singing bird w/head comb, unsigned but probably Massachusetts, large slightly indented stack mark on back, ca. 1870, 1 gal., 7" h. (ILLUS.) **633**

Small Crock with Orchid Decoration

Crock, cylindrical w/molded rim & eared handles, dark cobalt blue slip-quilled large ribbed orchid decoration below impressed mark "N.A. White & Son - Utica, NY," ca. 1870, 1 gal., 7" h. (ILLUS.) **330**

Norton Crock with Leaf Cluster

Crock, cylindrical w/molded rim & eared handles, cobalt blue slip-quilled large dotted & stylized leaf cluster below the impressed mark "E. & L. P. Norton - Bennington, VT," couple of minor interior rim chips, clay separation line in front left handle, ca. 1880, 1 gal., 7 1/2" h. (ILLUS., bottom previous page) **495**

Norton & Co. Crock with Plume Design

Crock, cylindrical w/thick molded rim & eared handles, cobalt blue slip-quilled dotted & stylized large plume design below the impressed mark "F.B. Norton and Co. - Worcester, Mass.," interior clay separation on the back, overall excellent condition, ca. 1870, 1 gal., 7 1/2" h. (ILLUS.).. **275**

Advertising Crock with Tulip Decoration

Crock, cylindrical w/wide molded flat rim & eared handles, large cobalt blue brushed tulip & leaves design, advertising-type, blue-trimmed impressed store mark of C.A. Becker, Wilkes Barre, Pennsylvania, attributed to the Sipe factory in Williamsport, Pennsylvania, professional restoration to overall glaze flaking, ca. 1870, 1 gal., 7 1/2" h. (ILLUS.).................... **143**

Pail-shaped Crock with Flower & Leaves

Crock, tapering cylindrical pail-shaped w/thick molded rim & eared handles, cobalt blue brushed simple flower & leaves, impressed & blue-trimmed mark "D. Mooney - Ithaca, NY," rare mark, somewhat overglazed in firing, ca. 1862, 8" h. (ILLUS.).. **330**

Six-quart Crock with Horse Picture

Crock, cylindrical w/molded rim & eared handles, cobalt blue brushed & sponged picture of a standing horse below an impressed "6," probably New York State, stone ping below left handle, minor use wear, ca. 1870, 6 qt., 8" h. (ILLUS.).......... **4,400**

Crock, wide ovoid form tapering slightly to a flat molded rim flanked by eared handles, cobalt blue slip-quilled word "Bread" framed by three large tornado designs on the front & the word "Bread" w/a dotted dragonfly design on the reverse, unsigned, Midwest origin, large X-shaped spider crack below one handle, mottled clay color from firing, ca. 1870, 8 gal., 15" h. (ILLUS. center with eagle-decorat-

ed churn & other unsigned crock, bottom
page 21) **1,595**

Early Albany Crock with Blue Number

Crock, wide ovoid body tapering to a wide
flat mouth flanked by eared handles,
brushed cobalt blue "1" below the impressed & blue-trimmed mark of Tyler &
Dillon, Albany, New York, minor crow's
foot spider crack under right handle, ca.
1825, 1 gal., 8 1/2" h. (ILLUS.) **248**

E.S. Fox Crock with Bird Decoration

Crock, cylindrical w/eared handles, slip-
quilled cobalt blue bird on the front, impressed mark for E.S. Fox, Athens
trimmed in blue, Athens, New York, professional restoration to two long tight
hairlines on front, couple of rim chips,
overall tan color clay, ca. 1840, 2 gal.,
9" h. (ILLUS.) **578**

Crock, cylindrical w/molded rim, cobalt blue
slip-quilled stylized fishing lure design
flanked by S-scrolls, unsigned but Midwestern origin, mottled clay color from
the firing, ca. 1880, 2 gal., 9" h. (ILLUS.,
top next column) **385**

Midwestern Crock with Fishing Lure Design

Crock with Large Feather Wreath Decor

Crock, cylindrical w/molded rim & eared
handles, cobalt blue slip-quilled large
feather wreath enclosing a numeral "2,"
impressed mark for Burger & Co., Rochester, New York, minor use staining, ca.
1877, 2 gal., 9" h. (ILLUS.) **495**

Crock with Fluffy-tailed Bird Decor

Crock, cylindrical w/molded rim & eared handles, cobalt blue slip-quilled bird w/long fluffy tail on a serpentine branch, impressed mark "Brady & Ryan - Ellenville, NY - 2," professional restoration to a few tight hairlines at base, ca. 1885, 2 gal., 9" h. (ILLUS., bottom previous page) 550

Crock with Large Singing Bird Design

Crock, cylindrical w/molded rim & eared handles, cobalt blue slip-quilled large singing bird on a scroll twig, impressed vendor mark "E. & N. Brownson - Troy, NY - 2," probably from Fort Edward Pottery, very minor glaze spider in front, minor stone ping on back, ca. 1870, 2 gal., 9" h. (ILLUS.) 605

Crock with Nice Pecking Hen Design

Crock, cylindrical w/molded rim & eared handles, cobalt blue slip-quilled design of

a hen pecking at corn on the ground, unsigned, professional restoration to tight hairline on front, some minor surface chipping, ca. 1870, 2 gal., 9" h. (ILLUS.) 688

Crock with Stenciled Starburst & Number

Crock, cylindrical w/molded rim & eared handles, cobalt blue stenciled starburst centering a large "2" on the front, probably Ohio origin, chip on back, ca. 1880, 2 gal., 9" h. (ILLUS.) 121

Crock with Blue Dotted Orchid Design

Crock, cylindrical w/molded rim & eared handles, dark cobalt blue slip-quilled large dotted orchid decoration, impressed mark "White & Wood - Binghamton, NY - 2," some minor staining & interior rim chip, ca. 1885, 2 gal., 9" h. (ILLUS.)... 303

Cortland, New York Crock with Fancy Flower & Stem Design

Crock, cylindrical w/molded rim & eared handles, fancy cobalt blue slip-quilled curly stems w/four flowers below impressed mark "Cortland - 2," Cortland, New York, ca. 1860, 2 gal., 9" h. (ILLUS.) **688**

Stained Crock with Tulips Decoration

Crock, cylindrical w/molded rim & eared handles, large bold brushed cobalt blue leafy stem w/two large tulip blossoms flanked by two "2" numerals below the impressed mark "Lyons," Lyons, New York, use staining & tight hairline through the design, ca. 1860, 2 gal., 9" h. (ILLUS.)... **165**

Early Repaired Crock with Vine Design

Crock, ovoid body w/a short wide flat neck flanked by heavy incurved loop handles, deeply incised & cobalt blue-trimmed vine design on the front & back, blue accents on handles, unsigned, ca. 1830, professional restoration to surface chips, one handle replaced, 1 gal., 9 1/2" h. (ILLUS.)... **143**

flower side w/a stack mark, glaze drip, very minor surface chip under glaze, Albany, New York, ca. 1807, 1 1/2 gal., 9 1/2" h. (ILLUS.) **2,530**

Bennington Crock with Fancy Leaf Design

Crock, wide ovoid body tapering slightly to a wide flat molded rim flanked by eared handles, cobalt blue slip-quilled large scrolling stylized leaf decoration below the impressed mark "J. & E. Norton & Co. - Bennington, VT," minor glaze drip & interior rim chip, ca. 1855, 1 1/2 gal., 9 1/2" h. (ILLUS.) **358**

Advertising Crock with Large Hen

Crock, advertising-type, cylindrical w/molded rim & eared handles, slip-quilled cobalt blue large hen pecking at corn, impressed advertising for Cornells & Mumford, Providence, Rhode Island, above a "2", unsigned Norton of Bennington pieces, ca. 1865, 2 gal., 9 1/2" h. (ILLUS.)... **3,300**

Early Cinnamon Red Cushman Crock

Crock, wide ovoid body w/a wide flat mouth flanked by eared handles, brushed cobalt blue accents through the deeply impressed mark at handles, a three-petal lightly brushed blue flower on the back, further enhanced w/a deeply tooled diamond & leaf design around the rim, cinnamon-colored clay color in the making,

Ovoid Crock from Short-lived Pottery

Crock, bulbous ovoid body tapering to a wide flaring flat mouth flanked by eared handles, simple brushed cobalt blue leaf design below the blue-trimmed impressed mark of J. Clark & Co., Troy, New York, short-lived factory, couple of surface chips at rim, ca. 1826, 2 gal., 9 1/2" h. (ILLUS.) **358**

Crock with Fanned Plume Decoration

Crock, cylindrical w/molded rim & eared
handle, dark cobalt blue slip-quilled
fanned triple plume decoration below impressed mark "Geddes, NY - 2," some
use staining, ca. 1870, 2 gal., 9 1/2" h.
(ILLUS.).. **248**

Unsigned Crock with Hen Pecking Corn

Crock, cylindrical w/molded rim & eared
handles, cobalt blue slip-quilled hen
pecking at corn, unsigned but probably
Poughkeepsie or Ellenville, New York,
overall use staining, ca. 1870, 2 gal.,
9 1/2" h. (ILLUS.) **413**
Crock, cylindrical w/molded rim & eared
handles, cobalt blue slip-quilled large
ribbed scrolling "antler" design, marked
by Edmands & Co., chip at rim, overall
dark use staining, couple of old spider
lines at sides & backs & a short hairline at
rim on back, ca. 1870, 3 gal., 9 1/2" h.
(ILLUS., top next column) **99**

Stained Crock with Unusual Design

Unique Crock with a Camel Scene

Crock, wide cylindrical form w/molded rim &
eared handles, cobalt-blue slip-quilled
decoration of a standing camel w/palm
trees & a pyramid in the distance, impressed mark of Wm. A. Macquoid & Co.,
Little Wst. 12th St., New York, New York,
small rim chip on front, tight full-length
hairline on back, ca. 1870, 1 1/2 gal.,
10" h. (ILLUS.) **12,650**

Fat Bird & Leaf Decor on Three-gallon Crock

Crock, cylindrical w/molded rim & eared handles, cobalt blue slip-quilled fat bird w/head up perched on a small leafy sprig, impressed mark "Ottman Bros. & Co. - Fort Edward, NY - 3," professional restoration to full-length hairline on front, ca. 1870, 3 gal., 10" h. (ILLUS., bottom of previous page) **209**

Crock with Large Pinwheel Flower Design

Crock, cylindrical w/molded rim flanked by eared handles, cobalt blue large slip-quilled pinwheel flower on leafy stem, impressed mark "C.W. Braun - Buffalo, N.Y. - 3," stone ping on right side, somewhat mottled clay color, minor glaze use wear, ca. 1870, 3 gal., 10" h. (ILLUS.) **220**

Norton Sons Crock with Large Dove

Crock, cylindrical w/thick molded rim & eared handles, cobalt blue slip-quilled large dove perched on a long slender sprig below the impressed mark "F.B. Norton Sons - Worcester, Mass. - 3," significant design fry in blue, minor surface wear & use staining, ca. 1886, 3 gal., 10" h. (ILLUS.) **330**

Crock, cylindrical, w/cobalt decoration of long-beaked bird on a cherry branch, impressed "6," 10" h. **495**

Ft. Edward Crock with Stylized Design

Crock , cylindrical w/a molded rim & eared handles, cobalt blue slip-quilled large stylized scrolling leaf & flower cluster, impressed mark of Haxton, Ottman & Co., Fort Edward, NY, overglazed in the making, very minor staining, ca. 1870, 3 gal., 10 1/2" h. (ILLUS.) **110**

Crock with Large Triple-leaf Decoration

Crock, cylindrical w/molded flat mouth & eared handles, dark cobalt blue slip-quilled large triple-leaf design w/the large leaf enclosing the numeral "3," impressed mark "Burger & Co. - Rochester, NY," use staining, ca. 1869, 3 gal., 10 1/2" h. (ILLUS.)...................................... **248**

Crock, cylindrical w/molded rim & eared handle, dark cobalt blue slip-quilled slender bird w/crest perched on a leafy sprig design below the impressed mark "E. & L. P. Norton - Bennington, VT - 3," small stone ping in the design w/minor stain, stabilized hairline from rim on the back, ca. 1880, 3 gal., 10 1/2" h. (ILLUS., top next page) **633**

Bennington Crock with Slender Bird

F.B. Norton Crock with Hen Decoration

Crock, cylindrical w/molded rim & eared handle, dark cobalt blue slip-quilled hen pecking at corn design below the impressed mark "F. B. Norton & Co. - Worcester, Mass. - 3," fairly rare, somewhat overall dry glaze, ca. 1870, 3 gal., 10 1/2" h. (ILLUS.) **3,850**

Crock with Large Fancy Floral Design

Crock, cylindrical w/molded rim & eared handles, cobalt blue slip-quilled large stylized ribbed & dotted floral design, impressed mark of Ottman Bros., Fort Edward, New York, quarter-size surface chip at front rim, small rim chips over handle, in-body glaze spider line, cinnamon clay color, ca. 1870, 3 gal., 10 1/2" h. (ILLUS.).. **165**

Crock with Bold Bird in Brush Decoration

Crock, cylindrical w/molded rim & eared handles, very dark, large & bold cobalt blue slip-quilled decoration of a large bird hiding in brush, probably New York state, overall design fry, ca. 1870, 3 gal., 10 1/2" h. (ILLUS., bottom previous page) **3,190**

Fine Stag Design on Whites Crock

Crock, cylindrical w/molded rim flanked by eared handles, dark cobalt blue slip-quilled standing stag looking back over his shoulder below the blue-trimmed impressed mark "Whites Utica - 3," in-the-making dry glaze, slight design fry, minor use staining, ca. 1865, 3 gal., 10 1/2" h. (ILLUS.).. **3,190**

Crock Decorated with a Large Robin

Crock, cylindrical w/thick molded rim & eared handles, cobalt blue slip-quilled design of a large robin perched on a leafy plume below the impressed mark "Haxstun & Co. - Fort Edward, NY - 3," some minor use staining, ca. 1870, 3 gal., 10 1/2" h. (ILLUS.) **1,430**

Crock with Rare Paul Cushman Mark

Crock, wide ovoid body w/a wide flat mouth flanked by eared handles, a large block letter mark impressed at the shoulder & washed in cobalt blue reading "Paul: Cushman Stoneware Factory," only known piece w/this style mark, large stone ping through part of the mark, restoration to a full-length hairline, Albany, New York, ca. 1807, 1 gal., 11" h. (ILLUS.).. **1,980**

Norton Crock with Long Bird Design

Crock, wide ovoid body tapering slightly to a wide flat molded rim flanked by eared handles, cobalt blue slip-quilled long-bodied bird on sprig below the impressed mark "J. Norton & Co. - Bennington, VT - 2," professional restoration to hairlines in front, ca. 1861, 2 gal., 11" h. (ILLUS.) **358**

Crock with "Dancing Flower" Design

Woodruff Crock with Double Blossoms

Crock, cylindrical w/molded rim & eared handles, cobalt blue brushed design of two blossoms on stem below impressed mark "M. Woodruff & Co. - Cortland - 3," Cortland, New York, glued surface chip above right handle, ca. 1870, 3 gal., 11" h. (ILLUS.) **165**

Crock, cylindrical w/molded rim & eared handles, cobalt blue slip-quilled "dancing flower" design & numeral "4" below the impressed mark "Burger Bro's & Co. - Rochester, NY," long J-shaped hairline from rim on the back, some use staining, ca. 1869, 4 gal., 11" h. (ILLUS.) **220**

Advertising Crock with Hen Decoration

Crock with Large Singing Bird Design

Crock, cylindrical w/molded rim & eared handles, advertising-type, cobalt blue slip-quilled hen pecking at corn decoration below impressed name "Thos. Losee Jr. - Grocer. - Dobbs Ferry. N.Y.," professional restoration to extensive cracking in back, ca. 1870, 4 gal., 11" h. (ILLUS.) **468**

Crock, cylindrical w/molded rim & eared handles, cobalt blue slip-quilled large singing bird on dotted plume design, lightly impressed mark of T.F. Connolly Manufacturer, New Brunswick, New Jersey, overall use stain, ca. 1870, 4 gal., 11" h. (ILLUS.) **523**

Crock with Unusual Noah's Ark Decoration

Crock, cylindrical w/molded rim & eared handles, cobalt blue slip-quilled unusual Noah's Ark design below the impressed mark "A.O. Whittemore - Havana, N.Y. - 4," some use staining, chip below right handle, minor stone ping on front, ca. 1870, 4 gal., 11" h. (ILLUS., above) **3,080**

mark "N.A. White & Son - Utica, NY - 4," professional restoration to long hairlines throughout, ca. 1870, 4 gal., 11" h. (ILLUS.) **385**

White & Son Crock with Large Bird

Crock, cylindrical w/molded rim & eared handles, dark cobalt blue slip-quilled large bird w/large paddle tail & perched on a flowering leafy sprig, impressed mark "N.A. White & Son - Utica, NY - 4," professional restoration to large chip at front base, some overall use staining, ca. 1870, 4 gal., 11" h. (ILLUS.) **798**

Crock with Large Paddle-tailed Bird

Crock, cylindrical w/molded rim & eared handles, dark cobalt blue slip-quilled large bird w/large paddle tail & perched on a flowering leafy branch, impressed

Double Blossoms on Three-gallon Crock

Crock, slightly tapering cylindrical body w/molded rim & eared handles, cobalt blue slip-quilled double blossoms on a curly stem below the impressed mark "M. Woodruff - Cortland - 3," few minor surface chips at rim, minor use staining, ca. 1870, 3 gal., 11 1/2" h. (ILLUS.)............... **220**

Crock with Bold Triple Flower Design

Crock, cylindrical w/molded rim & eared handle, dark cobalt blue slip-quilled large triple spade-shaped floral design beside a numeral "4" & below impressed mark "W.H. Farrar - Geddes, NY," full-length glued hairlines all around, ca. 1850, 4 gal., 11 1/2" h. (ILLUS.) **330**

Crock with Fancy Leaf & Blossom Design

Crock, cylindrical w/flared molded rim & eared handles, cobalt blue slip-quilled ornate scrolling dotted leaf & blossom design across the front, impressed mark "Troy, NY - Pottery - 4," some glaze flake spots, couple of very tight spider lines in design, surface wear at rim & some stack marks, ca. 1870, 4 gal., 11 1/2" h. (ILLUS.).. **220**

Crock with Large Double Flower Design

Crock, cylindrical w/molded rim & eared handles, cobalt blue slip-quilled large double spiral blossoms & fancy dotted leaves below the impressed mark "Haxstun & Ottman - Fort Edward, NY - 4," tight full-length spidered lines on side & back, ca. 1870, 4 gal., 11 1/2" h. (ILLUS.).. **110**

Crock with Elegant Tulip Decoration

Crock, cylindrical w/molded rim & eared handles, cobalt blue slip-quilled large tulip on leafy stem w/a numeral "4" to one side, impressed mark for Burger Bros. & Co., Rochester, New York, minor chip at front base, very minor staining, ca. 1869, 4 gal., 11 1/2" h. (ILLUS.)............................. **330**

Crock, cylindrical w/thick molded rim & eared handles, cobalt blue slip-quilled parrot flanked by large plumes below the impressed mark "F.B. Norton & Co. - Worcester, Mass. - 4," professional restoration to tight freeze line around base &

sides, interior surface rim chips, ca. 1870, 4 gal., 11 1/2" h. (ILLUS., below).... **1,210**

Crock with Large Parrot & Plumes Design

Crock, cylindrical w/thick molded rim & eared handles, cobalt blue slip-quilled folk art scene of a crudely drawn two-story house w/a sidewalk & steps leading to a large fir tree, front of house w/number "4" for size designation, impressed mark of C.W. Braun, Buffalo, New York, very tight hairline on front into design, several in-the-making stack marks, surface chipping around rim, ca. 1870, 4 gal., 11 1/2" h. (ILLUS., bottom of page) **7,425**

Crock with Folk Art House & Tree Design

Crock with Double Blossoms Design

Crock, cylindrical w/molded rim & eared handles, cobalt blue brushed & slip-quilled arched blossoms on a leafy stem decoration below the impressed mark "A.O. Whittemore - Havana, N.Y. - 5," some use staining & minor rim chip, ca. 1870, 5 gal., 11 1/2" h. (ILLUS.)................... **275**

Crock with Large Crossed Lovebirds

Crock, cylindrical w/molded rim & eared handles, cobalt blue slip-quilled large crossed lovebirds on leafy crossed branches below an impressed "5," no factory mark, professional restoration to a freeze line all around the base, full-length hairline to left of design, ca. 1870, 5 gal., 12" h. (ILLUS.) **1,100**

Covered Crock with Flower Decoration

Crock, cov., cylindrical w/molded rim & eared handle, domed cover w/brown Albany slip trim lightly impressed "Burger - 3," base decorated w/a cobalt blue slip-quilled five-petal flower above leaves & a script "3" w/the impressed mark "Burger Bro's & Co. - Rochester, NY," cover probably not original, restoration to very minor cover chip, base w/some rim chips, ca. 1869, 3 gal., 12" h. (ILLUS.)......................... **358**

Simple Early Paul Cushman Crock

Crock, ovoid body w/a short wide cylindrical neck w/flat rim flanked by eared handles, undecorated, made by Paul Cushman, Albany, New York, ca. 1807, professional repair to tight lines from bottom & halfway up sides, 1 1/2" gal., 12 1/2" h. (ILLUS.)...... **743**

Crock with Rare Spread-winged Bird & Wreath Decoration

Crock, cylindrical w/molded rim flanked by eared handles, unusual dark cobalt blue brushed decoration of a large spread-winged bird within a floral wreath, impressed mark of N.A. White & Son, Utica, New York, professional restoration to tight lines on front, ca. 1870, 5 gal., 12 1/2" h. (ILLUS., above)......................... **3,960**

Six-gallon Crock with Large Bird Decor

Crock, cylindrical w/molded rim & eared handles, cobalt blue slip-quilled large bird on a thick ribbed branch, impressed mark "Weston & Gregg - Ellenville, NY - 6," short-lived mark, Y-shaped line along the bottom that extends to left handle, ca. 1869, 6 gal., 12 1/2" h. (ILLUS.) **1,155**

Boldly Decorated John Bell Crock

Crock, cov., ovoid w/eared handles & a wide molded rim, heavy brushed cobalt blue bands of leafy flowering vines around the sides & on the cover, also blue-slip date "1874" under each handle, impressed mark of John Bell, Waynesboro, Pennsylvania, tightly glued hairline behind right handle, small piece reglued, ca. 1874, 4 gal., 13" h. (ILLUS.).. **11,550**

Crock with Very Rare Decoration

Crock, cylindrical w/eared handles & molded rim, slip-quilled cobalt blue extremely detailed scene of a large reclining stag & fence in the foreground & a large house & tree in the distance, impressed mark of J. & E. Norton, Bennington, Vermont, & a "5," minor surface chipping to rim interior, very tight minor hairline in left handle, ca. 1855, 5 gal., 13" h. (ILLUS., at left)........ **23,650**

Crock, ovoid w/flared mouth & eared handles, incised w/horizontal lines & two codfish on front, "Boston" & "JF" on reverse, Jonathan Fenton, Boston, ca. 1794-97, minor chips, 13" h. **6,000-6,500**

Crock, ovoid w/wide flat molded rim & loop shoulder handles, deeply incised around the shoulder w/a clamshell swag accented w/cobalt blue, impressed mark "N. York - Corlears - Hook - Commeraws" trimmed in blue, stack mark on one side w/minor surface wear along base, ca. 1805, approx. 2 gal., 13" h. (ILLUS., bottom of page).. **5,390**

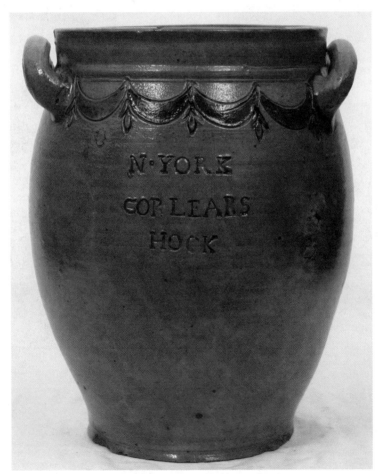

Rare Early New York Stoneware Crock

side, ca. 1870, 5 gal., 13" h. (ILLUS., be-low) 330

Crock with Large Double-flower Design

Crock, cylindrical w/molded flat mouth & eared handles, dark cobalt blue slip-quilled large two-flower on leafy stem design below a numeral "5" & the impressed mark "J. Burger, Jr. - Rochester, NY," some use staining, tight in-body hairline, some design fry, ca. 1885, 5 gal., 13" h. (ILLUS.).. **550**

Crock with Ribbed Flower & Leaves

"Lyons" New York Decorated Crock

Crock, cylindrical w/molded rim & eared handles, cobalt blue delicate slip-quilled script word "Lyons," blue script "5," impressed mark of J. Fisher, Lyons, New York, some surface roughness at rim, overall light tan clay, ca. 1880, 5 gal., 13" h. (ILLUS.) **275**

Crock, cylindrical w/molded rim flanked by eared handles, cobalt blue large slip-quilled ribbed flower blossom on a stem above four large leaves, impressed mark "C.W. Braun - Buffalo, N.Y. - 5," minor stack marks on front, stone ping on

Large Stencil-decorated Crock

Crock, tall cylindrical body tapering slightly to the molded rim flanked by eared handles, ornate stenciled decoration w/a large rose blossom & leaves above a large "5" over a large spread-winged eagle, a brushed cobalt blue band around the shoulder, faint marking but probably from the Star Pottery, mottled clay color from the firing, ca. 1880, 5 gal., 15 1/2" h. (ILLUS.).. **605**

Very Rare Crock with Great Folk Art Landscape

Crock, wide slightly ovoid body w/a wide flat mouth & eared handles, wonderful dark cobalt blue slip-quilled folk art design w/a large palm tree, standing dotted stag & fir tree below a numeral "6" & the impressed mark "John Burger, Rochester," Rochester, New York, couple of minor surface rim chips, minor kiln burn, ca. 1865, 6 gal., 16" h. (ILLUS.) **48,950**

Large Crock with Bold Peacock in Tree Decoration

Crock, cylindrical w/thick molded rim above a narrow crimped raised band & eared handles, unusual cobalt blue slip-quilled large dotted peacock perched in a large leafy tree below an upper zigzag & dotted upper band, unsigned but possibly by Martin White, Fort Dodge, Iowa, or Monmouth Pottery, Monmouth, Illinois, few minor interior & surface rim chips, ca. 1870, 10 gal., 16" h. (ILLUS., bottom previous page).. **15,950**

Nicely Stenciled Large Stoneware Crock

Crock, slightly swelled cylindrical body tapering slightly to a molded rim flanked by eared handles, large cobalt blue stenciled design w/a spread-winged American eagle w/shield surrounded by the marking "T.F. Reppert - Eagle Pottery - Greensboro, PA," free-hand blue band of foliate scrolls around the shoulder & "10" at the bottom front, imperfections, late 19th c., 10 gal., 21" h. (ILLUS.)................ **2,875**

Marked Three-gallon Crock Cover

Crock cover, round w/the middle in a dark brown Albany slip glaze, molded in relief "Hart Bros. - Fulton, NY - 3," excellent condition, ca. 1870, 11" d. (ILLUS.).............. **33**

Dark Brown Stoneware Lion Doorstop

Doorstop, figural, model of a low crouching lion on a heavy rectangular block base, overall dark brown Albany slip glaze, novelty piece attributed to the Lyons Factory, New York, surface wear to face, tail or back apparently either broken off or left unglazed, ca. 1870, 9" l., 5" h. (ILLUS.)... **55**

Drying or cooling rack, a wide flat-bottomed round form w/low flat sides raised on four tapering tab feet, a thick high arched handle from side to side, the entire inner bottom pierced w/rows of thin oblong holes, Bristol glaze w/a wide blue band on the handle, impressed mark of The Hansom & Van Winkle Co., ca. 1890, 11" d., 9" h. (tight crack through rim just to left of name, glued hairline at base of left handle end) **468**

Flask, figural, model of a standing pig, Bristol glaze w/applied brown mottled glaze, probably from Ohio, minor glaze spider crack, rare form, ca. 1900, 5" l. **523**

Flask, figural, model of a recumbent pig, applied brown alkaline glaze, one side incised "St. Louis R.R. & R. Guide with a little fine old bourbon," other side incised w/map of a railroad line & "Anna Pottery," anatomically correct bottom incised w/"Cincinnati - Ohio River," Anna, Illinois, late 19th c., excellent condition, 7 1/2" l., 3 1/2" h.. **6,325**

Flask, flattened ovoid body tapering sharply to a small molded mouth, undecorated, probably New York state origin, unusual small size, ca. 1830, 6" h. (somewhat overglazed in firing, age crazing to glaze) **413**

Simple Early Stoneware Flask

Flask, flattened ovoid body w/small neck, light tan, unsigned & undecorated, some staining from use, stone chip at shoulder, ca. 1830, 1 pt., 7" h. (ILLUS.)....... **154**

Early Dark-glazed Stoneware Flask

Flask, flattened ovoid body tapering to a molded mouth, unsigned, overall dry dark tan glaze, small remnants of original paper label on shoulder, minor surface chip on mouth, ca. 1830, 1 pt., 7 3/4" h. (ILLUS.)... **99**

Early Flattened Stoneware Flask

Flask, flattened ovoid form tapering to a small molded mouth, undecorated & unsigned, ca. 1830, 1 pt., 7 3/4" h. (ILLUS.)... **143**

Flask, flattened ovoid body w/small neck, light tan, unsigned & undecorated, age spider cracks from use, ca. 1830, 1 pt., 8" h. (ILLUS. middle with two other early flasks, top next page)..................................... **77**

Flask, flattened ovoid body w/small neck, overall dark brown alkaline glaze w/dark glaze accent band around the body, unsigned, ca. 1830, 8" h. (ILLUS. right with two other early flasks, top next page) **209**

Early Brown-glazed Stoneware Flask

Flask, thin flattened ovoid body w/small neck, overall dark brown alkaline glaze, minor surface wear at neck, ca. 1830, 7" h. (ILLUS.) **176**

Three Early Stoneware Flasks

Flask, flattened ovoid body w/small neck, tan mottled clay, undecorated, unsigned, ca. 1830, 8" h. (ILLUS. left with two other early flasks, above) **176**

Long, Flattened Early Stoneware Flask

Flask, long flattened ovoid body w/small neck, light tan, unsigned & undecorated,

crazing spiders around base, possibly from the making, ca. 1830, 8" h. (ILLUS.) **88**

Flask, tall slender flattened ovoid form tapering to a small molded mouth, decorated down the shoulder w/four repeated cobalt blue brushed long fern-like leaves, unsigned, design attributed to the Remmy factory of Philadelphia, ca. 1830, 8" h. (stack mark in blue design on one side, signs of overglazing on one side, professional restoration to mouth chip, long surface chip on bottom).................... **1,650**

Tall Slender Early Stoneware Flask

Flask, tall thin flattened ovoid form tapering to molded mouth, undecorated & unsigned, excellent condition, ca. 1830, 1 pt., 9" h. (ILLUS.) **275**

Flowerpot & attached underplate, tapering cylindrical form w/a deep underplate, overall mustard yellow alkaline glaze, ca. 1880, 7 1/2" h. (dime-sized chip at rim) **55**

Stoneware Brown & Tan Flowerpot

Flowerpot w/attached saucer base, wide tapering cylindrical form w/a tooled rope band near the rim, dark brown glaze accented w/a light tan pyramid design inside & out, unsigned, probably New York state origin, excellent condition, ca. 1880, 5 1/2" h. (ILLUS.) **88**

Flowerpot w/attached underplate, flaring cylindrical form w/wide low cylindrical underplate, overall dark brown mottled alkaline glaze, impressed mark of Haxstun & Co., Fort Edward, New York, very minor rim wear on underplate, ca. 1870, 2 gal., 11" d., 9" h. (ILLUS. right with crock & preserve jar made in Fort Edward, New York, top page 47) **303**

Flowerpot w/attached underplate, wide tapering cylindrical form w/deep underplate, brushed decoration of two stylized ochre flowers on the side, unsigned, uncommon form & color, use staining but overall excellent condition, ca. 1860, 5" h. (ILLUS. second from right with vase, crock, shard & jar, bottom page 36) **385**

Flowerpot w/attached underplate, inverted bell-shape w/deep flared underplate, overall nut brown alkaline glaze, molded relief drape designs at the rim w/molded flowers around body, impressed marks on front & back for West Troy Pottery, New York & number "3," excellent condition, ca. 1880, 8" d., 7" h. (ILLUS. far left with three other varied pieces, top page 37) **248**

Garden ornament, figural sewer tile-type, modeled as a realistic snapping turtle w/fine detailing, dark brown glaze, probably early 20th c., 9 1/2" l., 3 1/2" h. (minor surface wear) **209**

Humidor, cov., nearly spherical Bristol-glazed body molded w/an overall delicate diamond design background w/a high-relief figure of a hunting dog trimmed in cobalt blue on the front, a few minor glaze flakes, minor flake on domed cover, ca. 1900, 6 1/2" h. (ILLUS. second from right with two bean pots & other humidor, top page 14)...................... **132**

Humidor, cov., swelled base tapering to cylindrical sides, Bristol glaze w/overall delicate molded diamond background & a molded wave & shell design trimmed in cobalt blue around the swelled base, low domed cover w/a small figural finial of a snake w/a man's head also trimmed in blue, professional restoration to surface chips on cover, ca. 1900, 7 1/2" h. (ILLUS. second from left with two bean pots & other humidor, top page 14) **176**

Humidors & a match holder, three bulbous nearly spherical humidors, two w/domed covers, two molded in relief w/a hunting dog decorated in cobalt blue & the third smaller one w/a molded blue-decorated horse head, the tapering cylindrical match holder decorated around the base w/a blue band, 19th c., the group (ILLUS. second row down at the left side with the full page of various other stoneware pieces, page 27)...................... **235**

Ink bottle, small cylindrical body w/short conical neck & molded mouth, impressed mark of The Henry Stephens Ink Company, unsigned by maker, late 19th c., 5 1/2" h. (mottled clay color from firing, ink-stained) **11**

Inkwell, short flattened cylindrical form w/a large center hole in the top surrounded by three small holes, cobalt blue brushed accents on sides & on the impressed mark of M. Tyler, Albany, New York, Manufacturer, ca. 1840, 4 1/2" d., 1 3/4" h. (two large chips on side through the mark).. **275**

Inkwell, small cylindrical body w/flattened shoulder centered by a small molded neck, mottled brown glaze, minor surface wear & staining, 19th c., 2" d. (ILLUS. far left with three other inkwells, bottom of page)... **55**

Row of Early Stoneware Inkwells

Two Unsigned Jars & a Decorated Pitcher

Inkwell, low wide cylindrical form w/a flat top pierced w/a large center hole & two smaller holes to one side, blue decoration on the top, accented with four impressed snowflake or star designs, attributed to M. Woodruff, Cortland, New York, chips at base, some tight hairlines up from base, ca. 1850, 3 1/2" d., 1 1/2" h. (ILLUS. far right with three other inkwells, bottom previous page) **440**

Inkwell, wide low cylindrical form, the flat top pierced w/a large central hole & three smaller holes along one edge, unsigned & undecorated, few body chips, tight glaze spider crack on bottom, ca. 1830, 3 1/2" d., 1 3/4" h. (ILLUS. second from left with three other inkwells, bottom previous page) **33**

Inkwell, low wide cylindrical form w/a molded reeded band around the body, redware w/a dark brown mottled glaze, minor surface wear, ca. 1850, 4" d., 1 1/2" h. (ILLUS. second from right with other inkwells, bottom previous page) **99**

Jar, cov., advertising-type, wide cylindrical form w/rounded shoulder to a cupped rim w/inset cover, impressed on the shoulder "Geo. E. Wales - Newton Centre Mass.," unsigned by maker, short hairlines & long glued rim chip on back, surface rim chip at front, some use staining, ca. 1870, 1 pt., 6" h. (ILLUS. far right with vase, crock, shard & flowerpot, bottom page 36) **55**

Jar, bulbous ovoid body tapering to a wide flat mouth, cobalt blue large brushed four-leaf sprays around the sides, unsigned but probably Pennsylvania or Virginia, ca. 1830, 1/2 gal., 8" h. (mottled clay color from firing, some surface chipping along base, two minor hairlines down from rim) **132**

Jar, wide ovoid body tapering to a very wide flat mouth flanked by large eared handles, cobalt blue large triple flower on stem design, brushed size number on the back, unsigned but attributed to Ingell factory, Taunton, Massachusetts, mottled clay color, short glaze spider at base, interior glaze wear from use, ca. 1840, 1/2 gal., 8" h. (ILLUS. left with other unsigned jar & pitcher, top of page) **495**

Jar, wide ovoid body tapering to a very wide flat mouth flanked by large eared handles, cobalt blue small three-petal flower on leafy stem on one side, brushed size number on the back, unsigned but attributed to the Ingell factory, Taunton, Massachusetts, overall use stain, ca. 1850, 1/2 gal., 8" h. (ILLUS. right with other 1/2 gallon jar & decorated pitcher, above) **495**

Jar, nearly cylindrical form w/narrow molded flat rim, thin overall vertical ribbing around the sides typical of Southern pottery, dark glaze, impressed size number, unsigned but probably Carolina origin, ca. 1900, 3 qt., 9 1/4" h. (chip at base of back) **55**

Jar, cylindrical tapering slightly to a molded rim & eared handles, cobalt blue brushed stylized tulip blossom on stem, attributed to Elizabeth Bell, daughter of John Bell, Waynesboro, Pennsylvania, 1 gal., 7 1/4" h. **978**

Jar, simple ovoid body tapering to a thick flat molded rim flanked by large eared handles, cobalt blue brushed design of a delicate leaf band around the shoulder, unsigned but probably southern Pennsylvania or Virginia origin, ca. 1830, 1 gal., 8 1/4" h. (stack marks at center of body on one side) **798**

Early Decorated Utica Jar & Two Large Jugs

Jar, wide ovoid body tapering to a short flared neck flanked by eared handles, cobalt blue large swirled stylized flower on leafy stem, impressed & blue-trimmed mark on neck for D. Roberts & Co., Utica, New York, surface chips on rim, three tight hairlines from rim, chip on right handle, ca. 1828, 1 gal., 9" h. (ILLUS. center with two 2-gallon jugs, above)........... **248**

Jar, nearly cylindrical tapering slightly to a thin molded flat mouth, cobalt blue scattered brushed plume designs around the rim, impressed mark of W.H. Lehew & Co., Strasburg, Pennsylvania, ca. 1880, 1 gal., 9 1/2" h. (couple of rim chips, broken into two pieces & reglued).................... **110**

Jar, simple ovoid body tapering to a molded rim, cobalt blue brushed band of upswept leaves alternating w/blossoms around the shoulder, unsigned, ca. 1850, 1 gal., 9 1/2" h. (large kiln burn spot on one side, mottled clay color from firing, minor chipping at base) **187**

Jar, wide ovoid body tapering to a narrow molded rim flanked by eared handles, dark cobalt blue brushed design decorated w/two wide leafy stems ending in rounded blossoms arching away from each other above a thick horizontal cluster on front & back, unsigned but Shenandoah Valley, Pennsylvania,

origin, ca. 1850, 1 gal., 10" h. (some very old surface chips & roughness along base)... **935**

Jar, bulbous ovoid body tapering to a small molded mouth & strap handle, cobalt blue brushed "spitting" flower on leafy stem design typical of this factory, impressed & blue-trimmed mark of G. Heiser, Buffalo, New York, stack marks at shoulder, chips at mouth & underneath handle, clay discoloration from the firing, early Buffalo potter, ca. 1838, 1 gal., 11" h... **550**

Jar, cov., wide cylindrical form tapering to a low wide molded rim w/flat inset cover w/disk finial, eared handles, cobalt blue large slip-quilled stylized flowerpot w/looping flowers below an impressed size number, unsigned, 19th c., 2 gal. (ILLUS. third row down, far right, w/full page of various other stoneware pieces, page 27)................. **323**

Jar, swelled cylindrical body tapering to a wide flat & flared mouth flanked by eared handles, cobalt blue slip-quilled large scrolling plume design, blue-tinted impressed mark of C. Hart & Son, Sherburne, New York, couple of rim chips, ca. 1860, 2 gal., 10 1/2" h. (ILLUS. right with two jugs made in New York state, bottom of page)... **385**

A Jar & Two Jugs Made at Various New York State Potteries

Three Decorated Jars from Lyons, New York

Jar, wide bulbous ovoid body tapering to a flat narrow & slightly flared neck flanked by eared handles, lightly brushed cobalt blue "2" below the blue-washed impressed mark of N. White, Utica, New York, long surface glazed-over chip at left rim, few other surface chips on rim, ca. 1840, 2 gal., 10 1/2" h. (ILLUS. center with two crocks by various New York potters, top page 40) **275**

Jar, cylindrical body tapering gently to a wide short flared mouth flanked by eared handles, cobalt blue slip-quilled stylized large mustached & bearded man's face on the front below the impressed & blue-washed mark of A. MacQuoid & Co., Little West, 12th St., New York, mid-19th c., 10 5/8" h. (repaired, minor interior rim chips).. **1,528**

Jar, cylindrical body tapering slightly to a flat, flared rim flanked by eared handles, dark cobalt blue brushed large double flower on stem w/large leaves below a size number & the blue-tinted mark "Lyons," Lyons, New York, tight hairline down from rim, large base chip on back,

minor design fry, ca. 1860, 2 gal., 10 3/4" h. (ILLUS. left with two other Lyons, New York, jars, top of page)................. **413**

Jar, bulbous ovoid body tapering to a low flaring rim flanked by eared handles, cobalt blue brushed leaf sprig & size number below the blue-brushed impressed mark for N. Clark & Co., Lyons, New York, some surface chipping around rim, some pitting on base front, some surface wear & use staining, ca. 1850, 2 gal., 11" h. (ILLUS. center with two other decorated jars from Lyons, New York, above)............................. **165**

Jar, gently tapering cylindrical body w/a wide short cylindrical neck flanked by eared handles, dark cobalt blue large fancy slip-quilled flowers on a leafy stem beside a size number below the impressed mark of F. Stetzenmeyer & G. Goetzman, Rochester, New York, very tight hairline through the bottom & up the sides, short surface chip at base on one side, ca. 1857, 2 gal., 11" h. (ILLUS. right with two other decorated pieces from Rochester, New York, bottom of page).. **1,430**

Three Rare Decorated Pieces Made in Rochester, New York

Early New England Jar & Jugs

Jar, wide cylindrical body tapering slightly to a molded rolled rim flanked by eared handles, cobalt blue slip-quilled large dotted poppy blossom on a tall curved dotted leafy stem, impressed mark of N. White & Co., Binghamton, New York, ca. 1860, 2 gal., 11" h. (spider crack on left side, long in-body spider crack on the back, minor surface wear, use staining) 110

Jar, cylindrical body tapering slightly to a rolled rim flanked by eared handles, unusual dark cobalt blue double-heart design w/blue accents at the handles, impressed "22" at the rim, unsigned, probably New York state origin, minor stone ping in the design, minor chip at base, some use staining, ca. 1870, 2 gal., 11 3/4" h. 743

Jar, cov., bulbous ovoid body tapering to a small cylindrical neck & inset cover w/button finial, eared shoulder handles, cobalt blue stylized flower & leaf design on the shoulder w/blue accents on the handles, three hand-inscribed squiggle lines at the shoulder & rim, unsigned, some surface chipping around the rim, stained from use, early piece, ca. 1830, 2 gal., 12" h. 853

Jar, cylindrical tapering gently to a short flared neck flanked by eared handles, cobalt blue slip-quilled leafy wreath enclosing a size number below the impressed oval & blue-tinted mark of Burger & Lang, Rochester, New York, ca. 1870, 2 gal., 12" h. (some use staining, couple of surface chips on rim, minor glaze spider crack) 303

Jar, cylindrical tapering to a thick molded rim flanked by eared handles, cobalt blue slip-quilled double bull's-eye design below the impressed mark of F.B. Norton & Co., Worcester, Massachusetts, some use staining, ca. 1870, 2 gal., 12" h. (ILLUS. right with decorated crock & jug, bottom page 38) 275

Jar, cov., bulbous ovoid body tapering to a short neck w/inset cover w/knob finial flanked by open loop handles, impressed mark "Boston," ochre or dark brown accents at base & shoulder, attributed to Frederick Carpenter, a few chips at rim & base, ca. 1805, 2 gal., 13" h. (ILLUS. right with two early New England jugs, top of page)... 468

Stoneware Jug, Strainer & Washboard

Two Early Jars & a Smaller Jug

Jar, large bulbous ovoid body tapering to a wide cylindrical neck flanked by lug handles, simple cobalt blue brushed flower design w/blue handle accents, impressed mark of Gilson & Co., Reading, Pennsylvania, a very rare potter, tan clay color, dry glaze from the making, extensive surface wear on back, some use staining, tight hairline up from base on front, ca. 1840, 2 gal., 13" h. (ILLUS. left with strainer & washboard, bottom of previous page) **440**

Jar, wide ovoid body tapering to a short cylindrical neck flanked by eared handles, cobalt blue brushed large pointed blossom & leaves on front, very impressed mark of W. Smith, Greenwich, New York, early New York City, deep glaze flake spots on back, some kiln burns, ca. 1833, 2 gal., 13" h. (ILLUS. left with other larger jar & smaller jug, top of page) **688**

Jar, very bulbous ovoid body tapering sharply to the base & small molded mouth, strap handle, cobalt blue brushed underlined large "2" on the shoulder, impressed & blue-trimmed mark of Whites, Utica, New York, tan clay color & dray glaze from firing, chip at front base, some use staining, ca. 1850, 2 gal., 13 1/2" h. **330**

Jar, cylindrical tapering slightly to a molded rim & eared handles, cobalt blue slip-quilled decoration of a spotted bird on a branch, impressed mark of Edmands & Co., Charlestown, Massachusetts, ca. 1850-55, 2 gal., 14 3/8" h. **529**

Jar, wide cylindrical body tapering to a thin flat molded mouth, eared handles, cobalt blue large brushed wreath branches enclosing a slip-quilled tornado & pointed feather design w/further thin sprigs above & below, unsigned, 19th c., 3 gal. (ILLUS. top row, right, w/the full page of various stoneware pieces, page 27) **147**

Jar, cov., gently tapering cylindrical form w/molded rim, inset cover & eared handle, cobalt blue large slip-quilled singing bird on a slender twig, impressed mark of Riedinger & Caire, Poughkeepsie, New York, long chip on rim, horizontal clay separation below design, ca. 1870, 3 gal., 13" h. (ILLUS. center with two other bird-decorated pieces, top page 29) **358**

Unsigned Decorated Jar & Two Preserve Jars

Jar, wide ovoid body tapering to a wide flat mouth, eared handles, slightly domed cover w/disk handle, cobalt blue large stylized flowers & leafy vines around the sides, impressed size number on front, unsigned, use staining, ca. 1850, 3 gal., 13 1/2" h. (ILLUS. right with two decorated unsigned preserve jars, bottom of previous page).. **495**

Jar, bulbous ovoid body tapering to a wide rolled rim flanked by eared handles, large bold cobalt blue brushed decoration of three large tulip blossoms issuing from a small leafy stem w/long vertical leaves below & slender fern-like leaves flanking script size numbers around the top blossom, impressed & blue-washed mark of Wm. Farrar & Co., Geddes, New York, 19th c., 4 gal. (ILLUS. top row, center, with full page of various stoneware pieces, page 27).. **646**

Jar, advertising-type, slightly swelled cylindrical form w/a thin molded mouth & eared handles, cobalt blue brushed thin bands at top & around base w/another serpentine band near the top above a large, long horizontal serpentine feathery leafed band, script size number near the front base below the stenciled mark reading "Runpoint & McCormick - Dry Goods, - Groceries and - Notions. - Meyersville, W. Va.," unsigned by maker, ca. 1870, 4 gal., 14 1/2" h. (couple of very minor surface chips at base of rim, overglazed in firing at front left) **990**

Jar, cylindrical w/rounded shoulders tapering to a short wide neck w/molded rim, eared shoulder handles, cobalt blue slip-quilled design of a large long-tailed singing bird perched on a large tree stump, impressed mark of Riedinger & Caire, Poughkeepsie, New York, ca. 1870, 4 gal., 14 1/2" h. (minor use staining & kiln burns at base) **2,310**

Jar, ovoid body tapering to a molded mouth flanked by eared handles, cobalt blue overall brushed vines & flowers, impressed size number under each handle, unsigned, mottled clay & somewhat misshapen in the firing, two stack marks touching flowers on one side, ca. 1850, 4 gal., 15" h. (ILLUS. left with rare John Bell covered crock, bottom page 55)............ **495**

Jar, wide ovoid body tapering to a short cylindrical neck flanked by eared handles, cobalt blue brushed four-lobed frame around the impressed mark of C. Crolius, Manufacturer, New York City, brush blue swag design on other side w/blue accents on handles, an incised "X" on the shoulder on back & an incised triangle, surface chipping around rim, short hairline down from rim, stone pings, some chipping around base, ca. 1800, 4 gal., 16 1/2" h. (ILLUS. center with other early jar & smaller jug, top page 84) **1,925**

Jar, cylindrical tapering slightly to a molded rim & eared handles, cobalt blue stenciled decoration of tulip-like flowers & free-hand lines, also stenciled mark of T.F. Reppert, Greensboro, Pennsylvania, mid-19th c., 5 gal., 15 3/4" h. (hairline) **460**

Jar, wide cylindrical body w/a rounded shoulder tapering to a short wide neck w/rolled rim, cobalt blue brushed large horizontal tulip on a leafy stem, attributed to Elizabeth Bell, daughter of John Bell, Waynesboro, Pennsylvania, late 19th c., 7 1/4" h... **978**

Bulbous Jar from Pennsylvania Potter

Jar, wide bulbous ovoid body tapering to a wide flaring mouth, cobalt blue simple brushed flower & leaves design, impressed mark of Sipe & Sons, Williamsport, Pennsylvania, some use staining, three spider cracks from base, ca. 1870, 1 gal., 8" h. (ILLUS.) **176**

Four Southern Stoneware Pieces

Jar, wide ovoid body tapering to thin incised lines at the shoulder below the wide cupped rim, mottled dark brown alkaline glaze, possibly by Jesse P. Bodie, Edgefield District, South Carolina, ca. 1870, small glaze nick near bottom & top rim, 8 1/2" h. (ILLUS. far right with other Southern jugs & preserve jar, bottom of previous page) **546**

pressed mark of S. Blair, ca. 1830, a few stone pings on back, tight hairline up the back from the base, 1 gal., 9" h. (ILLUS.) **248**

S. Blair Jar with Simple Flower Design

Jar Made in Washington, D.C.

Jar, bulbous ovoid body tapering to a wide flat & slightly flared mouth, applied eared handles, simple stylized brushed cobalt blue flower below the blue-trimmed im-

Jar, cylindrical w/molded rim, mottled clay color from the firing, lightly impressed mark "P.F??? - & Co. - Washington, D.C.," ca. 1870, 1 gal., 9 1/2" h. (ILLUS.) **165**

Large Ovoid Jar with Stylized Flower Design

Jar, bulbous ovoid body tapering to a flat cylindrical neck & eared handles, large cobalt blue brushed "lollipop" flower & blue accents, impressed mark of N. Clark & Co., Lyons, New York, stack mark on back & sides, minor surface chip at right handle, ca. 1850, 1 gal., 10 1/2" h. (ILLUS., bottom of previous page) **688**

Two-Gallon Jar with Large Flower

Jar, cylindrical tapering to a short upright rim & eared handles, slip-quilled cobalt blue large stylized flower & leaves w/a number "2" beside them, impressed mark of F. Stetzenmeyer & G. Goetzman, Rochester, New York, washed in blue, very tight line through bottom, surface chip at base of right handle, ca. 1857, 2 gal., 11" h. (ILLUS.) **1,430**

Jar, bulbous ovoid body tapering to a molded band below the short rolled neck, overall light greenish brown alkaline glaze, possibly by John or Amos Landrum, Edgefield District, South Carolina, ca. 1840, 13" h. (missing handles, two small rim chips) **690**

Tall Virginia-made Stoneware Jar

Jar, flat-bottomed ovoid body tapering to a cylindrical neck w/molded rim, eared handles, cobalt blue brushed swag & leaf design around the shoulder & on the neck, mark of J. Keister & Co., Strasburg, Virginia, fairly uncommon maker, misshaping & minor overglazing, some specks of white overpaint, ca. 1880, 2 gal., 13" h. (ILLUS.) **2,420**

Jar, slightly swelled cylindrical body w/lightly molded rings below the rounded shoulder & wide flared mouth, eared shoulder handles, drippy dark brown alkaline glaze, impressed "2," by W.F. Hahn, Trenton, South Carolina, ca. 1880, 2 gal., 13" h. (stable hairline crack) **690**

Jar, bulbous ovoid body tapering to a rolled rim & eared handles, overall dark brown alkaline glaze, marked "2," possibly Alabama, 19th c., minor rim nick, 13 1/2" h. **230**

Jar, wide squatty ovoid body tapering to a wide rolled mouth & eared shoulder handles, overall running dark brown alkaline glaze, by Thomas Owenby, Union District, South Carolina, ca. 1860, chip on rim, 13 3/4" h. (ILLUS. center w/other storage jars, top next page) **575**

Jar, cov., wide ovoid body w/a wide flat rim & eared handles, domed cover w/pointed knob finial, cobalt blue free-form quilled designs around the top of the base & the cover, hairline in the side, some cover chips on flange, unsigned, late 19th c., 14" h. **863**

Early Ovoid Jar Probably from Ohio

Jar, wide ovoid body tapering to a flat flaring rim & eared handles, impressed bluewashed mark of L.H. Worbs, probably from Ohio, glaze burns & stack marks, Albany slip glaze drip on side, overall dry peppery glaze, surface chipping on rim, some glaze wear, ca. 1860, 4 gal., 14" h. (ILLUS.) **633**

Three Stoneware Storage Jars

Extraordinary "Poem" Jar by the Slave Potter "Dave"

Jar, poem-type, very wide bulbous ovoid body tapering to a rolled rim missing a large chunk flanked by eared handles, one w/a chip, overall greenish brown alkaline glaze, produced by the noted slave potter "Dave," who inscribed the shoulder w/the following poem: "Whats better than wishing while we both are at fishing," also signed "Febry 10, 1840. Mr. L. Miles, Dave," Edgefield District, South Carolina, unique & extremely rare, 15" h. (ILLUS.)... **155,250**

Jar, wide bulbous ovoid body tapering to a short rolled mouth flanked by eared handle, mottled overall greenish brown alkaline glaze, stamped "5," possibly by John or Amos Landrum, Edgefield District, South Carolina, ca. 1860, chip on one handle, 5 gal., 16 1/2" h. (ILLUS., next column) **920**

Jar, large bulbous ovoid body tapering to a rolled mouth flanked by eared handles, overall dark greenish brown alkaline glaze, by Ritchie or J.F. Seagle, Catawba Valley, North Carolina, ca. 1880, re-

paired rim & shoulder, 17" h. (ILLUS. right w/other storage jars, top of page) **316**

Large Early Southern Stoneware Jar

Jar, large bulbous ovoid body tapering to a rolled mouth flanked by eared handles, overall dark brown alkaline glaze, indistinct stamped mark on handle, Catawba Valley, North Carolina, late quarter 19th c., 17 1/4" h. (ILLUS. left w/other storage jars, top of page) **316**

Jardiniere, large wide simple ovoid body tapering to a fairly small molded flat mouth flanked by large eared handles, dark cobalt blue wide swagging leaf & flower vine around the upper body w/a unique framed potted flower under each handle, unsigned but probably Pennsylvania origin, ca. 1830, 3 gal., 13 1/2" h. (professional restoration to tight freeze crack around bottom)... **413**

Jug, miniature, beehive shape w/small mouth & strap handle, overall dark brown Albany glaze, incised on the front "Little Brown Jug," attributed to the Norton factory, Bennington, Vermont, ca. 1870, 3" h. **121**

Rare Decorated Miniature Tanware Jug

Jug, miniature, wide ovoid body tapering to a short neck & large loop strap handle, tanware profusely decorated w/dark brown vines & floral trees up each side w/brown accents at the base, mouth & handle, from western Pennsylvania, some overall staining, ca. 1870, 3 1/4" h. (ILLUS.)... **1,210**

Jug, miniature, beehive-shaped, overall dark brown Albany slip glaze incised in script on the front "Little Brown Jug," attributed to a Norton factory, Bennington, Vermont, excellent condition, ca. 1870, 3 1/2" h. **88**

Dark Brown Miniature Handled Jug

Jug, miniature, wide ovoid body tapering to a small mouth & strap handle, dark brown

dry glaze, chip at the mouth, ca. 1860, 3 1/2" h. (ILLUS.) **33**

Jug, miniature, beehive shape tapering to a small molded mouth & strap handle, overall dark brown Albany glaze, darker brown accent stripe around the middle, mid-19th c., 4" h. **33**

Early Miniature Stoneware Jug

Jug, miniature, wide bulbous ovoid body tapering to a short cylindrical neck w/molded rim, applied strap handle, brushed cobalt blue accents on the shoulder, probably New York state or New Jersey origin, very tight old hairline all around the center, ca. 1810, 4" h. (ILLUS.) **523**

Miniature Virginia Whiskey Jug

Jug, miniature, advertising-type, cylindrical w/rounded shoulder tapering to a small cylindrical neck, Bristol glaze w/blue stenciled advertising "Phill. G. Kelly - R - Straight Whiskey - Richmond, VA," ca. 1900, 4 1/2" h. (ILLUS.) **110**

Small Brown Souvenir Jug

Jug, wide flat-bottomed cylindrical body w/a wide shoulder tapering to a small cylindrical neck, front incised "Kickapoo Swizzle - Niagara's 9th Annual Convention," nut brown alkaline glaze, excellent condition, probably early 20th c., 5 1/2" h. (ILLUS.) **33**

Blue-stenciled Mini Advertising Jug

Jug, miniature, advertising-type, cylindrical w/rounded shoulder to the small neck, Bristol glazed w/blue stenciled advertising "Phill. G. Kelly - R - Straight Whiskey - Richmond, VA," excellent condition, ca. 1900, 4 1/2" h. (ILLUS.) **154**

Miniature Ohio Whiskey Advertising Jug

Jug, miniature, advertising-type, ovoid body tapering to a tall cylindrical neck, white Bristol glaze w/blue stenciled marking "Down On The Farm - Farmmato - C.W. Rodefer Co. - Shadyside, Ohio," overall age crazing, ca. 1900, 6 1/2" h. (ILLUS.)..... **121**

Miniature Comic Motto Whiskey Jug

Jug, miniature, motto-type, cylindrical w/conical shoulder to a small neck & strap handle, Bristol glaze w/dark brown upper half & grey lower half decorated w/a stenciled picture of a droopy looking hound dog looking at a whiskey jug above wording "His Master's Breath," excellent condition, ca. 1900, 5" h. (ILLUS.) **44**

Jug, advertising-type, cylindrical w/rounded shoulder to a small cylindrical neck, strap handle, dark brown-glazed shoulder & neck & a band around the bottom, the main body in unglazed tanware stenciled w/"S.T. Suit, - Suitland, MD - Little Brown Jug - The Whiskey in this jug was - made 1869 - and filled by me in 1879," ca. 1870, 7" h. (minor surface wear).................. **578**

Jug with Rare Applied Grape Clusters

Jug, ovoid body tapering to a short neck w/molded mouth & strap handle, dark brown alkaline glaze w/rare applied grape cluster & leaf designs around the sides, unsigned, probably New York state, minor surface chipping at base, ca. 1860, 7 1/2" h. (ILLUS.) **440**

Jug, simple ovoid form tapering to a narrow neck & small mouth & strap handle, overall chocolate brown alkaline glaze, unsigned, probably New York state origin, ca. 1840, 8" h. (minor age crazing to glaze) **132**

Jug, cylindrical body w/wide conical shoulder centered by a small flared neck, loop strap handle from neck to edge of shoulder, overall medium brown alkaline glaze, W.F. Hahn, Trenton, South Carolina, ca. 1880, chip on neck & rim, 8 1/4" h. (ILLUS. second from right with other Southern jug, jar & preserve jar, bottom page 85) **690**

Jug, grotesque face-type, wide bulbous ovoid form molded & incised w/exaggerated facial features including a large grinning mouth w/inset white rock teeth below a wide nose & large oval inset white eyes, large side ears, a small neck at the top & strap handle at the back shoulder, overall dark brown alkaline glaze, by Lanier Meaders, Southern folk artist, Georgia, mid-20th c., slight chipping to one tooth, small firing crack under one tooth on lip, 8 1/4" h. **2,760**

Jug, bulbous ovoid body tapering to a small molded mouth & strap handle, cobalt blue brushed folk art-style stick figure man w/walking stick carrying a tree branch, blue-tinted mark of J. Duntz Manufacturer, New Haven, Connecticut, overall use stain, very tight long old crack up from the base, ca. 1835, 9" h. (ILLUS., top next column) **1,100**

Early Jug with Folk Art Stick Figure

Jug, grotesque-type, wide flat bottom w/bulbous ovoid sides boldly tooled & shaped into a grotesque face w/open mouth, large nose, inset eyes & molded ears, short cylindrical mouth & strap handle at the top, overall green ash running glaze, from Edgefield, South Carolina, handle reglued, ca. 1860s, 9" h. (ILLUS., top next page) **24,725**

Dark Brown South Carolina Jug

Jug, wide swelled cylindrical body w/a wide flattened shoulder centered by a short rolled neck & strap handle, overall very dark brown alkaline glaze, possibly by Baynham, Miles Mill, South Carolina, ca. 1870, 10 1/2" h. (ILLUS.) **489**

Rare Early South Carolina Grotesque Face Jug

Large Stoneware Jug with Man's Face

Jug, wide cylindrical beehive-shaped w/impressed bands around the shoulder, small molded cylindrical neck & small loop shoulder handle, overall light greenish brown alkaline glaze, D.F. Landrum, Edgefield District, South Carolina, ca. 1870, 11" h. (ILLUS. second from left with other Southern jug, jar & preserve jar, bottom page 85) **748**

Jug, cylindrical w/rounded shoulder to a short neck & strap handle, cobalt blue large brushed folk art crescent-shaped feather enclosing the profile of a man, possibly a version of the man-in-the-moon, unsigned, 19th c., 11 5/8" h. (ILLUS., left) **4,888**

Jug, ovoid body tapering to small mouth & strap handle, overall brown alkaline glaze, possibly by J.G. Baynham, North August, South Carolina, ca. 1920, 13 3/4" h.. **316**

Jug, bulbous ovoid body tapering to a small molded neck & stump of broken-off handle, overall dark brown alkaline glaze, B.F. Landrum Sr., Horsecreeke Valley, Edgefield District, South Carolina, ca. 1850, 15 1/2" h... **604**

Small Jug and Group of Blue-banded Mugs

Jug, flat-bottomed wide ovoid body tapering to a small mouth & strap handle, overall dark brown alkaline glaze, impressed mark "Chelsea," Chelsea, Massachusetts, excellent condition, ca. 1840, 1 qt., 6 1/2" h. (ILLUS. third from right with group of mugs) **154**

Four Early Simple Stoneware Jugs

Jug, ovoid body tapering to a small molded mouth & strap handle, undecorated & unsigned, overall tan color, stone ping in handle, ca. 1830, 1 qt., 8 1/2" h. (ILLUS. far right with three other simple early jugs) **121**

A Small Jug, Pitcher, Syrup Pitcher & Storage Jar

Jug, narrow ovoid body tapering to a small molded mouth & strap handle, undecorated except for blue trim at the handle & on the impressed mark of D. Goodale, Hartford, Connecticut, some age spidering in glaze on back, few minor glaze flakes at base, some minor use staining, ca. 1826, 1 qt., 9 1/2" h. (ILLUS. far left with pitcher, syrup pitcher & storage jar) **275**

Jug, beehive-shaped tapering to a warped molded mouth & strap handle, cobalt blue large brushed stylized anchor & flower design across the front, impressed mark of the Clinton Pottery, New York state, probably rarest of New York state pottery marks, professional restoration to several cracks, ca. 1847, 1/2 gal., 7 1/2" h. **715**

Early Unsigned New York Jug

Jug, bulbous ovoid body tapering to a short cylindrical neck w/molded rim, applied strap handle, brushed cobalt blue simple stylized flying bird design, unsigned, probably New York state origin, kiln burn & chip on back base, ca. 1830, 1/2 gal., 8 1/2" h. (ILLUS.) **303**

Later New York Advertising Jug

Jug, advertising-type, cylindrical sides w/rounded shoulder tapering to a molded mouth, applied strap handle, slip-quilled cobalt blue angled wording "Doran - 92 West Main St.," a Rochester, New York store, unsigned by maker, some use staining, somewhat overglazed in the making, ca. 1880, 1/2 gal., 9" h. (ILLUS.) **88**

Jug, beehive-shaped tapering to a small molded mouth & strap handle, cobalt blue brushed antler design, unsigned but attributed to the Cortland, New York pottery, ca. 1860, 1/2 gal., 9" h. (surface chip at mouth, dark tan clay color from firing) **248**

Four Inscribed & Marked Advertising Jugs

Jug, advertising-type, cylindrical tapering to a tapered neck & strap handle, brushed cobalt blue advertising on front for "John O'Neil - Whitehall, - N.Y.," unsigned by maker, professional restoration to neck, long hairline up side from base, ca. 1870, 1/2 gal., 9 1/2" h. (ILLUS. second from left with three other marked advertising jugs).. **198**

Half-gallon New Jersey Advertising Jug

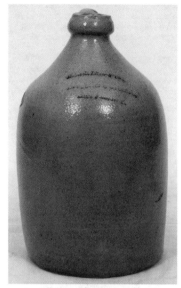

Jug with Impressed Advertising

Jug, flat-bottomed beehive shape tapering to a/small cylindrical mouth & strap handle, advertising-type w/cobalt blue script inscription reading "P.H. Corish - 63-67 Lexington St - Newark - N.J., " glossy Bristol glaze, significant glaze wear & shoulder & handle w/some use staining, ca. 1890, 1/2 gal., 9 1/2" h. (ILLUS.).................................. 132

Jug, ovoid body tapering to a small molded mouth & strap handle, brown & ochre accents at top & base, signed "Charleston," attributed to Frederick Carpenter, Charleston, Massachusetts, long chip at mouth, stack marks, ca. 1805, 1/2 gal., 9 1/2" h. (ILLUS. second from left with three other simple early ovoid jugs, center page 93)... 275

Jug, ovoid body tapering to a small molded mouth & strap handle, cobalt blue brushed plume accent on the shoulder & another accent on the handle, unsigned by possibly Albany, New York, potter, ca. 1830, 1/2 gal., 9 1/2" h. (ILLUS. far left with three other early ovoid jugs, center page 93).. 220

Jug, swelled wide cylindrical body tapering to a small molded mouth & strap handle, advertising-type, unsigned but impressed blue-tinted working "Babcock, Litner & Co. - Druggist & Grocers - Little Falls, N.Y.," stack mark on left shoulder, ca. 1880, 1/2 gal., 9 1/2" h. (ILLUS., top next column)........ 248

Jug, bulbous sharply ovoid body tapering to a small molded mouth & strap handle, redware w/a bold orange & dark brown speckled glaze, unsigned, mid-19th c., 1 gal. (ILLUS. second row down, far right, with full page of various other stoneware pieces, page 27)... 411

Early Jug with Applied Girl Figure

Jug, ovoid body tapering to a short cylindrical neck, applied with a realistic figure of a young African-American girl with one arm wrapped around the neck & shooing a fly with her other hand, when inverted the open skirt reveals anatomic features, hand-incised "Shoo Fly" & "Original Package," overall dark brown glossy glaze, professional restoration to some skirt chipping, Anna M., ca. 1860, 1 pt., 6 1/2" h. (ILLUS.) 7,150

Jug, advertising-type, wide beehive-shaped w/small mouth & strap handle, impressed & blue-tinted mark for "Struven & Wacker - Grocers & Ship Chandlers - Cor. Alice Ann & Chester St. - Baltimore, MD," unsigned by maker, rare inscription, professional restoration to mouth & base chips, replaced handle, ca. 1850, 1 gal., 8 1/2"h. **248**

Early Cylindrical Advertising Jug

Jug, cylindrical w/tapering shoulder to molded small mouth, advertising-type, unsigned by maker, blue-trimmed impressed advertising "C.J. Sturcke & D. Bornman - Grocery & Liquor Stones - 110 South St. and 379 Water Cor Oliver St. N.Y.," overall dark tan clay color, stack mark indent on side, ca. 1840, 1 qt., 8 1/2" h. (ILLUS.) **220**

Simple Plain Early Ovoid Stoneware Jug

Jug, bulbous ovoid body tapering to a short cylindrical neck w/molded rim, applied strap handle, unsigned & undecorated, glaze burn on front, stack marks on shoulder, ca. 1830, 1 gal., 9" h. (ILLUS.)..... **121**

Late Bristol-glazed Advertising Jug

Jug, advertising-type, beehive-shaped w/raised center band & molded handle holes on the shoulder flanking the small neck, Bristol glaze w/cobalt blue printed advertising reading "F. Randel - Utica, N.Y.," blue molded leaf decor at handle holes, wire bail handle w/turned wood grip, ca. 1890, 1 gal., 9 1/2" h. (ILLUS.)....... **132**

Very Early Boston Stoneware Jug

Jug, ovoid body tapering to a small neck w/incised rings, applied strap handle, overall mottled tan clay w/ochre accents, impressed mark for Boston, Massachusetts, large piece of mouth broken & reglued, minor stack mark, ca. 1805, 1 gal., 9 1/2" h. (ILLUS., bottom previous page)..... **248**

Jug, beehive-shaped w/a rounded molded mouth & strap handle, cobalt blue slip-quilled squatty bird w/droopy tail perched on a small twig, blue-tinted impressed mark of Whites, Utica, New York, overall use staining, couple of chips at the shoulder, ca. 1865, 1 gal., 10" h. (ILLUS. center with rare White & Son crock & other Whites jug, center page 46).................... **633**

Jug, beehive-shaped w/small molded mouth & strap handle, dark cobalt blue slip-quilled dotted double flower & leaves design, blue-tinted impressed mark of the Troy Pottery, Troy, New York, some surface chipping at mouth, some staining on side, tight hairline through at the base of the handle, ca. 1870, 1 gal., 10" h. (ILLUS. right with rare crock & larger jug made in Troy, New York, center page 51)................... **165**

Jug, bulbous beehive form tapering to a small molded mouth & strap handle, cobalt blue slip-quilled large arched double flowers flanking central leaf design below the impressed mark "Standish & Wright," Taunton, Massachusetts, rare maker, glaze burn on left side, some use staining & glaze flakes w/short clay separation line up from base, ca. 1855, 1 gal., 10" h. (ILLUS., top next column) **248**

Jug, bulbous ovoid body tapering to a small molded mouth & strap handle, cobalt blue crudely brushed butterfly design on the shoulder below the impressed & blue-tinted mark of Smith & Day manufacturers, Norwalk, Connecticut, overall use staining & glaze crazing, ca. 1845, 1 gal., 10" h. **248**

Standish & Wright Jug with Flowers

Jug, cylindrical w/rounded shoulder tapering to a small molded mouth & strap handle, cobalt blue slip-quilled small long-tailed bird on a leafy sprig, impressed & blue-tinted mark of W. Roberts, Binghamton, New York, ca. 1860, 1 gal., 10" h.. **1,018**

Jug, ovoid body tapering to a small molded mouth & strap handle, tooled incised line at the shoulder, signed "Boston," probably Jonathan Fenton factory, Boston, Massachusetts, crudely potted, overall use stain, some surface chipping at base, ca. 1795, 1 gal., 10" h. (ILLUS. second from right with three other simple early jugs, bottom page 93) **358**

Three Advertising Jugs of Various Shapes

Jug, wide beehive shape tapering to a small molded mouth & strap handle, cobalt blue brushed large drooping flowers flanking a fern-like leaf on the shoulder, impressed mark of Standish & Wright, Taunton, Massachusetts, glaze burn on left side, some use staining, couple of glaze flakes & a short separation line up from the front base, ca. 1855, 1 gal., 10" h. (ILLUS. left with Gardiner crock & Edmans & Co. preserve jar, bottom page 37) **440**

Jug, advertising-type, beehive-shaped tapering to a short neck & strap handle, cobalt blue slip-quilled script advertising for "H. &. Q. - Auburn - NY," impressed mark of J. Fisher & Co., Lyons, New York, minor glaze burning, some use staining, ca. 1880, 1 gal., 10 1/2" h. (ILLUS. right with two other advertising jugs, bottom previous page) **220**

Jug, advertising-type, beehive-shaped tapering to a short neck & strap handle, cobalt blue slip-quilled script advertising for "Chas. Seitz - 492 Rhode Island St - Buffalo - N.Y.," impressed mark of J. Fisher, Lyons, New York, cinnamon clay color, ca. 1870, 1 gal., 10 1/2" h. (ILLUS. left with other beehive & shouldered advertising jugs, bottom of previous page) **248**

Beehive Jug with Rye Advertising

Jug, advertising-type, beehive-shaped w/Bristol glaze, printed cobalt blue script advertising "Pure Neversink Rye," unsigned by maker, probably New Jersey

origin, minor glaze flakes on neck, minor stone ping on back, ca. 1880, 1 gal., 10 1/2" h. (ILLUS.) **209**

Jug with Unusual Inscription

Jug, advertising-type, cylindrical body tapering to a rounded shoulder & molded mouth, applied strap handle, slip-quilled cobalt blue script wording "C.D. Coons - Nunda, N.Y.," impressed mark of E.W. Farrington, Elmira, New York, inscription may be phonetic racial slur, the town is near the birthplace of the Ku Klux Klan, ca. 1890, 1 gal., 10 1/2" h. (ILLUS.) **523**

Jug, beehive-shaped tapering to a small molded mouth & strap handle, cobalt blue slip-quilled vertical leafy twig below the impressed & blue-tinted mark of E. & L.P. Norton, Bennington, Vermont, ca. 1880, 1 gal., 10 1/2" h. (some use staining) **187**

Jug, beehive-shaped tapering to a small molded mouth & strap handle, cobalt blue brushed crude short plume design below the impressed & blue-washed mark of J. Norton & Co., Bennington, Vermont, ca. 1861, 1 gal., 10 1/2" h. (overall use staining) **198**

Jug, bulbous ovoid body tapering to a small molded mouth & strap handle, dark cobalt blue brushed large curved flower on a leaf stem below the impressed & blue-washed mark of C. Boynton & Co., Troy, New York, dark mottled use stain, glaze drip on side, ca. 1825, 1 gal., 10 1/2" h. **440**

Decorated Jug from Short-lived Firm

Early D. Roberts Ovoid Jug

Jug, bulbous ovoid body tapering to a small molded mouth & strap handle, brushed cobalt blue stylized flower on the shoulder below the impressed mark of D. Roberts & Co., Utica, New York, minor in-the-making stack mark, short hairline under glaze at mouth, surface chip on bottom, ca. 1828, 1 gal., 10 1/2" h. (ILLUS.)............................. 495

Jug, bulbous ovoid body tapering to a small molded mouth & strap handle, unusual & beautiful design w/a slip-quilled dotted rectangle enclosing the date "1838" above a small shore bird at the middle of the side, blue accents at handle & on the impressed mark of Clark & Fox, Athens, New York, stack mark on tail of bird, very tight hairline at base of handle, some use staining & minor surface chip at front base, ca. 1838, 1 gal., 10 1/2" h. 3,080

Jug, cylindrical w/rounded shoulder to a short molded mouth & strap handle, cobalt blue crude brushed floral design below blue-trimmed impressed mark "J.B. Magee - Ithaca," New York, short-lived firm, minor in-the-making glaze burn, 1853-55, 1 gal., 10 1/2" h. (ILLUS., top next column)... 468

Jug, flat-bottomed beehive shape w/small cylindrical mouth & strap handle, advertising-type w/cobalt blue script inscription reading "Morris Fischler. - New Brunswick, N.J., " glossy Bristol glaze, very minor surface wear, ca. 1890, 1 gal., 10 1/2" h. (ILLUS., right) 220

New Jersey Advertising Jug

Jug, gently swelled cylindrical body w/a rounded shoulder to the small mouth & strap handle, cobalt blue stenciled diamond & dot band across the front, unsigned but design attributed to the Donaghho factory of Pennsylvania, stack marks in front & at shoulder, mottled clay color, ca. 1880, 1 gal., 10 1/2" h. (ILLUS. second from left with canister & two unsigned preserve jars, page 30) 165

Three Jugs Made by S. Hart, Fulton, New York

Jug, wide flat base & bulbous sides tapering sharply to a small molded mouth & strap handle, fancy cobalt blue brushed floral vine design across the front enclosing the word "one" written twice, impressed mark of S. Hart, Fulton, New York, in-the-making stack marks & a glaze drip, interior chip on mouth, ca. 1875, 1 gal., 10 1/2" h. (ILLUS. center with two other S. Hart, Fulton jugs, above) **660**

Three Stoneware Advertising Jugs

Jug, advertising-type, beehive-shaped tapering to a small cylindrical neck & strap handle, cobalt blue slip-quilled advertising for "Glens Falls Wine Co." across front, cinnamon clay color, large stone ping on front above first word, unsigned by maker, ca. 1880, 1 gal., 11" h. (ILLUS. left with two other advertising jugs, above) **154**

Jug, advertising-type, beehive-shaped tapering to a small neck & strap handle, light cobalt blue slip-quilled script inscription "J.C. Brophy - Liquor Dealer - Waterloo - N.Y.," impressed mark of F. Ohmann, Lyons, New York, slight burned over glazed at shoulder, ca. 1880, 1 gal., 11" h. **248**

Jug, advertising-type, beehive-shaped w/a small molded mouth & strap handle, impressed twice on shoulder & bluetrimmed mark "A.F. Parr & Co. Liquor Dealers - 38 West St. - Syracuse, NY," unsigned by maker, glaze spots all around the body, ca. 1880, 1 gal., 11" h. **33**

Jug, advertising-type, beehive-shaped w/a small molded mouth & strap handle, deeply impressed & blue-tinted inscription for "Fine Sirups (sic) & Extracts - From the Firm of John Matthews - First Ave 26th & 27th St. - New York," unsigned by maker, very tight spider crack on left side of shoulder, ca. 1880, 1 gal., 11" h. **132**

Jug, advertising-type, beehive-shaped w/small cylindrical neck & strap handle, cobalt blue script inscription across the front "Whitehead & Co. - Wholesale Liquor Dealer - Amsterdam - N.Y.," impressed mark of G.S. Guy & Co., Fort Edward, New York, minor surface flakes at rim, some use staining, ca. 1885, 1 gal., 11" h. **330**

Advertising Jug with Impressed Wording

Jug, advertising-type, cylindrical body tapering to a rounded shoulder & cylindrical mouth, applied strap handle, impressed & cobalt blue-trimmed wording "M Zunder & Sons - New Haven - CT - This Jug Can Not Be Sold" on shoulder, impressed store logo in shield below, un-

signed by maker, ca. 1875, 1 gal., 11" h. (ILLUS.).. **198**

Advertising Jug From Lyons, New York

Jug, advertising-type, cylindrical sides w/rounded shoulder tapering to a short cylindrical neck, applied strap handle, slip-quilled cobalt blue wording "S. Reals - Lyons, N.Y.," unsigned by maker, signs of over-paint on back, ca. 1880, 1 gal., 11" h. (ILLUS.) **132**

New York State Advertising Jug

Jug, advertising-type, cylindrical sides w/rounded shoulder tapering to a short cylindrical neck, applied strap handle, slip-quilled cobalt blue wording "Doran - 92 West Main St. -Rochester," by F. Ohmann, Lyons, New York, some use staining, large chip at base under the glaze, ca. 1880, 1 gal., 11" h. (ILLUS.) **176**

Jug, advertising-type, cylindrical tapering to a tapered neck & strap handle, brushed cobalt blue advertising on front for "John Rauber - Rochester, N.Y.," impressed mark for potter J. Fisher, Lyons, New York, couple of surface chips on neck, ca. 1880, 1 gal., 11" h. (ILLUS. far right with three other advertising jugs, bottom of page 94) **220**

Inscribed Texas Pottery Advertising Jug

Jug, beehive-shaped tapering to a small cylindrical neck & strap handle, cobalt blue slip-quilled stylized pine tree design, impressed mark of N.A. White & Son, Utica, New York, ca. 1870, 1 gal., 11" h. (amateur repair to large neck chip, overglazed at the shoulder in-the-making) **248**

Jug, beehive-shaped tapering to a small molded mouth & strap handle, advertising-type, undecorated but w/original paper label reading "Guaranteed Pure Cider Vinegar - WW Smith - Smyrna, New York," impressed mark of C. Hart & Son, Sherburne, New York, ca. 1870, 1 gal., 11" h. (some surface wear, use staining, couple of glaze spider cracks) **55**

Jug, beehive-shaped tapering to a small molded mouth & strap handle, cobalt blue slip-quilled large spade-shaped ribbed blossom on a stem w/smaller ribbed leaves, impressed mark of Whites, Utica, New York, ca. 1865, 1 gal., 11" h. (some overall staining, two chips at the base, minor surface wear on the mouth) **154**

Jug, beehive-shaped tapering to a small molded mouth & strap handle, cobalt blue crude brushed plume design on the shoulder below the impressed mark "Lyons," Lyons, New York, overall use staining, ca. 1860, 1 gal., 11" h. **187**

Jug, beehive-shaped tapering to a small molded mouth & strap handle, cobalt blue slip-quilled small long-tailed bird perched on a short squiggle twig, impressed mark of J. & E. Norton, Bennington, Vermont, ca. 1855, 1 gal., 11" h. (mottled clay color from firing, some minor surface wear at mouth, minor chip at base) **495**

Cooperative Pottery Advertising Jug

Jug, advertising-type, swelled cylindrical body tapering to a rounded shoulder & molded mouth, applied strap handle, slip-quilled cobalt blue wording "S. Reals - Lyons, N.Y.," upside down stamped mark of the Cooperative Pottery Company, Lyons, New York, somewhat overglazed, ca. 1880, 1 gal., 11" h. (ILLUS.) **132**

Jug, advertising-type, swelled cylindrical body w/rounded shoulder to short neck & applied strap handle, overall dark brown Albany slip glaze w/hand-inscribed advertising "Marshall Pottery Products - Contain Nothing Harmful - Use them with - Confidence," from the long-running Marshall Pottery of Texas, ca. 1910, 1 gal., 11" h. (ILLUS., top next column) **248**

Jug, advertising-type, tall narrow cylindrical form w/rounded shoulder & small mouth, strap handle, the front shoulder impressed & trimmed in blue w/"Gabriel Gerstley - Liquor Dealer - 512 W. Franklin St. - Baltimore, MD," unsigned by maker, overall age crazing, stack marks at shoulder, ca. 1850, 1 gal., 11" h. **358**

Two Fine Jugs & a Pitcher Made in Fort Edward, New York

Jug, beehive-shaped tapering to a small molded mouth & strap handle, cobalt blue slip-quilled long-tailed bird perched on a long squiggle twig, impressed mark of J. & E. Norton, Bennington, Vermont, ca. 1855, 1 gal., 11" h. (minor surface chip at mouth & at left base) **523**

Jug, beehive-shaped tapering to a thick rounded mouth & strap handle, cobalt blue slip-quilled plump running bird w/a drooping tail perched on a squiggled twig, impressed mark of Whites, Utica, New York, ca. 1865, 1 gal., 11" h. (dry overglaze at the shoulder, stain spots, surface chip at base on the side) **440**

Jug, beehive-shaped w/a molded mouth & strap handle, cobalt blue slip-quilled design composed of a large diamond formed w/four pointed pine tree designs surrounding a rectangular panel w/a small paddle-tailed bird on a flowering branch, very unusual design, impressed mark of N.A. White & Son, Utica, New York, some use staining, minor surface chip on mouth, few minor glaze chips around base, ca. 1870, 1 gal., 11" (ILLUS. right with rare White & Son crock & other White & Son jug, center page 46) **770**

Jug, beehive-shaped w/a small molded mouth & strap handle, cobalt blue large slip-quilled date across the front "1860" below the blue-tinted impressed mark of the Fort Edward Pottery Co., Fort Edward, New York, excellent condition, ca. 1860, 1 gal., 11" h. (ILLUS. center with other jug & pitcher made in Fort Edward, New York, top of page) **825**

Jug, cylindrical body tapering to a molded mouth & strap handle, cobalt blue slip-quilled stylized dotted dragonfly design, impressed mark "Ithaca, NY," ca. 1880, 1 gal., 11" h. (ILLUS., next column) **209**

Jug, cylindrical body w/rounded shoulder tapering to a molded mouth, applied strap handle, unusual bold slip-quilled cobalt blue four-petal starburst w/arrows & dots design, impressed mark of Cortland, New York, minor glaze wear, surface chip on back base, ca. 1860, 1 gal., 11" h. (ILLUS., next column) **578**

Jug with Stylized Dragonfly Design

Cortland, New York Jug with Starburst Design

Jugs with Goony Bird & Large Poppy Flower

Jug, cylindrical tapering to a small molded mouth & eared handle, cobalt blue slip-quilled long-necked goony-looking dotted bird near bottom, impressed mark of W. Roberts, Binghamton, New York, stack mark at front base, some use staining, in-the-making base chip, ca. 1860, 1 gal., 11" h. (ILLUS. right with jug with large delicate poppy flower, above) **688**

Jug, cylindrical w/rounded shoulder tapering to a cylindrical neck, applied strap handle, slip-quilled cobalt blue stylized pine tree design typical of the factory, impressed mark of N.A. White & Son, Utica, New York, glaze separation line at back of base, minor surface chip & staining on mouth, ca. 1870, 1 gal., 11" h. (ILLUS., below left)... **176**

White & Son Jug with Pine Tree Design   *Fine Whites, Utica Jug with Plump Bird*

A Group of Four Bird-decorated Bennington Jugs

Jug, cylindrical w/rounded shoulder tapering to a molded mouth, applied strap handle, slip-quilled cobalt blue large short plump rib-tailed bird on twig design, impressed mark of Whites, Utica, New York, minor stone ping, overall excellent condition, ca. 1865, 1 gal., 11" h. (ILLUS., bottom previous page) **1,155**

Jug, cylindrical w/rounded shoulder to a small molded mouth & strap handle, cobalt blue slip-quilled long bird perched on a twig below the blue-tinted impressed mark of J. & E. Norton, Bennington, Vermont, minor staining along base, ca. 1855, 1 gal., 11" h. (ILLUS. second from right with three other bird-decorated Bennington jugs, top of page) **468**

Jug, cylindrical w/rounded shoulder to a small molded mouth & strap handle, cobalt blue slip-quilled long bird perched on a squiggle twig below the blue-tinted impressed mark of J. & E. Norton, Bennington, Vermont, minor rim surface wear, ca. 1855, 1 gal., 11" h. (ILLUS. second from left with three other bird-decorated Bennington jugs, top of page) **715**

Jug, flat-bottomed beehive shape tapering to a/small cylindrical mouth & strap handle, advertising-type w/cobalt blue script inscription reading "Constine & Wolhow - W. Barre - Pa.," impressed factory mark of James Ryan, Pittston, Pennsylvania, glossy Bristol glaze, ca. 1890, 1 gal., 11" h. (ILLUS.) **176**

One-gallon Pennsylvania Advertising Jug

Advertising Jug Made in Lyons, New York

Jug, flat-bottomed beehive shape tapering to a/small cylindrical mouth & strap handle, advertising-type w/cobalt blue script inscription reading "C. Person's Sons - 390 Elm St - Buffalo, N.Y., " made in Lyons, New York, ca. 1870, minor chip in handle, 1 gal., 11" h. (ILLUS.) **220**

Three Decorated Jugs with Various Designs

Jug, flat-bottomed cylindrical body tapering to a small molded mouth & strap handle, cobalt blue slip-quilled small silhouetted bird perched on a fuzzy branch, impressed mark of North Bay Pottery, North Bay, New York, minor tight body clay separation line at name & another at back, stone ping on back, ca. 1870, 1 gal., 11" h. (ILLUS. center w/two larger decorated jugs) **1,540**

Three Jugs Made & Decorated by Whites, Utica, New York

Jug, flat-bottomed cylindrical form tapering to a small molded mouth & strap handle, dark cobalt blue slip-quilled stylized pine tree design below the impressed mark of N.A. White & Son, Utica, New York, surface chip & minor crazing at front base, ca. 1870, 1 gal., 11" h. (ILLUS. right with two other Whites, Utica decorated jugs) **330**

Two Decorated Jugs Made by Whites, Utica, New York

Jug, flat-bottomed wide tapering rounded body w/small molded mouth & strap handle, cobalt blue slip-quilled long slender leafy stem w/round blossom up the front below the impressed mark for Whites, Utica, New York, stack mark just at top of design, ca. 1865, 1 gal., 11" h. (ILLUS. right with other Whites jug, top of page)....... **303**

Jug, ovoid body tapering to a small molded mouth & strap handle, cobalt blue brushed stylized flower below the impressed mark of Wm. Moyer, Harrisburg, Pennsylvania, rare maker, tight spider crack on left side, some use staining, ca. 1858, 1 gal., 11" h. (ILLUS., bottom left)...... **358**

Early New York Jug with Staining

Jug, ovoid body tapering to a small molded mouth & strap handle, long bold brushed cobalt blue plume design down the front,

Jug by Rare Pennsylvania Pottery

blue accent at handle, probably New York state, ca. 1830, stack mark at shoulder, stone ping at back of mouth, stained w/some surface chipping along base, 1 gal., 11" h. (ILLUS.)...................................... **358**

Very Early Massachusetts Jug

Jug, sharply ovoid body tapering to a short small neck & mouth & strap handle, ochre accents at top & base, attributed to Frederick Carpenter, Charlestown, Massachusetts, minor surface wear at base, some minor use staining, ca. 1805, 1 gal., 11" h. (ILLUS.)...................................... **385**

Sipe & Sons Jug with Flower Design

Jug, swelled cylindrical body w/rounded shoulder to a short molded mouth, applied strap handle, brushed cobalt blue

simple large flower, impressed mark of Sipe & Sons, Williamsport, Pennsylvania, some use staining, ca. 1870, 1 gal., 11" h. (ILLUS.)... **165**

Tall Cylindrical Jug with Single Flower

Jug, tall slender cylindrical body w/a rounded shoulder to the ringed mouth, applied strap handle, small brushed cobalt blue stylized flower at the shoulder, impressed mark of J.B. Magee, Ithaca, New York, Albany slip glaze drip on side, mottled clay color, ca. 1853, 1 gal., 11" h. (ILLUS.) **165**

Jug From Last Utica, New York Pottery

Jug, wide cylindrical body w/rounded shoulder to a cylindrical neck, applied strap handle, stenciled cobalt blue mark "1 - C.N.Y.P. - Utica, N.Y.," mark of the Central New York Pottery, the last stoneware potter in Utica, ca. 1890, 1 gal., 11" h. (ILLUS.) **110**

Typical Pine Tree on White & Son Jug

Jug, wide cylindrical body w/rounded shoulder to a cylindrical neck, applied strap handle, slip-quilled cobalt blue stylized pine tree design, impressed mark of N.A. White & Son, Utica, New York, glaze burn to right of design, professional restoration to large chip in handle, ca. 1865, 1 gal., 11" h. (ILLUS.)................................... **220**

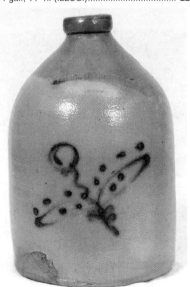

Jug with Unusual "Insect" Design

Jug, wide cylindrical body w/rounded shoulder to a molded mouth, applied strap handle, slip-quilled cobalt blue stylized unusual dotted spread-winged "insect" design, impressed mark of W. Roberts, Binghamton, New York, stack mark at front base, use staining at top, long surface chip at back of mouth, ca. 1860, 1 gal., 11" h. (ILLUS.) **143**

West Troy, New York Jug with Vine

Jug, wide cylindrical body w/rounded shoulder to a molded mouth, applied strap handle, slip-quilled cobalt blue stylized slender curling vine w/blossom design, impressed blue of Porter & Fraser, West Troy, New York, minor design fry, some stone pings, ca, 1855, 1 gal., 11" h. (ILLUS.) **143**

Jug, advertising-type, beehive-shaped tapering to a small cylindrical neck & strap handle, impressed & blue-trimmed advertising for "J. White & Co. - Wine & Spirit Merchants - 11 Ouellette Ave. - Windsor" on top of front shoulder, unsigned by maker, mottled clay color, ca. 1880, 1 gal., 11 1/2" h. (ILLUS. center with two other advertising jugs bottom page 100).. **55**

Jug, advertising-type, beehive-shaped tapering to a small cylindrical neck & strap handle, Bristol glaze stenciled on the front center "J. C. Bernhardt's Sons - 273 Washington St. - Buffalo, N.Y.," impressed "A1" on side of shoulder, minor glaze wear from use, few surface chips, ca. 1890, 1 gal., 11 1/2" h. (ILLUS. right with two other advertising jugs, bottom page 100).. **99**

Jug, advertising-type, cylindrical tapering to a tapered neck & strap handle, brushed cobalt blue advertising on front for "3. - J.H. Conners - 119 Hamilton St. - Boston," blue-trimmed impressed mark for potter Ottman Bros. & Co., Fort Edward, New York, short clay separation at base, stack marks, ca. 1870, 1 gal., 11 1/2" h. (ILLUS. far left with three other advertising jugs, bottom page 94)............................. **154**

New York Jug with Impressed Advertising

Jug, advertising-type, ovoid body tapering to a small molded mouth, applied strap handle, blue-tinted impressed shoulder advertising "J. Cochrane. - Wholesale & Retail Dealer in - Groceries & Provisions - Wines & Liquors & C. & C. - No 28 Main St. Rochester," from New York, unsigned by maker, ca. 1860, 1 gal., 11 1/2" h. (ILLUS.)....................................... **248**

Jug, beehive-shaped tapering to a small molded mouth & strap handle, cobalt blue slip-quilled large rounded blossom atop a tall stem w/feather-like leaves below the impressed & blue-tinted mark "Cortland," Cortland, New York, ca. 1860, 1 gal., 11 1/2" h. (professional restoration, handle replaced) **187**

Jug, beehive-shaped tapering to a small molded mouth & strap handle, cobalt blue large slip-quilled long-tailed bird perched on a thin scrolled twig below the impressed mark of J. Norton & Co., Bennington, Vermont, ca. 1861, 1 gal., 11 1/2" h. (badly stained, full-length crack running through design & mark) **248**

Jug, beehive-shaped w/a small molded mouth & strap handle, cobalt blue large slip-quilled pigeon-breasted bird perched on a slender scroll below the blue-tinted impressed mark of the Fort Edward Pottery Co., Fort Edward, New York, glaze discoloration from firing, ca. 1860, 1 gal., 11 1/2" h. (ILLUS. left with other jug & pitcher made in Fort Edward, top page 103)... **1,018**

Jug, bulbous ovoid body tapering to a short neck & strap handle, impressed mark "Boston," brown & ochre bands at shoulder & base, four incised accent lines at the neck, attributed to Frederick Carpenter, Boston, Massachusetts, couple of stack marks, ca. 1805, 1 gal., 11 1/2" h. (ILLUS. center with other jug & Boston-made jar, top page 83)................................. **798**

New York Jug & Fancy Preserve Jar

Rare Julius Norton Jug with Dove Among Flowering Branches

Jug, bulbous ovoid body tapering to a small molded mouth & strap handle, cobalt blue brushed & dotted large stylized flower on stem below the impressed mark of J. Heiser, Buffalo, New York, stack mark in the flower, early Buffalo potter, ca. 1852, 1 gal., 11 1/2" h. (ILLUS. left with Ithaca, New York preserve jar, bottom previous page) **330**

Jug, bulbous ovoid body tapering to a small molded mouth & strap handle, dark cobalt blue brushed fish design on the shoulder, unsigned but attributed to the Fenton factory in Massachusetts, professional restoration & handle replaced, very tight early horizontal line at the bottom & back, ca. 1800, 1 gal., 11 1/2" h. **1,155**

Jug, cylindrical body tapering to a small cylindrical mouth & strap handle, dark cobalt blue slip-quilled long-tailed bird below the impressed & blue-trimmed mark "Whites Utica," Utica, New York, very tight line in handle, short clay separation line at front base, ca. 1865, 1 gal., 11 1/2" h. (ILLUS., next column) **880**

Jug, cylindrical body tapering to a small molded mouth & strap handle, cobalt blue slip-quilled & incised large dove perched among flowering branches below the impressed mark "Julius Norton - Bennington, VT," probably a special order piece, minor stone ping on shoulder, some minor use staining, ca. 1848, 1 gal., 11 1/2" h. (ILLUS., top of page) **12,650**

Whites Utica Jug with Bird Decoration

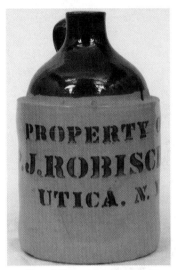

Grey & Brown Advertising Jug

Jug, cylindrical grey body w/glossy Bristol glaze & brown-glazed domed shoulder w/cylindrical neck & strap handle, advertising-type, stenciled in black around the body "Property of - P. J. Robischon - Utica, N.Y." & impressed "A1," couple of glaze spiders, ca. 1890, 1 gal., 11 1/2" h. (ILLUS.)...................... **33**

Jug, cylindrical tapering to a small cylindrical mouth & strap handle, tall cobalt blue brushed tulip blossom on a leafy stem, unsigned by probably the Farrington, Elmira, New York factory, stack mark at flower, ca. 1870, 1 gal., 11 1/2" h. (ILLUS. center with cream pot & crock, top page 33)................... **303**

Satterlee & Mory Jug with Bird Decor

Jug, cylindrical w/rounded shoulder to a small molded mouth, applied strap handle, slip-

quilled cobalt blue detailed bird on leafy stem, impressed blue-trimmed mark of Satterlee & Mory, Fort Edward, New York, very minor surface chip on mouth, ca. 1870, 1 gal., 11 1/2" h. (ILLUS.)................... **633**

Jug, cylindrical w/rounded shoulder to a small molded mouth & strap handle, cobalt blue slip-quilled long bird perched on a twig below the blue-tinted impressed mark of J. & E. Norton, Bennington, Vermont, staining from use, especially on upper half, ca. 1855, 1 gal., 11 1/2" h. (ILLUS. far left with three other bird-decorated Bennington jugs, top page 105)......................... **385**

Advertising Jug with Script Address

Jug, flat-bottomed beehive shape w/small cylindrical mouth & strap handle, advertising-type w/slip-quilled cobalt blue inscription reading "Aug. Baetzhold - 567 Michigan St. - Buffalo - N.Y., " impressed mark of J. Fisher, Lyons, New York, chip at base, some surface chipping at mouth, ca. 1880, 1 gal., 11 1/2" h. (ILLUS.).............................. **143**

Jug, flat-bottomed cylindrical form tapering to a small molded mouth & strap handle, dark cobalt blue slip-quilled stylized pine tree design below the impressed mark of N.A. White & Son, Utica, New York, stack marks on left side, in-the-making glaze drip above design, some surface chipping around mouth, ca. 1870, 1 gal., 11 1/2" h. (ILLUS. left with two other decorated jugs by Whites, Utica, bottom page 106)... **165**

Jug, flat-bottomed cylindrical form w/rounded shoulder to a short small neck & strap handle, cobalt blue slip-quilled very fat bird on a tiny sprig, blue-tinted impressed mark of Haxstun & Co., Fort Edward, New York, minor surface chip at base & one on neck, some use staining, ca. 1870, 1 gal., 11 1/2" h. (ILLUS. second from left with three other pieces made in Fort Edward, New York, top page 39)......... **523**

Jug, flat-bottomed wide tapering rounded body w/small molded mouth & strap handle, cobalt blue slip-quilled large stylized pine tree design below the impressed mark of N.A. White & Son, Utica, New York, very minor surface chips at front base, ca. 1870, 1 gal., 11 1/2" h. (ILLUS. left with other Whites, Utica jug, top page 107) **303**

N. White Utica Jug with Crude Flower

Jug, ovoid body tapering to a short neck w/molded mouth, applied strap handle, brushed cobalt blue large crude leaf-shaped flower, blue-trimmed impressed mark of N. White, Utica, New York, somewhat dry glaze & stack marks, some use staining, ca. 1840, 1 gal., 11 1/2" h. (ILLUS.) **385**

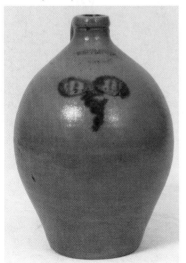

Early Seymour, Troy, New York Jug

Jug, ovoid body tapering to a small neck w/molded rim, applied strap handle, slip-quilled cobalt blue "elephant's head" design below impressed mark of I. Seymour, Troy, New York, one of New York's earliest factory marks, ca. 1820, 1 gal., 11 1/2" h. (ILLUS.) **358**

Early Thompson & Co. Jug

Jug, ovoid body tapering to a small neck w/molded rim, applied strap handle, brushed cobalt blue large pointed flower bud & two smaller buds on stem, impressed mark of Thompson & Co., Gardiner, Massachusetts, stone ping on left side, mottled clay color, ca. 1840, 1 gal., 11 1/2" h. (ILLUS.) **413**

Jug, swelled cylindrical form tapering to a small molded mouth & strap handle, brushed cobalt blue simple stick figure below the impressed mark of St. Johns Stoneware, St. Johns, Canada, use staining, some minor glaze wear, ca. 1870, 1 gal., 11 1/2" h. (ILLUS. left with other Canadian & Southern jugs, top of next page) **1,375**

Jug, beehive-shaped tapering to a small molded mouth & strap handle, cobalt blue simple stylized flower on leafy stem design below the impressed & blue-tinted mark of N. Clark, Jr., Athens, New York, kiln burn on left side, some minor surface wear at the base, ca. 1850, 1 gal., 12" h. **248**

Jug, beehive-shaped tapering to a small molded mouth & strap handle, dark cobalt blue slip-quilled large long-tailed bird perched on a long squiggle twig, impressed mark of J. & E. Norton, Bennington, Vermont, ca. 1855, 1 gal., 12" h. (professional restoration to chips on handle) **798**

A Southern & Two Canadian Jugs

12" h. (ILLUS. left with jug with goony bird design, top page 104) **413**

Jug, ovoid body tapering to a small neck & strap handle, undecorated except for light cobalt blue accents at the handle & impressed mark of D. Goodale, Hartford, Connecticut, large stack mark on very back, surface chipping around base, ca. 1836, 1 gal., 12" h. (ILLUS. center with table-top churn & other Hartford piece, top page 18) **165**

One-gallon Jug with Dotted Plume

Jug, cylindrical body tapering to a small mouth & strap handle, cobalt blue slip-quilled large dotted plume design, impressed mark for West Troy Pottery, West Troy, New York, ca. 1880, 1 gal., 12" h. (ILLUS.) **176**

Jug, cylindrical tapering to a small molded mouth & eared handle, cobalt blue slip-quilled oversized delicate poppy flowers on a tall leafy stem below the blue-trimmed impressed mark of N. White & Co., Binghamton, New York, kiln burn at very base of flowers, ca. 1860, 1 gal.,

Jug by Unlisted New York Maker

Jug, sharply ovoid body tapering to a small molded mouth & strap handle, brushed cobalt blue stylized design of a table holding a flowerpot below the impressed mark "P.V. Wiggins S. Springs," previously unlisted potter in Saratoga Springs, New York, some very tight spider lines up from the bottom, minor staining from use, ca. 1870, 1 gal., 12" h. (ILLUS.) 523

Jug, slim cylindrical form tapering to a rounded shoulder & small molded mouth, strap handle, overall dark brown alkaline glaze accented in blue at the shoulder w/script words "Whiskey" & "Ale" as well as a full-length stick figure of a man wearing a top hat & smoking a cigar, Southern U.S., very rare, ca. 1880, 1 gal., 12" h. (ILLUS. right with two Canadian jugs, top previous page) **1,375**

Simple Julius Norton Jug

Jug, tall cylindrical body w/rounded shoulder to a small molded mouth, undecorated, impressed blue-trimmed mark of Julius Norton, Bennington, Vermont, excellent condition, ca. 1848, 1 gal., 12" h. (ILLUS.) **132**

Jug, tall ovoid body tapering to a small molded mouth & strap handle, brushed cobalt blue scalloped design around the shoulder flanking the impressed mark of C. Crolius, Manufacturer, Manhattan Wells, New York, blue trim on name & handle, some minor surface chipping & age crazing to glaze, few stone pings, ca. 1830, 1 gal., 12" h. (ILLUS. left with flower-decorated crock & other jug, top page 43) **688**

Jug, advertising-type, cylindrical tapering to a tapered neck & strap handle, brushed cobalt blue advertising on front for "Moore & Hubbard - Syracuse. - N.Y.," impressed mark of Ottoman Bros. & Co., Fort Edward, New York, glaze flakes at neck & staining, ca. 1870, unusual 4 qt. mark, 12 1/2" h. (ILLUS. second from

right with three other advertising jugs, bottom page 94) **303**

Boston Advertising One-gallon Jug

Jug, flat-bottomed beehive shape tapering to a/small cylindrical mouth & strap handle, advertising-type w/cobalt blue script inscription reading "D.J. Long & Co - 306 Lincoln St. - Boston, " impressed factory mark of Ottoman Bros. & Co., Fort Edward, New York, stack mark just above name, surface chipping at mouth, some use staining, ca. 1870, 1 gal., 12 1/2" h. (ILLUS.)... **187**

Early Mount Morris, New York Jug

Jug, ovoid body tapering to a short neck w/molded mouth, applied strap handle, brushed cobalt blue underlined size number, Nathan Clark factory, Mount Morris,

New York, some use staining, ca. 1835, 1 gal., 12 1/2" h. (ILLUS.).............. **248**

Jug, tall ovoid body tapering to a small molded mouth & strap handle, incised long leafy branch design on the front shoulder, blue trim on handle, unsigned but probably early New York City origin, very minor surface chipping at base, overall use stain, ca. 1830, 1 gal., 13" h. (ILLUS. right with flower-decorated crock & other jug, top page 43)............... **523**

Jug, beehive-shaped tapering to a small molded mouth & strap handle, cobalt blue unusual slip-quilled bull's-eye & tornado design below size number, unsigned but attributed to an Albany, New York, potter, professional restoration to chips at mouth, shoulder & handle, ca. 1865, 1 1/2 gal., 12" h. (ILLUS. left with unsigned crock & pitcher, top page 42)........ **198**

Jug, cylindrical w/rounded shoulder to a small molded mouth & strap handle, cobalt blue slip-quilled large long "Benny" bird perched on a plume below the blue-tinted impressed mark of E. & L.P. Norton, Bennington, Vermont, somewhat overglazed at the shoulder, long hairline in right side just touching the plume, other spider lines, overall use staining, ca. 1880, 1 1/2 gal., 12" h. (ILLUS. far right with three other bird-decorated Bennington jugs, top of page 105) **358**

Jug, cylindrical body tapering to a small molded mouth & strap handle, cobalt blue slip-quilled design of a large dotted leaf cluster below the blue-tinted impressed mark of E. & L.P. Norton, Bennington, Vermont, glaze drip on back & mouth, very minor glaze flakes at mouth, ca. 1880, 1 1/2 gal., 13" h. (ILLUS. at right with Bennington-made advertising crock & other jug, bottom page 46).................... **248**

Jug, beehive-shaped tapering to a small molded mouth & strap handle, large dark cobalt blue slip-quilled design of a pair of large lobed blossoms among tightly scrolled leaves across the front & below the impressed & blue-tinted mark of J. & F. Norton, Bennington, Vermont, mid-19th c., some staining, 2 gal. (ILLUS. third row down, far left, with full page of other stoneware pieces, page 27)............... **529**

Jug, very wide bulbous body tapering sharply to a small molded mouth & strap handle, cobalt blue large brushed double flower & leaf up the front below the impressed mark of Jacob Caire, Main

Street, Poughkeepsie, New York, brushed size designation, extensive deep crazing in glaze, tight hairline from mouth through mark, ca. 1850, 2 gal., 10" h. (ILLUS. second from right with flowerpot & other various pieces, top page 37).. **523**

Beehive Jug with Printed Advertising

Jug, advertising-type, beehive-shaped w/Bristol glaze, printed cobalt blue size number above circle enclosed advertising "Masacaro - Tonique for the hair," unsigned by maker, ca. 1900, 2 gal., 11" h. (ILLUS.)... **132**

Jug, beehive-shaped tapering to a small molded mouth & strap handle, cobalt blue brushed double flower design below the impressed mark of Brown & Bros., Huntington, Long Island, New York, excellent condition, ca. 1890, 2 gal., 11 1/2" h. (ILLUS. left with Long Island crock with rare eagle, top page 46)............. **440**

Jug, beehive-shaped w/a wide flat bottom & small molded mouth & strap handle, cobalt blue slip-quilled drooping flower on leafy stem design below the blue-tinted impressed mark of A.O. Whittemore, Havana, New York, professional restoration to large chips & cracks overall, ca. 1870, 2 gal., 12" h. (ILLUS. right with Whittemore churn & crock, bottom page 19)......... **248**

Jug, bulbous ovoid body tapering to a small molded mouth & strap handle, impressed "2," unsigned & undecorated, 19th c., 2 gal., 12" h. **173**

Early Ovoid Jug with Stylized Tree

Jug, sharply ovoid body tapering to a small molded mouth & strap handle, brushed cobalt blue stylized tree & "2" on the shoulder below the blue-trimmed impressed mark "Thomas D. Chollar - Homer," Homer, New York, some staining from use, ca. 1835, 2 gal., 12" h. (ILLUS.) **908**

Nice Early Crolius Jug

Jug, bulbous sharply ovoid body tapering to a small molded mouth, applied strap handle, simple brushed cobalt blue drape design around the upper shoulder, additional blue accent on handle, mottled glaze, C. Crolius, New York, New York, ca. 1830, 2 gal., 12 1/2" h. (ILLUS.) **880**

Beehive Jug with Plume & Numbers

Jug, beehive-shaped w/wide flat bottom & molded mouth, applied strap handle, brushed cobalt blue small plume flanked by size numbers & impressed size number & mark of A.O. Whittemore, Havana, New York, stack marks on sides of design, very tight hairline up from front base, ca. 1870, 2 gal., 12 1/2" h. (ILLUS.) **154**

Jug with Double-poppy Decoration

Jug, cylindrical w/rounded shoulder tapering to a molded mouth & strap handle, large cobalt blue slip-quilled dotted double-poppy decoration w/dotted leafy stem below the impressed mark "Whites - Binghamton - 2," New York, professional restoration to a tight line along bottom & up front, ca. 1860, 2 gal., 12 1/2" h. (ILLUS.) **275**

Advertising Jug Made in Lyons, New York

Jug, flat-bottomed beehive shape w/small mouth & strap handle, advertising-type w/brushed cobalt blue inscription reading "R.H. Gilgallon - Scranton - Pa" & "2," made by Co-operative Pottery Co., Lyons, New York, cinnamon clay color in the making & some staining from use, ca. 1890, 2 gal., 12 1/2" h. (ILLUS.).................. **275**

Jug, wide flat base & bulbous sides tapering sharply to a small molded mouth & strap handle, fancy cobalt blue brushed tulip blossom on a swirling leafy stem below the impressed mark of S. Hart, Fulton, New York, professionally restored full-length hairline on left side of design, ca. 1875, 2 gal., 12 1/2" h. (ILLUS. right with two other S. Hart, Fulton jugs, top page 100)... **143**

S. Hart Jug with Unusual Bird Design

Jug, wide swelled cylindrical body w/rounded shoulder tapering to a molded mouth,

applied strap handle, large slip-quilled dark cobalt blue dotted bird on a curly vine beside size numbers, impressed mark of S. Hart, Fulton, New York, stone ping left of design, ca. 1875, 2 gal., 12 1/2" h. (ILLUS.) **550**

Advertising Jug with Bull's-eye Design

Jug, advertising-type, cylindrical body w/rounded shoulder to a small molded mouth, slip-quilled cobalt blue double bull's-eye design below the impressed size number & advertising reading "D. McCauley - NO. 53 Main St. - Springfield, Mass.," decoration associated w/the F. Norton factory of Bennington, tight spider crack at base of handle, T-shaped hairline up from base on back, couple of surface chips on mouth, ca. 1870, 2 gal., 13" h. (ILLUS.) **154**

Jug, advertising-type, shouldered-type w/cylindrical body stenciled in cobalt blue advertising for "James J. Duffy & Co. - 458-60 River St. - Troy, N.Y.," conical shoulder & small neck w/a dark brown alkaline glaze, unsigned by maker, ca. 1890, 2 gal., 13" h. (ILLUS. center with two beehive-shaped advertising jugs, bottom page 97)..................................... **198**

Jug, beehive-shaped tapering to a molded mouth & strap handle, cobalt blue brushed horizontal stylized scrolled & dotted drooping flower on a curved leafy stem, impressed & blue-tinted size number & mark of C. Hart & Son, Sherburne, New York, ca. 1870, 2 gal., 13" h. **495**

Jug, beehive-shaped tapering to a small mouth & strap handle, cobalt blue slip-quilled large bull's-eye above a tornado design on the front w/a small size number above, impressed mark of Albany, New York, unsigned by maker, clay separation line all around the base, dry glaze & tan clay color from the firing, ca. 1865, 2 gal., 13" h.. **275**

Jug, beehive-shaped w/a small molded mouth & strap handle, cobalt blue slip-quilled double plump lovebird design beside a large size number below the blue-tinted impressed mark of S. Hart, Fulton, New York, full-length glued hairline on back, ca. 1875, 2 gal., 13" h. (ILLUS. left with New York state jar & large jug, bottom page 81) **688**

Vermont Jug with Fireworks-like Design

Jug, beehive-shaped w/a small molded mouth & strap handle, cobalt blue slip-quilled unusual scrolling fireworks explosion-like design across the front, impressed blue-tinted mark of Ballard & Brothers, Burlington, Vermont, two short hairlines up from the back, very minor glaze flake on mouth, overglazing on left side, ca. 1860, 2 gal., 13" h. (ILLUS.) **688**

Jug, bulbous ovoid body tapering to a molded mouth & strap handle, cobalt blue brushed large plume below a large "2," impressed & blue-trimmed mark of S. Hart, Oswego Falls, New York, kiln burns at shoulder, ca. 1840, 2 gal., 13" h. (ILLUS. left with early Utica jar & other jug, top page 81) **330**

Two-gallon Jug with Floral Cluster

Jug, cylindrical body tapering to a small molded mouth & strap handle, cobalt blue slip-quilled flared cluster of stylized flowers, marked by Edmands & Co., mottled clay color, in-the-making kiln burns at base, ca. 1870, 2 gal., 13" h. (ILLUS.) **187**

Large Triple Tulip on Cortland, New York Jug

Jug, cylindrical body w/rounded shoulder tapering to a molded mouth, applied strap handle, unusual bold slip-quilled cobalt blue large triple tulip on ribbed stem design, impressed mark of Cortland, New York, some use staining, somewhat overglazed, ca. 1860, 2 gal., 13" h. (ILLUS.) **523**

J. Burger Jug with Leaf Cluster Design

Jug, cylindrical w/rounded shoulder to a cylindrical neck, applied strap handle, slip-quilled cobalt blue cluster of four oblong dotted leaves below the size number, impressed mark of J. Burger, Rochester, New York, entire hand print under the glaze below the design, minor use staining & surface chipping on mouth, ca. 1880, 2 gal., 13" h. (ILLUS., previous page) **176**

N. Clark Jug with Bold Double Flowers

Jug, wide cylindrical body w/rounded shoulder to a molded mouth, applied strap handle, brushed cobalt blue large double flowers on bold leafy stem design, impressed circle mark of N. Clark Jr., Athens, New York, some use staining, ca. 1850, 2 gal., 13" h. (ILLUS.) **358**

J. Norton Jug with Bird on Leaf Design

Jug, cylindrical w/rounded shoulder to a small molded mouth, slip-quilled cobalt blue long-tailed bird on tri-lobe leaf & sprig design typical of this factory, impressed size number & mark of J. Norton & Co., Bennington, Vermont, very minor surface chip on mouth, minor staining, ca. 1861, 2 gal., 13" h. (ILLUS.) **1,760**

Jug, flat-bottomed cylindrical body tapering to a small molded mouth & strap handle, cobalt blue brushed stylized tornado & dash design below the impressed mark of D.W. Graves, Westmoreland, New York, glued large break on back & glued break in handle, some use staining, ca. 1860, 2 gal., 13" h. (ILLUS. right with bird- and large flower-decorated jugs, top page 106) **110**

Jug, wide cylindrical body w/rounded shoulder tapering to a thin molded mouth & strap handle, cobalt blue slip-quilled plump hook-beaked bird looking over its shoulder & perched on a leafy stem w/rounded flower, impressed & blue-washed mark of Whites, Utica, New York, ca. 1865, 2 gal., 13" h. (some use staining, professional restoration to mouth chip) **743**

Graves Jug with Tornado Design

Jug, wide cylindrical body w/rounded shoulder to a short cylindrical neck, applied strap handle, brushed cobalt blue tornado & sprig design below the blue-trimmed impressed mark of D.W. Graves, Westmoreland, New York, professional restoration to long cracks on back, ca. 1860, 2 gal., 13" h. (ILLUS.) **132**

Three Decorated Jugs Made in Olean, New York

Jug, wide ovoid body tapering to a small molded mouth & strap handle, cobalt blue brushed large double tulip blossoms on leafy stem, impressed mark of E. A. Montell, Olean, New York, spider crack at mouth, stack mark on right, faint hairline in handle, ca. 1870, 2 gal., 13" h. (ILLUS. center with two other decorated Olean, New York jugs, top of page)......................... **413**

Jug, wide ovoid body tapering to a small molded mouth & strap handle, cobalt blue brushed antler design repeated three times around shoulder, blue trim on handle, marked by C. Crolius, New York City, cinnamon clay color, some use staining, ca. 1800, 2 gal., 13" h. (ILLUS. right with two early decorated jars, top page 84)... **2,310**

Buffalo, New York Advertising Jug

Jug, advertising-type, swelled cylindrical body tapering to a rounded shoulder & molded mouth, applied strap handle, slip-quilled cobalt blue wording "C. & S. - 368 Seneca St. - Buffalo, NY," impressed mark of C.W. Braun, Buffalo, New York, some use staining, minor chip on spout & base, stack marks at shoulder, ca. 1870, 2 gal., 13 1/2" h. (ILLUS.) **99**

Jug, beehive-shaped w/a small molded mouth & strap handle, cobalt blue slip-quilled design of a large lyre flanked by long feather scrolls, impressed mark of J.M. Pruden, Elizabethtown, New Jersey, couple of minor surface chips, minor use staining, ca. 1870, 2 gal., 13 1/2" h. (ILLUS. left with New Jersey-made crock & other jug, top page 44) **275**

Jug, beehive-shaped w/a small molded mouth & strap handle, cobalt blue slip-quilled delicate parrot perched on a stump design below the impressed mark for Whites, Utica, tight spider crack up from base, some use staining, ca. 1865, 2 gal., 13 1/2" h. (ILLUS. right with two bird-decorated pieces from Whites, Utica, top page 51).. **495**

Jug, beehive-shaped w/a small molded mouth & strap handle, cobalt blue slip-quilled design of a large lyre above a looped squiggle, impressed mark of J.M. Pruden, Elizabethtown, New Jersey, couple of minor glaze spider lines, ca. 1870, 2 gal., 13 1/2" h. (ILLUS. right with New Jersey-made crock & other jug, top page 44).. **550**

Jug, bulbous ovoid body tapering to a molded mouth & strap handle, cobalt blue slip-quilled size number & blue-trimmed impressed mark & size number for L. Norton & Son, Bennington, Vermont, large stack mark on left side, smaller one on right shoulder, overall use stain, ca. 1835, 2 gal., 13 1/2" h. (ILLUS. right with Bennington crock & cylindrical jug, bottom page 52)... **358**

Jug with Bee Stinger Decoration

Jug, cylindrical body tapering to a short cylindrical neck & strap handle, cobalt blue slip-quilled stylized bee stinger design below a "2," impressed mark of J. Fisher & Co., Lyons, New York, minor glaze burning, large glaze drips at shoulder & back, ca. 1880, 2 gal., 13 1/2" h. (ILLUS.) **176**

Stoneware Jug with Large Plume Design

Jug, cylindrical body tapering to a small molded mouth & strap handle, cobalt blue slip-quilled large plume & scroll design, impressed mark "New York Stoneware Co. - 2," ca. 1870, 2 gal., 13 1/2" h. (ILLUS.) **275**

Jug, cylindrical body tapering to a small molded mouth & strap handle, cobalt blue slip-quilled design of a large petaled flower among leaves & dots, blue-tinted impressed mark of J. & E. Norton, Bennington, Vermont, excellent condition, ca. 1855, 2 gal., 13 1/2" h. (ILLUS. left with Bennington-made crock & other jug, bottom page 46) **1,375**

F.B. Norton Jug with Parrot Design

Jug, cylindrical body tapering to a small molded mouth & strap handle, cobalt blue slip-quilled long parrot perched on a vertical leafy sprig below the impressed mark "F.B. Norton and Co. - Worcester, Mass. - 2," excellent condition, ca. 1870, 2 gal., 13 1/2" h. (ILLUS.) **1,485**

Jug with Running Bird Decoration

Jug, cylindrical tapering to a small molded mouth & strap handle, cobalt blue slip-quilled running bird w/fanned tail, impressed Whites, Utica mark, very minor stack marks on sides, New York, ca. 1865, 2 gal., 13 1/2" h. (ILLUS., previous page).. **495**

Jug, cylindrical w/rounded shoulder tapering to a small molded mouth & strap handle, small cobalt blue slip-quilled long-tailed bird perched on a scrolling branch, possibly by Edmands & Co., Charleston, Massachusetts, stack mark on top of design, somewhat mottled clay color, ca. 1870, 2 gal., 13 1/2" h. (ILLUS. right with unusual bird-decorated small churn & Edmands crock, bottom page 18) **330**

Fine Norton, Bennington Jug with Bold Flower & Leaf Decoration

New York Stoneware Jug with Blossom

Jug, cylindrical w/rounded shoulder to a small cylindrical neck, applied strap handle, slip-quilled cobalt blue large ribbed & pointed blossom on a leafy stem below the impressed size number & mark of the New York Stoneware Co., Fort Edward, New York, minor clay separation at shoulder, minor surface chipping on the neck, ca. 1880, 2 gal., 13 1/2" h. (ILLUS.) **248**

Jug, cylindrical w/rounded shoulder to a small molded mouth, applied strap handle, slip-quilled cobalt blue very large stylized dotted & petaled flower among dense leaves & scrolls, impressed mark of J. & E. Norton, Bennington, Vermont, glaze drip on shoulder, minor stack mark on front, ca. 1855, 2 gal., 13 1/2" h. (ILLUS., top next column).. **1,925**

Jug Decorated with Double Tulips

Jug, flat base w/tapering sides to a small molded mouth & strap handle, cobalt blue brushed double tulip flowers below the impressed mark "E.A. Montell - Olean, NY - 2," minor use staining, couple of surface chips at mouth, ca. 1860, 2 gal., 13 1/2" h. (ILLUS.) **248**

Two Jugs & a Pitcher from Binghamton, New York Potteries

Jug with Canadian Advertising

molded mouth & strap handle, cobalt blue brushed stylized running rabbit design typical of this firm & below the blue-washed impressed mark of Norton & Fenton, East Bennington, Vermont, two stack marks, some spider cracks from minor stone ping on shoulder, surface chip at base & mouth, some use staining, ca. 1840, 2 gal., 13 1/2" h. (ILLUS. left with Bennington crock & other ovoid jug, bottom page 52) **1,155**

Jug, flat-bottomed cylindrical form tapering to a small molded mouth & strap handle, dark cobalt blue brushed large double fan-shaped flowers on a tall leafy stem below the blue-washed impressed mark of Whites, Utica, New York, overall dark use stain, minor surface wear, ca. 1865, 2 gal., 13 1/2" h. (ILLUS. center with two other decorated jugs by Whites, Utica, bottom page 106) **303**

Jug, flat-bottomed beehive shape w/small mouth & strap handle, advertising-type w/impressed cobalt blue inscription reading "Allan Turner & Co - Chemists & Druggists - Brookville, ONT," large simple brushed cobalt blue leaf-shaped blossom, some minor staining from use, unknown maker, ca. 1870, 2 gal., 13 1/2" h. (ILLUS.)...................... **165**

Jug, flat-bottomed cylindrical body tapering to a small neck & strap handle, cobalt blue slip-quilled running songbird on a leafy sprig, impressed size number & mark for White & Wood, Binghamton, New York, some use staining, very minor glaze age crazing, ca. 1885, 2 gal., 13 1/2" h. (ILLUS. right with other pieces from Binghamton, New York, top of page) **770**

Jug, flat-bottomed cylindrical body w/a rounded shoulder tapering to a small

Ovoid Jug with Great Sunflower Design

Jug, ovoid body tapering to a molded mouth, applied strap handle, large slip-quilled finely detailed cobalt blue sunflower on a leafy stem & size number, unsigned but attributed to the John Burger factory, Rochester, New York, excellent condition, ca. 1855, 2 gal., 13 1/2" h. (ILLUS., previous page) **743**

Jug with Blue Clover Leaf Design

Jug, ovoid body tapering to a small molded mouth & strap handle, large cobalt blue brushed clover leaf design below the impressed mark "Lyons," Lyons, New York, some overgrazing at shoulder & side, tight in-the-making clay separation in the handle, ca. 1865, 2 gal., 13 1/2" h. (ILLUS.) **165**

Tall Jug with Double-flower Design

Jug, ovoid body tapering to a small molded mouth & strap handle, large cobalt blue brushed double flower on stem below the impressed mark of J. Heiser, Buffalo, New York, indented stack mark on front into design & other stack marks on side, ca. 1852, 2 gal., 13 1/2" h. (ILLUS.) **303**

Fine N. Clark Jug with Bold Floral Design

Jug, swelled cylindrical body w/rounded shoulder tapering to a molded mouth, applied strap handle, unusual bold slip-quilled cobalt blue vine w/pairs of large rounded blossoms up the side, impressed mark of N. Clark Jr., Athens, New York, stack mark at shoulder, minor stone pings, ca. 1850, 2 gal., 13 1/2" h. (ILLUS.).. **688**

Charlestown Jug with Black Flower

Two Jugs & a Preserve Jar Made in Rochester, New York

Jug, tall cylindrical body w/a rounded shoulder to the small molded mouth, applied strap handle, brushed very dark black stylized flower above a dotted stem w/leaves, impressed mark of Charlestown, Massachusetts, incised "1/2 - 1/2" to right of design, ca. 1850, 2 gal., 13 1/2" h. (ILLUS., previous page).............. **495**

Troy, New York Jug with Blossom Design

Jug, wide cylindrical body w/rounded shoulder to a molded mouth, applied strap handle, slip-quilled cobalt blue stylized double blossom on leafy scrolled sprig, impressed mark of Troy, New York, deep incised line around the center, some use staining & kiln burn on left side, chip on mouth, ca. 1870, 2 gal., 13 1/2" h. (ILLUS.) **110**

Jug, wide flat bottomed cylindrical form w/a rounded shoulder to a small neck & strap handle, small cobalt blue slip-quilled scrolling plume design, lightly impressed mark of the New York Stoneware Co., Fort Edward, New York, overall use staining, long spot of glaze wear on right

side, ca. 1870, 2 gal., 13 1/2" h. (ILLUS. left with bird-decorated crock & another jug from Fort Edward, New York, top page 54).. **110**

Jug, beehive-shaped tapering to a small molded mouth & strap handle, dark cobalt blue large slip-quilled blossoms w/six ribbed petals surrounded by scrolls & dotted leaves, impressed & blue-tinted mark of Haxstun, Ottman & Co., Fort Edward, New York, ca. 1870, 2 gal., 14" h. (large glaze burn in center of design) **154**

Jug, beehive-shaped tapering to a small mouth & strap handle, cobalt blue slip-quilled unusual design of two large loop & feather flowers centered by a plume design & above two narrow fanned horizontal leaves, attributed to Albany, New York, some design fry, minor glaze flake spots at base, restoration to chip at mouth, ca. 1870, 2 gal., 14" h. **303**

Jug, beehive-shaped tapering to a small mouth & strap handle, dark cobalt blue slip-quilled large parrot perched on a long scrolling branch & a script size number near the mouth, impressed "Cornwall Ont.," design attributed to the Flack & Van Arsdale Pottery, Cornwall, Ontario, Canada, minor staining, somewhat dry glaze, short clay separation under handle, ca. 1870, 2 gal., 14" h. **633**

Jug, beehive-shaped tapering to a thick molded mouth & strap handle, cobalt blue slip-quilled delicate running bird w/a wide fanned tail on a squiggle twig near the front bottom, two incised shoulder bands form the impressed mark of Whites, Utica, New York, ca. 1865, 2 gal., 14" h. (minor chip on mouth)............... **853**

Jug, beehive-shaped w/a short cylindrical neck & strap handle, cobalt blue slip-quilled large five-petaled ribbed flower on a stem w/four ribbed leaves below a size number & the impressed mark of J. Burger, Jr., Rochester, New York, excellent condition, ca. 1885, 2 gal., 14" h. (ILLUS. left with other jug & preserve jar made in Rochester, New York, top of page)............. **495**

Jug, beehive-shaped w/a small molded mouth & strap handle, cobalt blue slip-quilled running bird on stem near front base, impressed mark of Whites, Utica, New York, stack marks on side, stack mark in breast of bird, chip at base below design, ca. 1865, 2 gal., 14" h. (ILLUS. left with bird- and owl-decorated pieces from Whites, Utica, top page 51)................. **440**

Two-gallon Jug with Leaf Sprig Decor

Jug, cylindrical body tapering to a small cylindrical mouth & strap handle, cobalt blue slip-quilled stylized leaf sprig decoration, impressed mark of New York Stoneware Co., Fort Edward, New York, minor glaze flake at mouth, ca. 1880, 2 gal., 14" h. (ILLUS.) **187**

N. Clark & Co. Jug with Plume Design

Jug, bulbous ovoid body tapering to a molded mouth, applied strap handle, brushed cobalt blue plume design & size number w/blue-trimmed impressed mark of N. Clark & Co., Lyons, New York, some staining & glaze spiders, stack marks & mottled clay color, ca. 1850, 2 gal., 14" h. (ILLUS.)...................... **385**

Jug, bulbous ovoid body tapering to a molded mouth & strap handle, cobalt blue brushed upturned ribbed leaf below the impressed & blue-tinted mark of N. Clark, Athens, New York, mottled clay, couple of stack marks on one side, ca. 1820, 2 gal., 14" h. (ILLUS. right with early Utica jar & other jug, top page 81)........................ **440**

Jug, bulbous ovoid body tapering to a short neck & strap handle, blue accents at handle & impressed ring around neck, unsigned, probably early Connecticut origin, large stack mark on right side & overglazing at shoulder, some use staining, ca. 1820, 2 gal., 14" h. (ILLUS. left with Boston-made jar & jug, top page 83)... **121**

Jug, bulbous ovoid body tapering to a small neck & strap handle, cobalt blue brushed stylized flower & leaf below the blue-washed impressed mark of L. Norton, Bennington, Vermont, stack marks, stone ping & mottled clay color from the firing, ca. 1830, 2 gal., 14" h. (ILLUS. center with a Vermont-made crock & another jug, top page 56) **660**

Tall Jug with Bold Bird & Branch Design

Jug, cylindrical body tapering to a small cylindrical mouth & strap handle, large dark cobalt blue slip-quilled paddle-tailed bird w/white head on a long leafy branch, impressed mark of N.A. White & Son, Utica, New York, kiln burn, very tight body hairline & stone ping on left side, ca. 1870, 2 gal., 14" h. (ILLUS., previous page) **1,595**

Jug, cylindrical body tapering to a small molded mouth & strap handle, cobalt blue large unusual double flower design w/large oblong leaves below the blue-tinted impressed mark of Ballard & Brothers, Gardiner, Maine, kiln burn at shoulder, professional restoration to chips on mouth, ca. 1855, 2 gal., 14" h. (ILLUS. left with decorated crock & jar, bottom page 38) **198**

Bennington Jug with Large Peacock

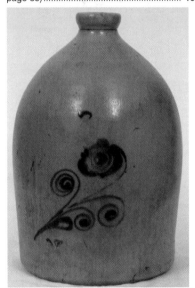

Unmarked Jug with Leaf Decoration

Jug, cylindrical body w/tapering shoulder to a small mouth & strap handle, cobalt blue slip-quilled bull's-eye leaf design, probably Albany, New York, some use staining & minor surface chip on mouth, ca. 1870, 2 gal., 14" h. (ILLUS.) **121**

Jug, cylindrical form tapering to a rounded shoulder & small molded mouth & strap handle, brushed cobalt blue large stylized triple flower on leafy stem, impressed mark of W. E. Welding, Brantford, Ontario, Canada, some use staining, ca. 1870, 2 gal., 14" h. (ILLUS. center with other Canadian & a Southern jug, top page 114) **550**

Jug, cylindrical tapering to a small molded mouth & strap handle, cobalt blue slip-quilled large peacock perched on a big tree stump, impressed mark of J. & E. Norton, Bennington, Vermont, minor stone ping on back near handle, ca. 1855, 2 gal., 14" h. (ILLUS., top next column) **4,950**

Whites Jug with Tall Bouquet Design

Jug, cylindrical w/rounded shoulder tapering to a molded mouth, applied strap handle, slip-quilled cobalt blue tall elegant bouquet of stylized flowers below the impressed mark of Whites, Utica, New York, tight glued U-shaped crack around design from just below the mouth to the base, stack mark touches one of the flowers, ca. 1865, 2 gal., 14" h. (ILLUS.) **303**

Running Bird on Whites, Utica Jug

Jug, cylindrical w/rounded shoulder tapering to a molded mouth, applied strap handle, slip-quilled cobalt blue running bird w/fanned tail near the front bottom, impressed & blue-trimmed mark of Whites, Utica, New York, some design fry, minor surface chip on mouth, ca. 1865, 2 gal., 14" h. (ILLUS.) **385**

Jug with Fancy Bird on Vine Decoration

Jug, cylindrical w/rounded shoulder tapering to cylindrical neck, applied strap handle, slip-quilled cobalt blue large paddle-tailed bird w/head raised & perched on a very long & scrolling flowering vine, impressed mark of N.A. White & Son, Utica, New York, some surface roughness &

minor chipping on rim, ca. 1870, 2 gal., 14" h. (ILLUS.) **1,925**

E. & L.P. Norton Jug with Bird Design

Jug, cylindrical w/rounded shoulder to a small molded mouth, applied strap handle, slip-quilled cobalt blue bird sitting at an angle on a plume-form leaf, impressed size number & mark of E. & L.P. Norton, Bennington, Vermont, tight in-body hairline just touching leaf, spider crack at shoulder, ca. 1880, 2 gal., 14" h. (ILLUS.)... **275**

J. & E. Norton Jug with Peacock Design

Jug, cylindrical w/rounded shoulder to a small molded mouth, applied strap handle, slip-quilled cobalt blue large peacock perched on a stump, impressed size number & mark of J. & E. Norton, Bennington, Vermont, overall use stain, ca. 1855, 2 gal., 14" h. (ILLUS.)..................... **2,310**

Floral Spray on E. & L.P. Norton Jug

Jug, cylindrical w/rounded shoulder to a small molded mouth, slip-quilled cobalt blue dotted stylized floral spray, impressed size number & mark of E. & L.P. Norton, Bennington, Vermont, very minor use staining, stack mark at front base, ca. 1880, 2 gal., 14" h. (ILLUS.)......... **275**

Jug, flat-bottomed cylindrical body tapering to a small molded mouth & strap handle, cobalt blue brushed & dotted oversized double flower on leafy stem design below the blue-trimmed impressed mark of C.E. Pharris & Co., Geddes, New York, minor stack mark in design, mottled clay color, ca. 1865, 2 gal., 14" h. (ILLUS. left with bird-decorated & tornado-decorated jugs, top page 106) **798**

Jug, flat-bottomed cylindrical body tapering to a small neck & strap handle, finely done cobalt blue slip-quilled large ribbed & dotted bird perched on a lacy branch, impressed mark for N.A. White & Co., Binghamton, New York, minor surface chip at base on back, stack marks at shoulder, ca. 1868, 2 gal., 14" h. (ILLUS. left with other jug & pitcher made in Binghamton, New York, top page 124) **1,210**

John Burger Jug with Triple Leaf Design

Jug, flat-bottomed ovoid body tapering to a molded mouth, applied strap handle, slip-quilled finely detailed cobalt blue triple ribbed leaf design below the size number, impressed mark of John Burger, Rochester, New York, stone ping at base, some minor use staining, ca. 1865, 2 gal., 14" h. (ILLUS.) **220**

Three Decorated Jugs Made in Lyons, New York

Three Decorated Jugs from Troy, New York

Jug, flat-bottomed ovoid body tapering to a small molded mouth & strap handle, cobalt blue slip-quilled plume design & number below the impressed mark of T. Harrington, Lyons, New York, stack marks on shoulders & front, short hairline in mouth, ca. 1850, 2 gal., 14" h. (ILLUS. center with two other decorated jugs from Lyons, New York, bottom previous page) **330**

Jug, flat-bottomed tapering body w/a small mouth & strap handle, large sideways cobalt blue brushed flower on leafy stem below the impressed mark of Clark & Fox, Athens, New York, centered by a size number, professional restoration & handle replaced, ca. 1838, 2 gal., 14" h. (ILLUS. center with two other flower-decorated crocks, center page 43) **176**

Jug, flat-bottomed tapering ovoid body w/a molded small mouth & strap handle, cobalt blue slip-quilled plume & dotted scroll design below the impressed mark of W.J. Seymour, Troy, New York, large stone ping on left side, some glaze flaking, some use staining, ca. 1855, 2 gal., 14" h. (ILLUS. center with two other Troy, New York, jugs, top of page) **99**

Jug, ovoid body tapering to a small molded mouth, applied strap handle, slip-quilled cobalt blue large fanned & petaled flower above a stem of long leaves & below the size number, impressed mark of F. Stetzenmeyer, Rochester, New York,

some use staining, otherwise excellent, ca. 1855, 2 gal., 14" h. (ILLUS., below)............. **1,650**

Large Fanned Flower on New York Jug

Bold Flower on Stetzenmeyer Jug

Jug, ovoid body tapering to a small molded mouth, applied strap handle, slip-quilled bold dark cobalt blue large fanned & petaled flower above a stem of long leaves & below the size number, impressed mark of F. Stetzenmeyer, Rochester, New York, stone ping & stack mark on shoulder, ca. 1860, 2 gal., 14" h. (ILLUS.)...................... **1,650**

Tall Two-gallon Jug with Flower

Jug, ovoid body tapering to a small molded mouth & strap handle, large cobalt blue slip-quilled blossom above two large oblong leaves & "2," possibly from the I.H. Wands Factory, Olean, New York, cinnamon-colored clay, some surface chipping at mouth & couple at base, long very tight spidering glued crack on right side, ca. 1860, 2 gal., 14" h. (ILLUS.)........................ **275**

White, Utica Jug with Brushed Design

Jug, ovoid body tapering to a small neck w/molded rim, applied strap handle, brushed cobalt blue crude curved flower on stem & star w/size number painted twice, impressed mark of White, Utica, New York, minor design fry, ca. 1840, 2 gal., 14" h. (ILLUS.) **550**

Jug, swelled cylindrical form tapering to a small molded mouth & strap handle, cobalt blue large brushed draping flower designs around the shoulder, unsigned by possibly a Shenandoah Valley potter, minor surface wear at mouth, kiln burn touching design & one on the left side, ca. 1850, 2 gal., 14" h. (ILLUS. left with decorated crock & preserve jar, top page 38).. **275**

Jug with Light Blue Brushed Flower

Jug, wide cylindrical body tapering to a small cylindrical mouth & strap handle, light cobalt blue brushed flower design below a numeral "2," Lyons, New York factory, brown orange peel glazing at shoulder & handle, ca. 1860, 2 gal., 14" h. (ILLUS., previous page) **248**

Whites Jug with Large Poppy Design

Jug, wide cylindrical body w/rounded shoulder to a molded mouth, applied strap handle, slip-quilled cobalt blue large stylized dotted poppy on a long leafy stem, blue-trimmed impressed mark of Whites & Co., Binghamton, New York, design fry, stack marks at shoulder, some use staining, ca. 1866, 2 gal., 14" h. (ILLUS.) **303**

Jug with Unusual Incised Bird Design

Jug, wide cylindrical body w/rounded shoulder to a molded mouth, applied strap handle, rare incised & blue-tinted design of a songbird perched on a large leaf, impressed size number on the shoulder, unsigned but probably New York State origin, minor spider crack around spout & minor glaze spider just above bird, ca. 1860, 2 gal., 14" h. (ILLUS.) **468**

Jug, wide flat bottomed cylindrical form w/a rounded shoulder to a small neck & strap handle, cobalt blue slip-quilled large triple ribbed-leaf design, impressed mark of the New York Stoneware Co., Fort Edward, New York, some use staining, small tight hairline up from base on back, ca. 1880, 2 gal., 14" h. (ILLUS. right with bird-decorated crock & other jug all made in Fort Edward, New York, top page 54) **143**

Jug, beehive-shaped tapering to a small molded mouth & strap handle, cobalt blue slip-quilled design of two graduated pair of oblong dotted wings joined by stylized tornados & bee stinger squiggles below the lightly impressed & blue-tinted mark of N. Clark, Jr., Athens, New York, ca. 1850, 2 gal., 14 1/2" h. (long age spider crack from a minor stone ping at the front shoulder) **468**

Jug with Fat Bird Cobalt Decoration

Jug, cylindrical body tapering to a small cylindrical neck & strap handle, cobalt blue slip-quilled fat bird perched on a squiggle branch, impressed mark "Ottman Bro's & Co. - Fort Edward, N.Y. - 2," stone pings & stack marks, ca. 1870, 2 gal., 14 1/2" h. (ILLUS.) **578**

Jug with Fancy Scrolling Floral Design

Jug, cylindrical body tapering to a small molded mouth & strap handle, cobalt blue slip-quilled large branched stylized scrolling floral design below the impressed mark "Fenton & Hancock - St. Johnsbury, VT," fairly uncommon mark, minor chip at bottom front, ca. 1852, 2 gal., 14 1/2" h. (ILLUS.)................................ **578**

Advertising Jug Made in New York

Jug, flat-bottomed beehive shape w/small cylindrical mouth & strap handle, advertising-type w/slip-quilled cobalt blue inscription reading "Moore, & Hubbard - Syracuse. - N.Y." below an impressed "2" & the mark of Ottmann Bros. & Co., Fort Edward, New York, tight spider line at mouth & handle, some glaze flake spots, ca. 1870, 2 gal., 14 1/2" h. (ILLUS.)................... **132**

Whites, Utica Jugs with Birds & a Flower

Jug, flat-bottomed cylindrical form tapering to a small molded mouth & strap handle, cobalt blue slip-quilled running bird design at the front base, impressed mark of Whites, Utica, New York, stack mark through tail of bird, minor surface chip on mouth, ca. 1865, 2 gal., 14 1/2" h. (ILLUS. center with bird- and flower-decorated jugs from Whites, Utica, bottom previous page)... **495**

Burger & Lang Jug with Daisy Design

Jug, flat-bottomed ovoid body tapering to a molded mouth, applied strap handle, slip-quilled finely detailed cobalt blue five-petal daisy on leafy stem design, impressed mark of Burger & Lang, Rochester, New York, some use staining, stack marks on shoulder, surface chip on mouth, ca. 1870, 2 gal., 14 1/2" h. (ILLUS.)................... **220**

Jug, flat-bottomed ovoid body tapering to a small molded mouth & strap handle, small cobalt blue brushed plume design & size number below the impressed mark "Lyons," Lyons, New York, large glaze burn & stack mark on back, ca. 1860, 2 gal., 14 1/2" h. (ILLUS. second from right with crock & other jugs made in Lyons, New York, page 44) **165**

Jug, flat-bottomed ovoid body tapering to a small molded mouth & strap handle, cobalt blue brushed plume design & size number below the impressed mark "Lyons," Lyons, New York, minor chip at mouth, ca. 1860, 2 gal., 14 1/2" h. (ILLUS. second from left with other Lyons, New York, jugs & crock, page 44) **358**

Jug, flat-bottomed ovoid body w/a molded mouth & strap handle, dark cobalt blue slip-quilled large feather leaf enclosing the size number below the impressed mark of John Burger, Rochester, New

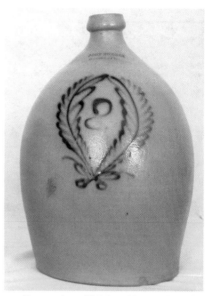

Burger Jug with Large Wreath Design

York, very minor surface chip at base on side, ca. 1865, 2 gal., 14 1/2" h. (ILLUS.) **440**

Burger Jug with Large Flower Design

Jug, flat-bottomed ovoid body w/a molded mouth & strap handle, dark cobalt blue slip-quilled large rose-like flower on a leafy stem below a size number & the blue-trimmed impressed mark of John Burger, Rochester, New York, some in-the-making clay separation, three hairlines up from base, stack mark on left, ca. 1865, 2 gal., 14 1/2" h. (ILLUS.) **468**

Great Flower-decorated New York Jug

Jug, ovoid body tapering to a molded mouth, applied strap handle, slip-quilled finely detailed cobalt blue large sunflower on leafy stem design, impressed blue-trimmed mark of Harrington & Burger, Rochester, New York, excellent condition, ca. 1853, 2 gal., 14 1/2" h. (ILLUS.)............................ **1,430**

J.W. Cowden Jug with Large Blossom

Jug, ovoid body tapering to a small molded mouth, applied strap handle, brushed cobalt blue large rounded petaled blossom below the blue-trimmed impressed size number & mark of J.W. Cowden, Harris-

burg, Pennsylvania, very minor glaze separation at base, hairline down from mouth, ca. 1861, 2 gal., 14 1/2" h. (ILLUS.) **303**

Stetzenmeyer Jug with Drooping Flower

Jug, ovoid body tapering to a small molded mouth, applied strap handle, slip-quilled cobalt blue large drooping ribbed flower above a stem of long leaves & below the size number, impressed mark of F. Stetzenmeyer, Rochester, New York, minor surface roughness on mouth, minor glaze wear on left side, ca. 1855, 2 gal., 14 1/2" h. (ILLUS.) **2,640**

Jug with a Large Stylized Flower

Jug, ovoid body tapering to a small molded mouth, slip-quilled cobalt blue large eight-petalled flower blossom w/fine shading & the number "2" above it, impressed mark of N. Clark & Co., Rochester, New York, washed in blue, couple of minor stack marks, ca. 1850, 2 gal., 14 1/2" h. (ILLUS.) **3,520**

Lyons, New York Jug with Leaf Design

Jug, ovoid body tapering to a small molded mouth & strap handle, large cobalt blue brushed leaf design beside a large "2," impressed mark "Lyons," Lyons, New York, stack marks at base & side, ca. 1860, 2 gal., 14 1/2" h. (ILLUS.).................. **220**

Early Ovoid Jug with Leaf Design

Jug, ovoid body tapering to a small molded mouth & strap handle, simple cobalt blue brushed large leaf design below the impressed mark of J. Clark & Co., Troy, New York, fairly uncommon potter, stack mark at top, stone ping just above mark, some use staining & minor surface chipping, ca. 1827, 2 gal., 14 1/2" h. (ILLUS.) **220**

Jug, ovoid body tapering to a small neck & molded mouth w/strap handle, unique large dark cobalt blue slip-quilled eight-petal blossom beside a size number & below the blue-tinted impressed mark of N. Clark & Co., Rochester, New York, couple of minor stack marks, ca. 1850, 2 gal., 14 1/2" h. (ILLUS. center with two other rare decorated pieces made in Rochester, New York, bottom page 82).... **3,520**

Seymour Jug with Bumblebee Design

Jug, sharply ovoid body tapering to a small molded neck, applied strap handle, cobalt blue slip-quilled stylized bumblebee design on shoulder below impressed blue-trimmed mark "I. Seymour Troy," Troy, New York, ca. 1830, overall staining from use, 2 gal., 14 1/2" h. (ILLUS.)....... **275**

Jug, wide cylindrical body tapering to a small neck & strap handle, super cobalt blue slip-quilled design of a very large peacock perched on a tall stump, blue-tinted impressed mark of Haxstun & Co., Fort Edward, New York, somewhat dry glaze, mottled clay color, ca. 1870, 2 gal., 14 1/2" h. (ILLUS. center with two other bird-decorated pieces from Fort Edward, New York, top page 49) **2,090**

Whites, Utica Jug with Running Bird

N. Clark Jug with Stylized Flowers

Jug, wide cylindrical body w/rounded shoulder to a molded mouth, applied strap handle, brushed cobalt blue stylized flowers on a leafy stem, impressed circle mark of N. Clark Jr., Athens, New York, two stack marks on shoulder, lamp hole drilled in base at back, ca. 1850, 2 gal., 14 1/2" h. (ILLUS.) **165**

Jug, beehive-shaped w/a short molded neck & strap handle, cobalt blue slip-quilled tulip blossom on a leafy stem below a script size number & the blue-tinted impressed mark of Burger & Lang, Rochester, New York, stack mark but overall excellent condition, ca. 1870, 2 gal., 15" h. (ILLUS. right with other jug & preserve jar made in Rochester, New York, top page 126) **413**

Jug, bulbous ovoid body tapering to a small molded mouth & strap handle, cobalt blue slip-quilled large dotted tulip on leafy stem design, blue-tinted impressed mark of N. Clark & Co., Lyons, New York, ca. 1850, 2 gal., 15" h. (ILLUS. right with very rare Lyons butter churn & cream pot, top page 21) **1,100**

Jug, cylindrical w/rounded shoulder tapering to a molded mouth, applied strap handle, slip-quilled cobalt blue running bird w/fanned tail near the front bottom, impressed & blue-trimmed mark of Whites, Utica, New York, design fry, ca. 1865, 2 gal., 15" h. (ILLUS.) **385**

Jug, flat-bottomed ovoid body tapering to a small molded mouth & strap handle, cobalt blue brushed tulip on leafy stem design & size number below the impressed mark "Lyons," Lyons, New York, dry glaze & clay discoloration, stack mark on front below flower, minor use staining at base, ca. 1860, 2 gal., 15" h. (ILLUS. far left with two other Lyons jugs & a crock, bottom page 44) **209**

Jug, flat-bottomed tapering ovoid body w/a molded small mouth & strap handle, cobalt blue slip-quilled squatty bird on a scroll below the impressed mark for the West Troy Pottery, Troy, New York, very minor surface chip on mouth, long X-shaped spider crack from stone ping on shoulder, clay separation line at mouth on back, ca. 1880, 2 gal., 15" h. (ILLUS. right with two other Troy, New York, jugs, top page 131) **385**

Early Jug with Head of Bearded Man

Jug, sharply ovoid body tapering to a small neck & strap handle, the shoulder deeply incised w/a bust portrait of a long-haired unshaven man, unsigned, probably New York or New Jersey, tight hairline down from neck, stack marks, ca. 1820, 2 gal., 15" h. (ILLUS.) **3,300**

Early Connecticut Ovoid Jug

Jug, ovoid body tapering to a small neck w/incised rings, applied strap handle, overall tan clay w/age staining, impressed mark of D. Goodale, Hartford, Connecticut, ca. 1826, 2 gal., 15 1/2" h. (ILLUS.)... **303**

Early Jug Possibly From Ohio

Jug, tall slender ovoid body w/short neck & molded mouth, applied strap handle, cobalt blue brushed "88" on the front, blue trim on handle, unsigned but possibly early Ohio origin, overall glaze pit spots, old professional restoration to spout, ca. 1830, 2 gal., 15 1/2" h. (ILLUS.) **132**

Jug, wide ovoid body tapering to a small molded mouth & strap handle, cobalt blue brushed stylized flowers on the shoulder below the blue-trimmed impressed mark for N. & R. Seymour, Rome, New York, very uncommon potter, mottled clay color, couple of minor stack marks, ca. 1820, 2 gal., 16" h. **440**

Large Jug with Double Love Birds

Jug, wide-bottomed ovoid body tapering to a small mouth & strap handle, cobalt blue slip-quilled double love birds design beside "3" below the impressed mark "S. Hart - Fulton," New York state, use staining, glued crack at back, ca. 1875, 3 gal., 13 1/2" h. (ILLUS., previous page) **495**

Jug, bulbous ovoid body tapering to a small mouth & strap handle, dark cobalt blue small brushed oval flower & leaf design just below the mouth, further incised w/four lines around the shoulder, unsigned, prominent stack marks in the making, ca. 1830, 3 gal., 14" h. **440**

Jug, tall ovoid body tapering to a very small mouth & strap handle, impressed blue-trimmed band at shoulder showing alternating incised bird & leaf design, impressed w/"Wine" at the shoulder above the band, attributed to Joseph Remmey, New Jersey, very early piece, stack mark & kiln burns at shoulder, large indented stack mark on back, virtually undamaged, ca. 1820, 3 gal., 14" h. **825**

Jug with Scroll & Number Design

Jug, wide-bottomed ovoid body tapering to a small mouth & strap handle, cobalt blue slip-quilled scroll & dot design below "3" below the impressed mark "S. Hart - Fulton," New York state, some minor use staining, ca. 1875, 3 gal., 14" h. (ILLUS.) **154**

Jug, advertising-type, cylindrical body w/rounded shoulder to the small molded mouth, applied strap handle, blue-trimmed impressed shoulder advertising "Peck's - Drug, Store - 34 & 39 - Colden - New Burgh," all above a slip-quilled cobalt blue large singing bird w/a wide fanned drooping tail, unsigned by maker but probably New York origin, minor glaze burn on very back of base, ca. 1880, 3 gal., 14 1/2" h. (ILLUS., top next column) **385**

Advertising Jug with Singing Bird Design

Jug, beehive-shaped tapering to a thin molded mouth & strap handle, cobalt blue slip-quilled large stylized design of two large rounded flowers below a fanned leaf cluster all on a long slender stem, impressed & blue-tinted size number & the mark of C. Hart, Sherburne, New York, a carved wood stopper included, ca. 1870, 3 gal., 14 1/2" h. (shoulder overglazed in-the-making, minor surface wear & stains) **187**

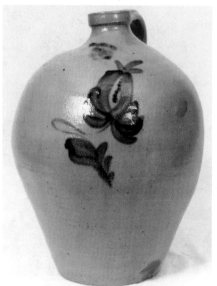

Ovoid Jug with Bold Tulip Decoration

Jug, bulbous ovoid body tapering to a short neck & molded rim, applied strap handle, brushed dark cobalt blue tulip on leafy stem decoration, impressed mark for Jordan, somewhat misshapen & overglazed on the back, ca. 1850, 3 gal., 14 1/2" h. (ILLUS., previous page) **440**

Early Bennington Jug with Flowers

Jug, cylindrical body tapering to a small molded mouth & strap handle, cobalt blue brushed stylized triple flower design below the impressed mark "Norton & Fenton - East Bennington, VT - 3," long surface chip on mouth, fairly uncommon maker, ca. 1840, 3 gal., 14 1/2" h. (ILLUS.) **176**

F.B. Norton Jug with Bird on Plume

Jug, cylindrical body w/rounded shoulder to a small molded mouth, slip-quilled cobalt blue large parrot on a plume leaf design, impressed mark of F.B. Norton & Co., Worcester, Massachusetts, overall use staining, ca. 1870, 3 gal., 14 1/2" h. (ILLUS.) **743**

Jug, wide cylindrical body tapering to a small molded mouth & strap handle, cobalt blue slip-quilled large parrot flanked by plumed leaves below the impressed mark of F.B. Norton & Co., Worcester, Massachusetts, clay separation line at base of handle, very minor glaze wear, ca. 1870, 3 gal., 14 1/2" h. (ILLUS. right with parrot-decorated F.B. Norton crock, bottom page 53) **1,540**

Jug, beehive-shaped tapering to a small molded mouth & strap handle, cobalt blue slip-quilled fancy design of two long-legged birds facing each other but looking back over their shoulders, perched on a flowering rose-type bush, impressed & blue-tinted mark of Whites, Utica, New York, ca. 1865, 3 gal., 15" h. (professional restoration to a stack mark at top of design, in-the-making variations in the cobalt blue application) **1,925**

Jug, bulbous ovoid body tapering sharply to a small molded mouth & strap handle, cobalt blue brushed small leaf design on the shoulder, heavy blue accents at the handle, unsigned but probably New York state origin, dark tan clay color from the firing, stack marks at the shoulder, a few minor glaze flakes, ca. 1830, 3 gal., 15" h.. **358**

Jug, bulbous ovoid body tapering to a small mouth & strap handle, deeply incised & blue-trimmed leaf design at the shoulder, unsigned, stack mark & kiln burns from the firing, mottled clay shading from grey to olive green, glaze spider crack on the side & hairlines in the handles, ca. 1820, 3 gal., 15" h. **209**

Plump Bird on Whites, Utica Jug

Jug, cylindrical w/rounded shoulder tapering to a molded mouth, applied strap handle, slip-quilled cobalt blue short plump rib-tailed bird on twig design, impressed mark of Whites, Utica, New York, stone ping just below mark, two stack marks on back, few spider cracks, ca. 1865, 3 gal., 15" h. (ILLUS., previous page) **413**

Large Peacock on Whites, Utica Jug

Jug, cylindrical w/rounded shoulder tapering to a molded mouth, applied strap handle, slip-quilled cobalt blue large long-tailed peacock perched on a long stump, impressed mark of Whites, Utica, New York, glaze burns on side & back, professional restoration to overall long hairlines, ca. 1865, 3 gal., 15" h. (ILLUS.) **633**

Plume on Norton Jug, Missing Handle

Jug, cylindrical w/rounded shoulder to a small molded mouth, slip-quilled cobalt blue dotted plume, impressed size number & mark of E. & L.P. Norton, Bennington, Vermont, some use staining, missing handle, ca. 1880, 3 gal., 15" h. (ILLUS.) **154**

Jug, flat-bottomed wide ovoid body tapering to a small molded mouth & strap handle, dark cobalt blue wreath enclosing the size number below the impressed & blue-tinted mark of J. Mantell, Penn Yan, New York, glaze drips on front, surface chip at front base, ca. 1860, 3 gal., 15" h. **330**

Jug by Rare New Jersey Maker

Jug, sharply ovoid body tapering to a small mouth & strap handle, brushed cobalt blue large flower below the impressed mark of Humiston & Stockwell, S. Amboy, New Jersey, one of the rarest early New Jersey marks, pinhead size flake on top of lip, stack mark on side, ca. 1830, 3 gal., 15" h. (ILLUS.) **1,870**

Jug, swelled cylindrical body w/rounded shoulder to a small molded mouth, applied strap handle, brushed cobalt blue man-in-the-moon enclosed in wreath design, impressed size number & mark of Cowden & Wilcox, Harrisburg, Pennsylvania, some minor design fry, ca. 1870, 3 gal., 15" h. (ILLUS., top next page) **7,700**

Jug, wide bulbous ovoid body tapering to a small molded mouth & strap handle, dark cobalt blue slip-quilled pair of three-petaled triangular flowers on a curly stem w/two oblong leaves, impressed & blue-washed mark of Mantell & Thomas, Penn Yan, New York, rare maker, excellent condition, ca. 1854, 3 gal., 15" h. **1,100**

Jug, wide ovoid body tapering to a small molded mouth & strap handle, cobalt blue slip-quilled large sunflower on leafy stalk design & a script size number below the impressed mark of I. H. Wands, Olean, New York, fairly uncommon maker, in-the-making glaze burn on right, some use staining, small clay separation line on back base, ca. 1858, 3 gal., 15" h. (ILLUS. left with two other Olean, New York jugs, top page 121)..................... **413**

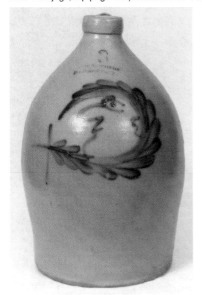

Cowden & Wilcox Man-in-the-Moon Jug

Advertising Jug with Unique Bird Design

Jug, advertising-type, cylindrical body w/rounded shoulder to the small molded mouth, applied strap handle, blue-trimmed impressed shoulder advertising "John Cavanagh - Wholesale - Wine & Liquor Store - Cor Atlas & Columbia Sts -

Brooklyn," from New York, all above a large slip-quilled cobalt blue bird w/dotted neck & long curling tail perched on a large blossom on a scrolling vine, unsigned by maker but probably New York origin, glued hairlines in handle & around shoulder, top probably knocked off but carefully glued back, minor use staining, ca. 1870, 3 gal., 15 1/2" h. (ILLUS.)......... **1,018**

Jug, beehive-shaped tapering to a small molded mouth & strap handle, cobalt blue slip-quilled plump bird w/a long, wide tail perched on a squiggled twig, impressed & blue-tinted mark for Whites, Utica, New York, ca. 1865, 3 gal., 15 1/2" h. (glaze drip spots, long in-body spider crack on shoulder, stack mark on back, overall dark use staining) **523**

Jug, beehive-shaped w/a small cylindrical neck & strap handle, cobalt blue slip-quilled stylized leaf cluster below the blue-tinted impressed mark of Brady & Ryan, Ellenville, New York, chip at front of neck, some use staining, ca. 1885, 3 gal., 15 1/2" h. (ILLUS. right with rare Brady & Ryan crock & other New York state crock, top page 50) **220**

Jug, beehive-shaped w/small molded mouth & strap handle, dark cobalt blue slip-quilled dotted large spread-winged eagle carrying a thin banner in its beak, blue-tinted impressed mark for W.J. Seymour, Troy, New York, minor glaze spider crack near handle, ca. 1855, 3 gal., 15 1/2" h. (ILLUS. center with rare Troy crock & smaller jug, center page 51) **1,705**

Early L. Norton Jug with Ochre Flower

Jug, bulbous ovoid body tapering to a small molded mouth, applied strap handle, rare ochre brushed flower design, tan background, impressed mark of L. Norton & Son, Bennington, Vermont, early mark, minor clay separation, ca. 1833, 3 gal., 15 1/2" h. (ILLUS.) **1,980**

Bennington Jug with Thistle Flowers

Jug, cylindrical body tapering to a small molded mouth & strap handle, cobalt blue slip-quilled large cluster of thistle flowers & scrolling leaves below the impressed mark "J. & E. Norton - Bennington, VT - 3," professional restoration to chips at back of mouth & handle, ca. 1855, 3 gal., 15 1/2" h. (ILLUS.).................. **468**

Plump Bird on Whites Utica Jug

Jug, cylindrical tapering to a small molded mouth & strap handle, cobalt blue slip-

quilled plump bird perched on a flowering branch, mark of Whites, Utica, New York, two small stone pings & glaze drip on front, some use staining, ca. 1865, 3 gal., 15 1/2" h. (ILLUS.) **715**

Gale Jug with Large Bold Flower

Jug, cylindrical w/rounded shoulder to a small molded mouth, applied strap handle, slip-quilled cobalt blue large rounded flowers above a pair of large leaves & a tall curlique stem, impressed size number & mark of F.A. Gale, Galesville, New York, minor horizontal glaze spider at base, long thin worn chip on base, ca. 1860, 3 gal., 15 1/2" h. (ILLUS.) **688**

Seymour Jug with Simple Flower

Jug, sharply ovoid body tapering to a small molded mouth & strap handle, simple brushed cobalt blue flower on the shoulder below the impressed mark accented w/blue, I. Seymour, Troy, New York, ca. 1825, minor in-the-making stack mark & clay separation at mouth, 3 gal., 15 1/2" h. (ILLUS., previous page).............. **303**

Jug, tall beehive-shaped w/a small molded mouth & strap handle, very large dark cobalt blue slip-quilled design of a large peacock perched on a tall, detailed tree stump, blue-tinted impressed mark of J. & E. Norton, Bennington, Vermont, minor glaze wear spot, filled-in lamp hole in base at back, ca. 1855, 3 gal., 15 1/2" h. (ILLUS. right with rare Bennington crock & a preserve jar, bottom page 51)............. **2,420**

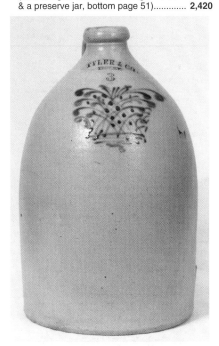

Jug From Short-lived New York Potter

Jug, wide cylindrical body w/rounded shoulder to a molded mouth, applied strap handle, slip-quilled cobalt blue dotted crown design right below the blue-trimmed impressed mark of Tyler & Co., Troy, New York, short-lived factory, very minor surface chip at side of base, ca. 1860, 3 gal., 15 1/2" h. (ILLUS.).................. **550**

Jug, wide ovoid body tapering to a small ringed mouth & strap handle, large cobalt blue crudely brushed flower & leaf design on the shoulder, more accents on handle, three deep scribe lines at shoulder, unsigned but probably New York state origin, possibly Capital district, stack mark

just touching the flower, minor surface chipping along base, ca. 1820, 3 gal., 15 1/2" h... **605**

Jug, advertising-type, tall beehive shape tapering to a tiny cylindrical neck & strap handle, cobalt blue brushed leaf sprig at shoulder above two undulating bands flanking a large script size number above the arched stenciled advertising near the base reading "Hyman Browarsky - Wholesale Liquor - Dealer - North 5th Ave. - Pittsburgh, PA," unsigned but typical of Greensboro, Pennsylvania, area potters, ca. 1870, 3 gal., 16" h. (stack marks at shoulder, dark clay color from firing)... **385**

Jug, beehive-shaped tapering to a small molded mouth & strap handle, cobalt blue slip-quilled bird w/very long narrow tail perched on a slim twig, impressed mark of Whites, Utica, New York, ca. 1865, 3 gal., 16" h. (extensive design fry leaving a brown color in the design, couple of glaze drips on side, some use staining) **275**

Bennington Jug with Compote of Flowers

Jug, cylindrical body tapering to a small molded mouth & strap handle, cobalt blue slip-quilled large compote of oversized flowers below the impressed mark of J. & E. Norton, Bennington, Vermont, professional restoration to a full-length J-shaped hairline, some use staining, ca. 1855, 3 gal., 16" h. (ILLUS.) **550**

Jug with Long-stemmed Daisy Decor

Jug, cylindrical body tapering to a small mouth & strap handle, cobalt blue slip-quilled tall leafy stem w/daisy blossom, impressed mark "3 - F.B. Norton Sons - Worcester, Mass.," overall use staining, restoration to chips at mouth & base, handle replaced, ca. 1886, 3 gal., 16" h. (ILLUS.).. **176**

Jug, cylindrical body tapering to a small mouth & strap handle, cobalt blue slip-quilled large fat bird perched on a looped twig, impressed mark "Fort Edward Stoneware Co. - Fort Edward, NY - 3," some glaze flaking around base, two stone pings in design, ca. 1884, 3 gal., 16" h. (ILLUS.) **550**

Jug, flat-bottomed cylindrical form tapering to a small molded mouth & strap handle, cobalt blue slip-quilled large angled bird running up a stem design, impressed mark of Whites, Utica, New York, over-glazing at shoulder, surface chip on mouth, some use staining, minor glaze spider on front, couple of back bottom chips, ca. 1865, 3 gal. 16" h. (ILLUS. left with other bird-decorated and a flower-decorated Whites, Utica jugs, bottom page 134)... **468**

Jug, flat-bottomed ovoid body tapering to a small molded mouth & strap handle, cobalt blue brushed & dotted large six-petaled flower on a very leafy tall stem w/size number below the impressed mark for N. Clark & Co., Lyons, New York, faint signs of old blue overpainting, excellent condition, ca. 1850, 3 gal., 16" h. (ILLUS. left with two other decorated jugs from Lyons, New York, bottom page 130)... **578**

Jug, flat-bottomed tapering ovoid body w/a molded small mouth & strap handle, cobalt blue slip-quilled long bird on a looped twig below the impressed mark for the West Troy, New York Pottery, mottled clay color, minor hairline up from base on side, some use staining, ca. 1880, 3 gal., 16" h. (ILLUS. left with two other Troy, New York, jugs, top page 131).................... **633**

Ft. Edward Jug with Fat Bird Design

Burlington, Vermont Jug with Iris Decor

Rare Fort Edward Pottery Jug with Outstanding Stag Decoration

Jug, tall cylindrical body w/rounded shoulder to a small molded mouth, slip-quilled cobalt blue small dotted iris design, impressed size number & mark of F. Woodworth, Burlington, Vermont, kiln burn on back, minor glaze spider on front, ca. 1875, 3 gal., 16" h. (ILLUS., previous page) **99**

Jug, bulbous ovoid body tapering to a small mouth & strap handle, large dark cobalt blue brushed snowball flower flanked by tall curved leaves forming a wreath, blue accents at handle, unsigned but probably New York state origin, stack mark touches wreath, surface chip at base on right, some use staining, ca. 1830, 3 gal., 16 1/2" h. **605**

Jug, cylindrical w/rounded shoulder to a small molded mouth, applied strap handle, slip-quilled cobalt blue large stag standing between stylized trees, impressed mark of the Fort Edward Pottery, Fort Edward, New York, professional restoration, handle replaced, minor stone ping, ca. 1870, 3 gal., 16 1/2" h. (ILLUS., top of page) **4,950**

Jug, flat-bottomed ovoid body tapering to a small molded mouth & strap handle, cobalt blue brushed & dotted large double flower design beside a size number below the impressed mark for N. Clark & Co., Lyons, New York, surface chipping at mouth interior, overall use staining, ca. 1850, 3 gal., 16 1/2" h. (ILLUS. right with two other decorated jugs from Lyons, New York, bottom page 130) **440**

Ovoid Jug with Large Petaled Flower

Decorated Whites, Utica Jug & Preserve Jar

Jug, ovoid body tapering to a small molded mouth, applied strap handle, slip-quilled cobalt blue large ribbed & petaled flower above a stem of long leaves & below the size number, impressed mark of F. Stetzenmeyer, Rochester, New York, some minor use staining, minor touch mark, ca. 1855, 3 gal., 16 1/2" h. (ILLUS., previous page) **2,860**

Jug, bulbous ovoid body tapering to a small molded mouth & strap handle, cobalt blue brushed small drape band at the top of the shoulder below the impressed & blue-tinted mark of I. Seymour, Troy, New York, excellent condition, ca. 1830, 3 gal., 17" h. **440**

Jug, flat-bottomed cylindrical form tapering to a small molded mouth & strap handle, cobalt blue brushed large double fanned blossoms on a leafy pointed stem below the impressed mark for Whites, Utica, New York & the impressed size number, overall dry glaze w/use staining, very tight long hairline up from base on left, ca. 1865, 3 gal., 17" h. (ILLUS. left with N.A. White plume-decorated preserve jar, top of page) **303**

Jug, flat-bottomed cylindrical form tapering to a small molded mouth & strap handle, cobalt blue slip-quilled very large drooping orchid blossom issuing from a pair of large leaves near the bottom, light blue-tinted impressed mark of N.A. White & Son, Utica, New York, stack mark just touching design, overall light tan use staining, ca. 1870, 3 gal., 17" h. (ILLUS. right with two bird-decorated Whites, Utica jugs, bottom page 134)............................ **440**

Jug, ovoid body tapering to a small molded mouth & strap handle, dark cobalt blue slip-quilled design of a very large flower w/four rounded, fanned & ribbed petals above a stem w/long oblong ribbed leaves, impressed & blue-tinted mark of F. Stetzenmeyer, Rochester, New York, ca. 1860, 3 gal., 17" h. (profession-

ally repaired rim chip, tight glaze spider crack just below mouth, very minor design fry, stone ping to left of flower) **2,035**

Jug, tall ovoid body tapering to a small ringed mouth & strap handle, very deeply incised pinwheel flower on the front below a row of eight small stars & the incised mark for Goodwin & Webster, Hartford, Connecticut, blue accents at name & handle, use staining, chipping at very base on front, ca. 1830, 3 gal., 17" h. (ILLUS. right with early New York City crock, bottom page 48) **1,650**

Unsigned Simple Midwestern Jug

Jug, cylindrical body w/rounded shoulder to the short neck w/molded rim, strap handle, cobalt blue slip-quilled squiggle at the front, large carved wooden stopper, unsigned, possibly Midwestern or Red Wing Potteries, two large chips on base, glaze drips on shoulder, ca. 1880, 3 gal., 20" h. (ILLUS.) **66**

Jug, wide flat base & bulbous sides tapering sharply to a small molded mouth & strap handle, fancy cobalt blue brushed tulip blossom on a swirling leafy stem below the impressed mark of S. Hart, Fulton, New York, stack mark below flower, minor use staining, ca. 1875, 4 gal., 15" h. (ILLUS. left with two other S. Hart, Fulton jugs, top page 100) **220**

Jug, beehive-shaped tapering to a molded mouth & strap handle, cobalt blue brushed stylized triple flower on leafy stem below the impressed & blue-washed mark of Lehman & Biedinger, Poughkeepsie, New York, ca. 1855, 4 gal., 15 1/2" h. (couple of minor base chips).. **330**

Decorated Massachusetts Jug

Large Fort Dodge, Iowa Stoneware Jug

Jug, domed beehive shape w/small molded mouth & strap handle, cobalt blue stenciled mark in rectangle on front "Fort Dodge Stoneware Co. - Manufacturers - Fort Dodge, Ia." & stenciled "4" w/sprigs on shoulder, late 19th c., 4 gal., 15 1/2" h. (ILLUS.).. **460**

Jug, wide cylindrical body w/rounded shoulder to a small cylindrical neck, slip-quilled cobalt blue large stylized dotted & ribbed flower amid scrolls across the front, impressed size number & mark of F.T. Wright & Son, Taunton, Massachusetts, design fry, some faint signs of old overpainting, some use staining, ca. 1870, 4 gal., 16" h. (ILLUS., top next column) **220**

Jug, wide ovoid body tapering sharply to a small molded mouth & strap handle, cobalt blue brushed large double flower design below the impressed mark of E.A. Montell, Olean, New York, overall use staining, overglazed in the making, small spider crack up from base, ca. 1870, 4 gal., 16" h. (ILLUS. right with two other Olean, New York jugs, top page 121) **303**

Haxstun, Ottman Jug with Large Bird

Jug, cylindrical w/rounded shoulder to a small cylindrical neck, applied strap handle, slip-quilled cobalt blue large bird perched on a wide leafy stem, blue-washed impressed mark of Haxstun, Ottman & Co., Fort Edward, New York, glaze drip on left side, some minor use staining, ca. 1870, 4 gal., 16 1/2" h. (ILLUS.).................................... **1,760**

Large Jug with Unusual Fighting Cock Scene

Jug, cylindrical tapering to a small molded mouth & strap handle, cobalt blue slip-quilled design of two large fighting cocks, professional restoration to tight in-body line, stone ping at shoulder, ca. 1865, 4 gal., 17" h. (ILLUS.).................................. **8,800**

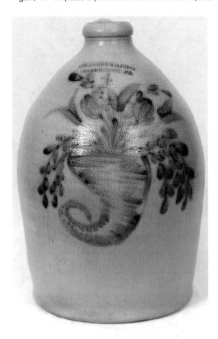

Extremely Rare Cowden & Wilcox Jug with Cornucopia Decoration

Jug, swelled cylindrical body w/rounded shoulder tapering to a small molded mouth, applied strap handle, brushed cobalt blue large cornucopia overflowing w/flowers across the front, impressed & blue-tinted size number & mark of Cowden & Wilcox, Harrisburg, Pennsylvania, rare decoration, some very minor staining, ca. 1870, 4 gal., 17" h. (ILLUS.).. **15,400**

Jug with Large Perched Bird

Jug, wide ovoid body tapering to a small molded mouth & strap handle, incised & blue-tinted large perched bird on the shoulder below a brushed size number, unsigned but probably Capitol District region of New York State, large stack marks & kiln burns on sides, heavy chipping on mouth, chip at base side, ca. 1820, 4 gal., 17" h. (ILLUS.) **1,760**

Jug, tall beehive shape tapering to a small molded mouth & strap handle, cobalt blue slip-quilled detailed design of a dandelion-like blossom above a long scrolling vine w/a large dotted leaf, impressed mark of Nicholas & Boynton, Burlington, Vermont, professional restoration to a tight crack around the shoulder, ca. 1855, 4 gal., 17 1/2" h. (ILLUS. right with Vermont-made crock & smaller jug, top page 56) **440**

Jug, ovoid body tapering to a small molded mouth, applied strap handle, unique brushed cobalt blue design of a large American shield flanked by American flags w/leafy branches below, impressed size number & mark of Cowden & Wilcox, Harrisburg, Pennsylvania, very minor staining, ca. 1870, 4 gal., 18" h. (ILLUS., top next page)... **8,800**

Very Rare Cowden & Wilcox Jug with Patriotic Shield & Flags Design

Large Flowers on Cowden & Wilcox Jug

Jug, ovoid body tapering to a small molded mouth, applied strap handle, slip-quilled cobalt blue design of a very large ribbed four-petaled flower w/a smaller blossom & rounded leaves, impressed size number & mark of Cowden & Wilcox, Harrisburg, Pennsylvania, some very minor use staining, ca. 1870, 4 gal., 18 1/2" h. (ILLUS.) **7,700**

Jug, flat-bottomed cylindrical form tapering to a small cylindrical neck & strap handle, cobalt blue large slip-quilled detailed

streamlined paddletailed bird on a long leafy stem, impressed mark of White & Wood, Binghamton, New York, couple of minor surface chips at base, ca. 1885, 5 gal., 18" h. (ILLUS. left with small & large crocks made in Binghamton, New York, bottom page 50) **2,420**

Bull's-eye & Flowers on Tall Jug

Jug, cylindrical tapering to a small molded mouth & strap handle, cobalt blue slip-quilled bull's-eye & flower design, impressed mark of New York Stoneware Co., surface roughness around lip, full-length J-shaped tight crack on right side, ca. 1870, 5 gal., 18 1/2" h. (ILLUS.) **209**

Unusual Two-handled Stoneware Jug

Jug, double-handled, cylindrical body tapering to a wide flat molded mouth, cobalt blue brushed bird perched beside a flower on leafy stem, ring-form impressed mark "N. Clark Jr. - Athens, NY - 5," very tight jagged hairline down from rim through mark, stack marks & clay separation at one handle & shoulder, ca. 1850, 5 gal., 18 1/2" h. (ILLUS.)................... **935**

Early Two-handled Jug with Tulip Design

Jug, double-handled, ovoid body tapering to a small molded mouth & handles, cobalt blue brushed design of a large stylized tulip on a leafy stem, attributed to I.M. Mead, Mogadore, Ohio, stack mark on left side, some spidering to glaze, ca. 1840, 5 gal., 18 1/2" h. (ILLUS.) **2,750**

Jug, beehive-shaped w/a small molded mouth & strap handle, advertising-type, cobalt blue slip-quilled large eight-arm scrolled & ribbed snowflake design below the blue-tinted impressed advertising on the shoulder for A.E. Allen, Massena Springs, New York, probably produced at the Ogdensburg Pottery, Ogdensburg, New York, very minor staining, ca. 1870, 5 gal., 19" h. (ILLUS. center with smaller New York state jug & jar, bottom page 81)... **2,145**

Jug, double-handled, tall ovoid body tapering to a tiny mouth, decorated around the shoulder w/a band of brushed cobalt blue paired leaves above the stenciled mark of C.L. Williams & Co., New Geneva, Pennsylvania above a large free-hand "5" near the bottom, some use staining, ca. 1897, 5 gal., 19" h. (ILLUS., below) **1,265**

Very Tall Brushed & Stenciled Jug

Jug-strainer, cylindrical body tapering to a molded wide mouth, never had a handle, the body incised all around & up the body w/closely spaced incised lines pierced through w/tiny holes, unsigned & undecorated, unusual form w/the wide mouth indicating possible use as an oyster strainer, probably New York state origin, very tight horizontal freeze line at the base halfway around, ca. 1870, 2 gal., 14 1/2" h. **798**

Jug/bank, miniature, beehive-shaped tapering to a small neck w/stopper, coin slot on back shoulder, decorated in an early salmon glaze painted w/brownish yellow leaf sprigs & white blossoms, ca. 1870, 4 1/4" h. (minor age staining) **77**

Keg, advertising-type, barrel-shaped w/four tiny knob feet at the bottom side & a small neck at the top center, molded in bold relief around the sides w/a stag & floral design w/scattered leaves all trimmed in cobalt blue, a spigot hole at one end, the other end molded w/center sprigs enclosed by the wording "Bardwell's Root Beer" in script, late 19th - early 20th c. (ILLUS. third row down, second from left, with the full page of various other stoneware pieces, page 27)................................. **558**

Rare Early "Brandy" Keg

Keg, barrel-shaped, molded pairs of horizontal bands trimmed in cobalt blue, top band hand-incised "BRANDY" trimmed in blue, the center band incised w/a scene of a rowboat & oars trimmed in blue, impressed mark of Tyler & Dillon, Albany, New York, chip on left to edge, hairline across from chip, short-lived pottery, ca. 1825, 2 gal., 13 1/2" h. (ILLUS.) **5,500**

Meat tenderizer, short cylindrical head covered w/small sharp points, embossed mark "Pat'd Dec. 25, 1877," a long narrow turned wood handle, ca. 1877, overall 10" l. (very minor chips to points) **110**

Milk pan, deep slightly flaring cylindrical sides w/a molded rim band w/a pinched spout, cobalt blue repeated brushed drooping flower & leaf design around the sides, unsigned but an impressed size number under the spout, interior stone ping, some overall glaze wear, ca. 1850, 1 gal., 11 1/2" d., 5" h. (ILLUS. left with signed decorated batter pail, top page 13)... **358**

Milk pan, wide flat-bottomed rounded bowl-form w/wide, thin molded rim, cobalt blue brushed large horizontal flower on a long leafy stem below the impressed mark of Cowden & Wilcox, Harrisburg, Pennsylvania, ca. 1870, 1 gal., 5 1/2" d., 11" h. (some rim chipping, few short hairlines down from rim)..................................... **413**

Milk pan, deep slightly flaring cylindrical sides w/thin molded rim w/pinched spout, eared handle, cobalt blue brushed large band of flowering vines around the sides, unsigned, right handle missing but probably in-the-making, stone ping chip in left handle, minor glaze burn, ca. 1850, 2 gal., 12" d., 6" h. (ILLUS. left with unsigned butter crock & covered cake crock, bottom page 26) **358**

Stoneware Milk Pan with Plume Decor

Milk pan, deep slightly flaring cylindrical sides w/a molded rim & pinched spout, decorated w/five small brushed cobalt blue plumes around the sides & three dashes under the spout, unsigned, size designation tooled just below the spout, X-shaped hairline at the base w/a grease stain, ca. 1850, 1 1/2 gal., 11 1/2" d., 6" h. (ILLUS.) **330**

Southern Stoneware Milk Pan & Oil Jug

Milk pan, very deep & wide slightly swelled cylindrical body w/a flattened rim band, dark brown glaze, Georgia, ca. 1880, 9 3/4" d., 8" h. (ILLUS. right with oil jug, above) **316**

Mottled Brown Stoneware Cat Figure

Model of a cat, recumbent animal on a thin oval base, hollow body, light & dark brown alkaline glaze, minor chip at base, glaze chip on ear, ca. 1900, 4 1/2" l., 2 1/2" h. (ILLUS.) **88**

Model of a cat, stylized, somewhat comical reclining cat w/tail wrapped around body & head raised w/ears pointed up, on a thin oval base, the body decorated over- all w/cobalt blue circles w/blue facial fea- tures, uncertain age but probably old, 8" l., 8" h. (overall dark black stains, pierced holes at front paws & body in-the- making) **688**

Small Stoneware Begging Spaniel Figure

Model of a dog, seated begging spaniel in cream w/dark bluish green applied ac- cents under the Bristol glaze, probably from Ohio, possibly early 20th c., minor surface wear, 5 1/2" h. (ILLUS.).................. **495**

Model of a dog, commemorative, seated spaniel on an oval base, overall dark brown Albany glaze, base molded in relief "Souvenir 1877 - F.M. King & Co. - 1897," King being a general merchant in Augusta, Illinois, probably produced by the Galesburg Pottery Company, Galesburg, Illinois, excellent condition, 7 1/2" h. **660**

Early Sewer Tile Pottery Lion Figure

Model of a lion, sewer tile-type, recumbent on a thick rectangular base, overall dark brown mottled glaze, hollow heavy body, overall chipping, ca. 1850, 9" l., 7 1/2" h. (ILLUS.) **198**

Mug, child's, tapering cylindrical form w/a C-form handle, overall reddish brown & green alkaline glaze, bottom impressed "TB" in a circle, attributed to Tode Brothers, a New York City vendor, ca. 1860, 2 3/4" h. **198**

Mug, cylindrical, two blue bands & an incised "2," hand-incised blue-trimmed German inscription "Gesundheit - Herr Noirban," brown Albany slip-glazed interior indicates American manufacture, unsigned, minor surface wear & use staining, ca. 1850, 4" h. (ILLUS. third from left with other mugs & small jug, top page 93) **248**

Mug, cylindrical salt-glazed body w/small C-form handle, incised blue-trimmed bands around body, applied brown Albany slip glazed interior, unsigned, probably New York state, ca. 1850, 4 1/4" h. (ILLUS. far left with other mugs & small jug, top page 93) **77**

Mug, cylindrical salt-glazed body w/small C-form handle, incised wide blue-trimmed bands around body, applied brown Albany slip glazed interior, unsigned, probably New York state, ca. 1850, 4 1/4" h. (ILLUS. far right with other mugs & small jug, top page 93) **121**

Mug, barrel-shaped salt-glazed body w/two incised & blue-trimmed body bands, unsigned but probably New York state origin, ca. 1850, 4 1/2" h. (ILLUS. second from right with other mugs & small jug, top page 93) **66**

Mug, slightly tapering cylindrical salt-glazed body w/large C-form handle, two incised & blue-trimmed narrow bands around the body, brown Albany slip-glazed interior,

unsigned but probably New York state origin, minor touch mark & glaze flake at base, ca. 1850, 4 3/4" h. (ILLUS. second from left with other mugs & small jug, top page 93) **66**

Oil jug, wide flat bottom & bulbous squatty body tapering to a short rolled neck & small cylindrical shoulder spout, overall very dark brown alkaline glaze, Miles Mill, South Carolina, ca. 1880, 5 1/2" h. (ILLUS. left with large, deep milk pan, top previous page) **374**

Early Marked Stoneware Oyster Jar

Oyster jar, wide cylindrical body tapering to a wide flat molded mouth, large deeply impressed & blue-tinted advertising "Tode Bros. - 972 Bower - New York," some staining from use, ca. 1868-79, 4" h. (ILLUS.) **413**

Maine Advertising Oyster Jar

Three Decorated Unsigned Stoneware Pitchers

Oyster jar, cylindrical handled body w/rounded shoulder to a short, wide cylindrical neck, advertising-type, blue-tinted impressed name "Bryant & Woodruf - Pittsfield, ME," maker unknown, overall use staining, some glaze grazing at base, ca. 1860, 1 qt., 7 1/2" h. (ILLUS., bottom previous page) **413**

Pipkin, wide flat bottom & bulbous rounded sides tapering slightly to a flared rim w/pinched spout, tapering cylindrical side handle, overall brown alkaline glaze, unsigned, ca. 1850, 5 1/4" h. (minor surface chipping at end of handle & on spout) **143**

Pitcher, large ovoid body w/a wide rolled rim, short angled cylindrical spout at front rim, strap handle at the back, elaborately decorated w/cobalt blue slip-quilled scrolling floral vines & squiggle bands flanking the spout & w/thin blue bands around the top & base, unsigned, 19th c., 1 gal. (ILLUS. second row down, second from right, with full page of various other stoneware pieces, page 27) **147**

Pitcher, 6 1/2" h., ovoid body tapering to a cylindrical neck w/molded rim & pinched spout, small C-form strap handle, cobalt blue brushed flowerpot on the front & another on the right side, the left side w/a swag design, scattered blue accents, unsigned, tight hairline up from the base on right & through the design, professional restoration to a surface chip at left rim, ca. 1850, 1 pt. (ILLUS. center with rare Cowden & Wilcox batter pail & larger pitcher, bottom page 12) **770**

Pitcher, 8" h., wide ovoid body tapering to a flaring neck w/molded rim & pinched spout, strap handle, cobalt blue brushed large design of two leafy forked stems topped by double blossoms on the front below the spout, two incised lines around the neck, unsigned, surface chips at base, a couple of long horizontal clay separation glaze lines, tight hairline running along the very bottom on side, ca. 1860, 1/2 gal. (ILLUS. left with rare Cowden & Wilcox batter pail & smaller pitcher, bottom page 12) **963**

Pitcher, 9" h., flat-bottomed ovoid body tapering to a cylindrical neck w/a pinched spout & strap handle, dark cobalt blue brushed design of two large triangular blossoms above a pyramidal leaf below the blue-framed spout, unsigned, probably Southern origin, Virginia or West Virginia, mottled clay color from the firing, three pierced holes at the rim probably for a hinge for a cover, tight spider crack off a stack mark on one side, ca. 1850, 1/2 gal. (ILLUS. center with two other unsigned pitchers, top of page) **468**

Pitcher, 9 1/2" h., wide flat-bottomed baluster-form body tapering to a cupped rim w/pinched spout & strap handle, cobalt blue slip-quilled small flower above forked leafy stems below the large impressed mark of Burger & Lang, Rochester, New York, surface chipping at spout, minor chip at back base, ca. 1870, 1 gal. (ILLUS. left with large pitcher & preserve jar made in Rochester, New York, bottom of page) **1,375**

Two Rare Pitchers & a Preserve Jar Made in Rochester, New York

Pitcher, 10 1/2" h., flat-bottomed wide squatty bulbous body tapering to a thick cupped rim w/pinched spout, strap handle, dark cobalt blue slip-quilled ribbed plume design across the front below the spout, unsigned, probably New York state origin, some use staining, chip at rim to right of spout, ca. 1870, 1 gal............. 275

Pitcher, 11" h., bulbous ovoid body tapering to a cylindrical neck w/a large pinched spout, strap handle, small cobalt blue slip-quilled plumed design below the spout, unsigned, professional restoration to chips at spout, some design fry, ca. 1870, 1 gal., 11" h. 275

Pitcher, 11" h., flat-bottomed ovoid body tapering to a cylindrical neck w/a pinched spout & strap handle, dark cobalt blue brushed design of an overall bold flowering leafy vine w/swag designs at the rim, spout & handle, a tooled circle w/the size number at the rim near the handle, unsigned but possibly the Remmey factory in New Jersey or Bell factory in Pennsylvania, very old surface chipping around the base in front, some old chips at rim, two large rim chips on the spout, ca. 1850, 1 gal. (ILLUS. right with two other unsigned pitchers, top previous page) 798

Pitcher, wide squatty bulbous tapering lower body below the wide gently flaring neck w/a deep molded rim w/a large pinched spout, strap handle, cobalt blue slip-quilled large dotted poppy blossoms on a long curled leafy stem, impressed & blue-tinted mark for Whites, Binghamton, New York, ca. 1860, 1 1/2 gal., 9 1/2" h. (overglazed in the making, clay separation line at base of handle) 743

Pitcher, 11" h., bulbous baluster-form body tapering to a flat rim w/pinched spout & strap handle, cobalt blue large slip-quilled dotted sunflower blossom above leaves, the impressed mark of F. Stetzenmeyer & G. Goetzman, Rochester, New York, in the middle front under the spout & below a slip-quilled long squiggle, some loss to cobalt blue in the firing, few surface chips in spout, very tight short hairline from rim near handle, ca. 1857, 1 1/2 gal. (ILLUS. right with smaller pitcher & preserve jar made in Rochester, New York, bottom previous page) **1,265**

Pitcher, 11" h., wide flat-bottomed baluster-form w/a wide molded rim w/pinched spout & strap handle, cobalt blue slip-quilled small long-tailed bird perched on a tree stump at the bottom front under the spout & below the impressed mark of Satterlee & Mory, Fort Edward, New York, professional restoration to a hairline on the right side, chips at rim & handle, minor glaze burn at bottom of design, glaze flake at rim, ca. 1870, 1 1/2 gal. (ILLUS. right with two jugs made in Fort Edward, New York, top page 103) **1,595**

Pitcher, wide flat-bottomed ovoid body tapering to a thick line-incised rim w/a large pinched spout, strap handle, thin incised shoulder bands & impressed size number & mark of F.T. Wright & Son Stone Ware, Taunton, Massachusetts, all trimmed in blue, fitted w/hand-made period wooden cover, ca. 1870, 2 gal., 13" h. (some use staining).................................... **413**

Pitcher, 13 1/2" h., tall baluster-form w/thin molded rim w/large pinched spout & strap handle, cobalt blue tall brushed tulip blossom on a leafy stem below the spout, blue swag accents around the rim, impressed size number below the spout, unsigned but probably the Remmey factory in New Jersey, clay separation at very bottom, professional restoration to a long crack in the front just touching the design, ca. 1850, 2 gal. (ILLUS. left with two smaller unsigned pitchers, top previous page) **385**

Pitcher, large ovoid lower body tapering to a tall cylindrical neck w/pinched spout, strap handle, cobalt blue slip-quilled small palm trees flanking a size numeral on the front below the spout decorated w/a Roman starburst design, unsigned, ca. 1850, 3 gal., 16" h. (professional restoration to hairlines down from rim) **440**

Pitcher, miniature, 3 3/4" h., simple baluster-form body w/a wide flat rim & pinched spout, strap handle, brown Albany slip-glazed interior, unglazed light brown exterior, unsigned, probably New York state origin, ca. 1850 .... **143**

Pitcher, 4 5/8" h., miniature, baluster-shaped w/a wide flat rim & large pinched spout, strap handle, decorated around the rim & middle w/incised sawtooth bands trimmed in cobalt blue, possibly an early piece from the N. Clark factory of Lyons, New York, ca. 1860 (couple of early chips at base)................................... **880**

Pitcher, 6" h., bulbous Bristol-glazed body w/a short cylindrical neck w/pointed spout, large C-form handle, the body molded in relief & trimmed in cobalt blue w/a continuous deer hunt scene, an impressed & blue-trimmed German verse on each side of the neck, minor glaze flake at spout, ca. 1900 (ILLUS. center with advertising cake crock & larger pitcher, top page 28) **248**

Pitcher, 7 1/2" h., bulbous Bristol-glazed body w/a short cylindrical neck w/pointed spout, large C-form handle, the body molded in relief & trimmed in cobalt blue w/a continuous deer hunt scene, an impressed & blue-trimmed German verse on each side of the neck w/a molded deer head under the spout, clay separation in the making, ca. 1900 (ILLUS. left with cake crock & smaller pitcher, top page 28) **143**

Pitcher, 8" h., flat-bottomed ovoid body tapering to a cylindrical neck w/pinched spout & strap handle, dark cobalt blue long fern-like leaves topped by blossoms branching across the front, further leaf sprigs around the neck & brushed size number on the back, attributed to the Ingell factory, Taunton, Massachusetts, overall use stain, ca. 1840, 1/2 gal. (ILLUS. center with two unsigned 1/2 gallon jars, top page 80) **1,375**

Brown-glazed Stoneware Pitcher

Pitcher, 8 1/2" h., footed bulbous body tapering to a tall neck w/molded rim & deeply molded spout, strap handle, unsigned, overall dark brown alkaline glaze, some very minor surface chipping at the back rim, ca. 1870, 1/2 gal. (ILLUS.) **303**

Pitcher, 8 1/2" h., footed waisted baluster-form body w/a molded ribbed spout down the front, strap handle, mottled brown overall glaze, impressed mark of Roberts, Binghamton, New York, old surface chipping at spout, ca. 1860, 1 gal.

(ILLUS. second from left with small jug, syrup pitcher & storage jar, bottom page 93) **330**

Tanware Pitcher with Albany Slip Trim

Pitcher, 9" h., tanware, baluster-shaped body w/flared neck & pinched spout, dark brown overall Albany slip dashes & squiggle lines decorating the body, attributed to western Pennsylvania, minor chip on rim, professional restoration to spout chip, ca. 1870 (ILLUS.) **825**

Penn Yan, New York Pitcher & Preserve Jars

Pitcher, 9 1/2" h., bulbous ovoid body tapering to a molded rim w/pinched spout & strap handle, cobalt blue slip-quilled three-ribbed leaf below spout, impressed mark for Penn Yan, New York pottery on left side, cinnamon clay color, glaze burn on front, couple of surface chips on rim & one on center of spout, very rare form for this factory, ca. 1860, 1 gal. (ILLUS. right with two other Penn Yan pieces, bottom previous page) **688**

Pitcher, 10" h., bulbous body w/slightly flared base & slightly tapered neck, applied strap handle, freehand cobalt foliage decoration starts at bottom below spout & extends back almost to handle, small fan or leaf designs near the top, wavy lines below the neck rim, incised line detail around the body, firing separations in side & bottom................................ **3,410**

Pitcher, 10" h., bulbous hexagonal baluster-form w/a wide arched spout & C-scroll handle, overall dark brown alkaline glaze, each panel molded in relief on the side & neck w/a spread-winged American eagle, rare form, probably from the Albany region of New York state, few flecks of missing glaze, overall excellent condition, ca. 1850, 1/2 gal. (ILLUS. left with stoneware coffeepot, top page 32)................................ **413**

Pitcher, 10 1/2" h., ovoid body tapering to a molded rim w/a pinched spout & strap handle, large cobalt blue brushed flowers on leafy stem, blue-trimmed impressed mark for Whites, Binghamton, New York, professional restoration to two hairlines down from rim flanking spout, ca. 1860, 1 gal. (ILLUS. center with two jugs made in Binghamton, New York, top page 124)........ **440**

Pitcher, 10 5/8" h., ovoid body w/raised ring base w/slightly flared rim, short cylindrical neck, applied handle, cobalt floral decoration & line detail around spout & handle (some pot stones) **880**

Pitcher, bulbous ovoid body w/molded base tapering to a wide cylindrical neck w/a deep pinched spout, applied strap handle, decorated w/cobalt blue brushed large feather leaves w/curled-back tips around the body & neck, unsigned, mid-19th c., 10 3/4" h. **881**

Pitcher, 11" h., buttermilk-type, loop shoulder handle, brown alkaline glaze, attributed to W.F. Outern, Catawba Crossroads, North Carolina, ca. 1920 (some minor chips around rim) **173**

Pitcher, 11" h., bulbous ovoid body tapering to a molded rim w/pinched spout & strap handle, cobalt blue stylized dotted leaf design below the spout, unsigned but probably New York state origin, rim chips & chip at tip of spout & on handle, ca. 1870, 1 gal. (ILLUS. right with unsigned crock & jug, top page 42) **495**

Tall Stoneware Pitcher with Cherries

Pitcher, 10" h., ovoid body tapering to a wide cylindrical neck w/pinched spout, impressed 3/4 capacity mark below the spout & above a cobalt blue brushed cluster of cherries decoration, unsigned but probably from New Jersey or Pennsylvania, glaze burn & mottled clay color, ca. 1850 (ILLUS.) **990**

Large Boldly Decorated Pitcher

Pitcher, 11 1/2" h., wide ovoid body tapering to a tall cylindrical neck w/a pinched spout, cobalt blue brushed tulip decoration from top to bottom, impressed mark "RCR Phila" & "1 1/2" impressed on the side, stack mark in design, overall dry glaze, cinnamon clay color from overfiring, ca. 1870, 1 1/2 gal. (ILLUS.).. **1,430**

Pitcher, 13" h., large flat-bottomed ovoid body tapering slightly to a wide cylindrical neck w/thin molded rim & pinched spout, strap handle, cobalt blue brushed tall double flower stems below the spout w/scattered blue accents, impressed size number below the spout, attributed to Peter Herrmann, Baltimore, Maryland, professional restoration to a Y-shaped tight hairline on left side, X-shaped crack on front, minor stack mark on front, ca. 1850, 2 gal. (ILLUS. right with unsigned ovoid crock, bottom page 40)...................... **743**

Swag-decorated Stoneware Pitcher

Two-gallon Tall Stoneware Pitcher

Pitcher, 13" h., very slightly tapering cylindrical body below the tall waisted neck w/a pinched spout, stenciled cobalt blue flower design & mark of Williams & Reppert, Greensboro, Pennsylvania, additional brushed blue accents at base, shoulder & rim, free-hand size designation, overall very dark tan clay color, age wear to glaze, ca. 1880, 2 gal. (ILLUS.)....... **990**

Pitcher, 13 1/2" h., wide ovoid body tapering to a cylindrical neck w/pinched spout, cobalt blue brushed swag & leaf design around the shoulder, blue accents on spout & handle, size designation impressed at rim, unsigned, professional restoration to chipping on spout, ca. 1870, 2 gal. (ILLUS., top next column)...... **1,045**

Tall Ovoid Pitcher with Molded Designs

Pitcher, 14" h., tall ovoid tankard-type w/pinched small rim spout, relief-molded bands trimmed w/cobalt blue at the top & base, large blue-tinted applied designs around the sides, one of a dancing girl, one of a stork standing among reeds & a third of a woman pouring wine, impressed "5" just above the applied handle, early work of Whites Pottery, Utica, New York, chip & short hairline at rim, ca. 1900 (ILLUS.).. **358**

Large Boldly Decorated Stoneware Pitcher

Pitcher, 14" h., wide-bottomed ovoid body tapering to a cylindrical neck w/large pinched spout, cobalt blue brushed triple blossom tulip on the front w/draping flowers around the shoulder & on the neck, blue accents on the handle, impressed mark of W.H. Lehew & Co., Strasburg, Virginia, tooled size designation, old chipping around base, chip in spout, ca. 1880, 2 gal. (ILLUS.) **3,520**

Pitcher & mug set: ovoid large pitcher w/a flat rim & pinched spout, angled handle, overall bumpy surface w/molded leaf bands at the top & oval panels w/molded flower sprigs on each side & an oblong panel below the spout molded w/the word "Prosit," molded designs all trimmed in cobalt blue, each of the tapering cylindrical mugs also molded w/"Prosit" & blue trim, 7 pcs. (ILLUS. of part, bottom row, second from left, in full page of various other stoneware pieces, page 27) **206**

Preserve jar, cov., cylindrical body tapering to a wide, low cupped rim w/inset flat cover w/button finial, overall mottled brown alkaline glaze, unsigned, ca. 1860, 1 qt., 5 1/2" h. (minor surface chipping around rim & on the cover)...................................... **55**

Preserve jar, cov., cylindrical body tapering to a wide, low cupped rim w/inset flat cover w/button finial, overall mottled olive green alkaline glaze, unsigned, ca. 1860, 1 qt., 5 3/4" h. (minor surface chipping at rim) **33**

Preserve jar, cylindrical w/indented neck ring below the thick molded rim, cobalt blue brushed drooping plume design repeated three times around sides, unsigned, glaze burn, mottled clay color, ca. 1850, 1 qt., 7" h. (ILLUS. far right with canister & two other unsigned pieces, bottom page 30) **198**

Preserve jar, cylindrical w/flat angled shoulder to a wide low cylindrical neck, overall warm brick red glaze, impressed mark of W. Smith, Greenwich, New York, ca. 1850, 1/2 gal., 8" h. (potter finger tip impressions at base, minor rim wear) **198**

Preserve jar, slightly swelled cylindrical form tapering slightly to a flat molded rim, unusual cobalt blue brushed & slip-quilled design w/a cluster of large brushed leaves & vines supporting large grape clusters, brushed size number on back, unsigned, ca. 1860, 1/2 gal., 9" h. (professional restoration to a full-length hairline to right of design)............................ **413**

Preserve jar, cov., cylindrical body tapering to a wide, low cupped rim w/inset flat cover w/button finial, overall mottled dark green alkaline glaze, unsigned, ca. 1860, excellent condition, 1 qt., 5 3/4" h. **55**

Preserve jar, cov., wide cylindrical form w/a rounded shoulder to the wide short cylindrical neck & inset cover w/disk finial, unusual cobalt blue arched dotted "serpent" design below the blue-trimmed impressed mark of John B. Caire & Co., Main St., Pokeepsie (sic), New York, short hairline down from rim on back & another short one up from back, some use staining, minor chip at base on back, minor glaze spider cracks, ca. 1850, 1 gal., 8" h. (ILLUS. far right with flowerpot & various other pieces, top page 37) **303**

Preserve jar, cylindrical w/flattened molded mouth, cobalt blue large brushed flowers on leaf stem around the top, unsigned, excellent condition, ca. 1870, 1 gal., 8 1/2" h. (ILLUS. second from right with canister & two other unsigned pieces, bottom page 30).. **385**

Preserve jar, cov., cylindrical body tapering slightly to a flared short flat neck, inset cover w/button finial, unusual cobalt blue slip-quilled lobster design below an impressed sunburst & "Cortland" mark, Cortland, New York, minor chip at rim, X-shaped tight line on back, ca. 1860, 1 gal., 9" h. (ILLUS. center with Cortland crock & other preserve jar, top page 41)...... **578**

Preserve jar, cov., slightly tapering cylindrical body w/a flared rolled rim & inset cover, eared handles, simple light cobalt blue brushed flower on leafy stem below the impressed & blue-tinted mark "Penn Yan," Penn Yan, New York, surface chip at rim on back, a few stone pings overall, ca. 1860, 1 gal., 9" h. **358**

Preserve jar, cov., swelled cylindrical body tapering to a molded rim flanked by eared handles, very rare cobalt blue slip-quilled swimming fish design below the blue-trimmed impressed mark of H.M. Whitman, Havana, New York, w/hand-wrought handled iron cover, excellent condition, ca. 1860, 1 gal., 9" h. (ILLUS. right with very rare crock with camel & another preserve jar, bottom page 42)......... **7,425**

Preserve jar, gently swelled cylindrical form tapering to a molded rim, cobalt blue stenciled arched mark for the Pallatine Pottery Co., Pallatine, West Virginia, a picture of a barking dog in the center of the mark, ca. 1875, 1 gal., 9" h. (surface roughness along wax seal rim, mottled dark grey clay from firing)............................ 660

Preserve jar, slightly tapering cylindrical form w/a rolled rim & eared handles, cobalt blue brushed stylized tulip below the impressed mark of the Penn Yan, New York factory, minor use staining & surface chip on interior back rim, ca. 1860, 1 gal., 9" h. (ILLUS. center with Penn Yan pitcher & other preserve jar, bottom page 158).. 303

Preserve jar, tapering cylindrical body w/a flat slightly flaring neck flanked by eared handles, cobalt blue large slip-quilled ovoid petaled blossom above large leaves & below the blue-tinted impressed mark of F. Stetzenmeyer & Co., Rochester, New York, professional restorations to a full-length hairline at left of design & a long horizontal line at the back, ca. 1860, 1 gal., 9 1/2" h. (ILLUS. center with two rare pitchers made in Rochester, New York, bottom page 156) 715

Preserve jar, cylindrical body tapering slightly to a low flared rim flanked by eared handles, cobalt blue large brushed "spitting" flower design w/matching accents under the handles & the size number below the blue-tinted impressed mark "Lyons," Lyons, New York, few minor rim chips, stack mark on left front, minor glaze flake on front base, overall use stain, ca. 1860, 1 gal., 9 3/4" h. (ILLUS. right with two other decorated jars from Lyons, New York, top page 82).................. 198

Preserve jar, cov., cylindrical body w/an indented band below the flared flat mouth w/an inset cover, cobalt blue crudely brushed cluster of three tulips on the front & back, unsigned but attributed to Peter Hermann, Baltimore, Maryland, small hairline down from rim, some surface chipping, ca. 1850, 1 gal., 10" h. (ILLUS. center with larger unsigned jar & preserve jar, bottom page 84) 143

Preserve jar, gently swelled cylindrical form tapering to a molded rim, cobalt blue stenciled arched mark for the Pallatine Pottery Co., Pallatine, West Virginia, a picture of a pear in the center of the mark, ca. 1875, 1 gal., 10" h. (minor stack mark on left side, mottled grey clay from firing).. 330

Preserve jar, nearly cylindrical body tapering slightly below the flat molded rim, cobalt blue brushed narrow scalloped band w/large scroll devices just below the rim, lightly impressed mark of S. Bell & Son, Strasburg, Pennsylvania, ca. 1850, 1 gal., 10 1/2" h. (Y-shaped hairline extending down from rim, long shallow chip in bottom reglued, overglazing from firing).................. 176

Preserve jar, nearly spherical form w/slightly tilted molded flat rim, dark cobalt blue large brushed pair of three-lobed blossoms above a four-lobed leaf cluster, impressed size number on shoulder, unsigned, ca. 1850, 1 gal., 10 1/2" h. (age lines in bottom & up the sides from freeze lines).................................. 110

Preserve jar, cov., cylindrical tapering slightly to flared rim flanked by eared handles, cobalt blue brushed tulip blossom design, impressed mark of W.A. Macquoid & Co. Pottery Works, Little West, 12th St., New York, some use staining & chip on base of right handle, ca. 1870, 1 1/2 gal., 10" h. (ILLUS. left with rare camel-decorated crock & fish-decorated preserve jar, bottom page 42).. 358

Preserve jar, wide flat bottom w/rounded sides tapering to a flat molded rim w/inset cover, eared handles, cobalt blue brushed flowers on leafy stem design beside a large size number below the impressed mark of A.O. Whittemore, Havana, New York, minor surface chips at rim, some design fry, ca. 1870, 2 gal., 9 1/2" h. (ILLUS. center with crock with cornucopia & other signed Whittemore piece, top page 55) 358

Preserve jar, cylindrical slightly tapering body w/wide short flat neck & eared handles, cobalt blue slip-quilled large dotted rounded blossom on a stem w/three long ribbed leaves, impressed & blue-tinted size number & mark of C. Hart, Sherburne, New York, ca. 1870, 2 gal., 10 1/2" h. (short hairline at rim behind left handle, another up from the base w/a surrounding stain spot on the right side)...... 165

Preserve jar, cov., wide slightly tapering cylindrical body w/a wide flaring neck, inset original cover, eared handles, cobalt blue slip-quilled pair of large painted blossoms on a spiraling dotted stem, impressed & blue-tinted mark "Cortland," Cortland, New York, ca. 1860, 2 gal., 10 1/2" h. (large surface chip on front rim, minor glaze spider crack on back) 358

Preserve jar, cov., wide gently tapering cylindrical body w/a narrow flared rim & inset cover, eared handles, dark cobalt blue large slip-quilled double flowers on a stem w/large ribbed leaves, impressed & blue-tinted mark of J. Mantell, Penn Yan, New York, tight in-body crack on the back, surface chip at leaf handle, couple of minor glaze spider cracks, ca. 1860, 2 gal., 11" h.. 1,485

Preserve jar, slightly swelled cylindrical shape tapering slightly to a rolled rim flanked by eared handles, cobalt blue brushed feathered tree-of-life design, an "X" & "2" below the blue-washed impressed mark of M. Woodruff, Cortland, New York, few minor surface chips, somewhat dry glaze & use staining, ca. 1870, 2 gal., 11" h. (ILLUS. left with Cortland crock & other preserve jar, top page 41) 248

Preserve jar, slightly tapering cylindrical body w/a thick molded rim & eared handles, cobalt blue slip-quilled design of a triple sunflower on a leafy stem, impressed & blue-tinted mark of the Pottery Works, Little West, 12th St., NYU, ca. 1870, 2 gal., 11" h. (use staining) 330

Preserve jar, wide cylindrical body tapering slightly to a wide short neck flanked by eared handles, finely detailed large incised & blue-tinted large double flower buds on a long leafy stem below the impressed mark of J.M. Mott & Co., Ithaca,

New York, rare potter, minor use staining, ca. 1855, 2 gal., 11" h. (ILLUS. right with Buffalo, New York ovoid jug, bottom page 110) **3,630**

Preserve jar, wide slightly tapering cylindrical form w/a flat flaring rim flanked by eared handles, large dark cobalt blue slip-quilled large double flowers on a winged-leaf stem below the impressed mark of the Penn Yan, New York factory, attributed to the short-lived partnership of Mantell & Thomas, some rim & handle chips, ca. 1854, 2 gal., 11" h. (ILLUS. left with other Penn Yan preserve jar & pitcher, bottom page 158) **633**

Preserve jar, advertising-type, gently swelled cylindrical form tapering to a molded rim, cobalt blue brushed double plain bands & squiggle band around the top & a single plain band around the base, the whole center of the side stenciled in cobalt blue w/inscription reading "From Ood's Hardpan Crockery - Lockhaven, PA," the oversized "C" & "Y" in "Crockery" flanking the center part of the inscription, a stenciled size number flanked by leafy scrolls below the inscription, unknown maker, excellent condition, ca. 1870, 2 gal., 11 1/2" h. **1,705**

Preserve jar, cov., wide cylindrical body tapering to a flared molded mouth flanked by eared handles, cobalt blue slip-quilled small flower on a leafy stem below a script size number & the blue-tinted impressed mark of Burger Bros. & Co., Rochester, New York, glued-in rim chip on the back, ca. 1860, 2 gal., 11 1/2" h. (ILLUS. center with two jugs made in Rochester, New York, top page 126) **330**

Preserve jar, cylindrical form tapering gently to the thick molded mouth flanked by eared handles, cobalt blue slip-quilled large bird on branch, impressed mark of J.A. & C.W. Underwood, Fort Edward, New York, two stone pings on front, some lime staining, long chip at bottom front, ca. 1865, 2 gal., 11 1/2" h. (ILLUS. center with a crock & flowerpot made in Fort Edward, New York, top of page 47) **385**

Preserve jar, wide swelled cylindrical body tapering to a raised molded rim flanked by eared handles, dark cobalt blue slip-quilled large floral spray below the blue-tinted impressed mark of E. & L.P. Norton, Bennington, Vermont, hairline in body at back, minor surface chipping at handles, ca. 1880, 2 gal., 11 1/2" h. (ILLUS. left with rare Bennington crock & jug, bottom page 51) **413**

Preserve jar, cov., cylindrical tapering to a rounded shoulder & flaring mouth & inset cover, cobalt blue large brushed double leaf design below the faint impressed mark partially reading "Peckslip, NY," significant design fry on design, replaced cover, ca. 1880, 2 gal., 12" h. (ILLUS. left with decorated crock & jug, top page 38) **303**

Preserve jar, cylindrical tapering gently to a narrow molded mouth flanked by eared handles, cobalt blue slip-quilled stylized floral spray on the side, impressed mark of E. & L.P. Norton, Bennington, Vermont, ca. 1880, excellent condition, 2 gal., 12" h. **605**

Preserve jar, cylindrical tapering gently to a short flared neck flanked by eared handles, dark cobalt blue slip-quilled large tulip-like flower on a leafy stem, impressed mark of Lyons, New York, ca. 1860, 2 gal., 12" h. (very minor spider crack on back)............... **275**

Preserve jar, cylindrical tapering slightly to a wide short cylindrical mouth & eared handles, dark cobalt blue slip-quilled very large sunflower on a leafy stem beside the size number & below the impressed mark of F. Stetzenmeyer & Co., Rochester, New York, very tight hairline on back, ca. 1860, 2 gal., 12" h. (ILLUS. left with two other rare decorated pieces made in Rochester, New York, bottom page 82).. **2,090**

Two Unique Cowden & Wilcox Preserve Jars

Preserve jar, cylindrical tapering to a thin molded mouth flanked by eared handles, cobalt blue large brushed flowers above leafy stems, impressed mark of Cowden & Wilcox, Harrisburg, Pennsylvania, two large chips on front rim, few minor glaze spots, very tight X-shaped crack at back base, some use staining, ca. 1870, 2 gal., 12" h. (ILLUS. left with very rare Cowden & Wilcox covered preserve jar, bottom previous page) **440**

Preserve jar, wide cylindrical body tapering gently to a molded flared mouth flanked by eared handles, cobalt blue tall slip-quilled ribbed wreath design above fancy scrolls down the front, impressed mark of Edmans & Co., Charleston, Massachusetts, rim chip above right handle, glaze spider on very bottom, minor glaze spider by right handle, ca. 1870, 2 gal., 12" h. (ILLUS. right with Gardiner crock & Standish & Wright jug, bottom page 37) **688**

Preserve jar, cylindrical tapering gently to a short flared neck flanked by eared handles, cobalt blue slip-quilled large plump dove facing down & perched on a large fern leaf, impressed mark of F.B. Norton & Co., Worcester, Massachusetts, ca. 1870, 2 gal., 12 1/2" h. (few minor glaze flakes, minor surface wear at interior rim, minor design fry) **853**

Preserve jar, cov., cylindrical gently tapering to a short flared neck flanked by eared handles, inset cover w/pointed knob finial, cobalt blue one-of-a-kind slip-quilled design of a large walking Texas longhorn below the blue-tinted impressed mark of Cowden & Wilcox, Harrisburg, Pennsylvania, overglazed in the making but otherwise excellent, ca. 1870, 3 gal., 12 1/2" h. (ILLUS. right with flower-decorated Cowden & Wilcox preserve jar, bottom previous page) **14,300**

Preserve jar, cov., flat-bottomed rounded cylindrical body tapering to a flat, flared low rim & original inset cover, eared handles, cobalt blue large slip-quilled feathered wreath enclosing the size number below the blue-trimmed impressed mark for Lyons, New York, decoration associated w/the Burger factory in Rochester, New York, but made in Lyons, fine piece, excellent condition, ca. 1855, 3 gal., 13" h. (ILLUS. left with two other rare decorated pieces made in Lyons, New York, bottom page 33).............................. **1,265**

Preserve jar, cov., wide gently tapering cylindrical body w/a thin molded rim & eared handles, original inset stoneware cover, dark cobalt blue slip-quilled design of small four-petaled & dotted flowers flanking a tall plume-like stem below the impressed & blue-tinted mark of Thompson & Tyler, Troy, New York, uncommon Capital District potter, only in business

one year, ca. 1858, 3 gal., 13" h. (a few grease stain spots)...................................... **605**

Preserve jar, cylindrical tapering slightly to a flared molded rim & eared handles, dark cobalt blue slip-quilled & brushed large plume design up from the front bottom, impressed mark of N.A. White & Son, Utica, New York, overglazed & glaze burn on shoulder, hairline above left handle, some interior rim chipping w/short hairline, some chipping on right handle, ca. 1870, 3 gal., 14" h. (ILLUS. right with flower-decorated Whites, Utica jug, top page 148)....................................... **358**

Preserve jar, wide cylindrical body tapering slightly to wide molded flat mouth, cobalt blue large brushed drooping tulip & leaves design repeated four times around the upper body, unsigned, impressed size number near rim, mottled cinnamon clay, long horizontal very tight hairline near the base, small stack mark in one of the flowers, overall use stain, ca. 1860, 3 gal., 15" h. (ILLUS. left with unsigned smaller preserve jar & large covered jar, bottom page 84)............. **165**

Preserve jar, cov., slightly tapering cylindrical body w/a short, flat flaring neck & eared handles, dark cobalt blue slip-quilled exceptional design of a very large rooster w/a dotted body, elaborate tail feathers & a distinctive comb & wide eye, two clumps of leaves below, the impressed & blue-tinted mark of C.W. Braun, Buffalo, New York, along w/the size number, ca. 1870, very rare, 4 gal., 14" h. (couple of short hairlines down from rim at back) **34,100**

Preserve jar, cylindrical body tapering to a molded rim flanked by eared handles, fine cobalt blue slip-quilled scene of a large reclining dotted stag between fir trees & rail fences, blue-tinted impressed mark of J. & E. Norton, Bennington, Vermont, surface wear on interior rim, few glaze flake spots on front, ca. 1855, 4 gal., 14 1/2" h. (ILLUS. center with two other rare Vermont-made pieces, bottom page 56)... **9,350**

Preserve jar, cylindrical tapering gently to a short flared neck flanked by eared handles, dark cobalt blue large flowers w/three large vertical petals beside one smaller rounded daisy-like flower, both above large oblong leaves, a script size number & the impressed & blue-tinted mark of John Burger, Rochester, New York, ca. 1865, 4 gal., 15" h. (overall glaze flakes, stone ping under the right handle)... **2,200**

Preserve jar, wide flat bottom below slightly swelled cylindrical sides tapering to a banded shoulder below the wide cupped rim, overall brown alkaline glaze, Edgefield District, South Carolina, ca. 1850,

7 1/2" h. (ILLUS. far left with other Southern jugs & jar, bottom page 85) **805**

Preserve Jar with Blue Inscription

Preserve jar, cov., cylindrical body tapering to a flaring flat neck & inset cover w/disk finial, large cobalt blue slip-quilled "2 Quarts" in script below a round blue-trimmed tooled & impressed circle mark for a Cortland, New York factory, ca. 1860, 2 qt., 7 1/2" h. (ILLUS.) **303**

Striped & Stenciled Preserve Jar

Preserve jar, slightly swelled cylindrical body tapering to a thick molded rim, eight cobalt blue brushed bands around the body dividing the stenciled marking for

Hamilton & Jones Star Pottery, Greensboro, Pennsylvania, full-length very tight glued hairline, ca. 1870, 1/2 gal., 8 1/4" h. (ILLUS.) **550**

Ribbed Leaf Cluster on Preserve Jar

Preserve jar, cylindrical body tapering to flaring molded rim & inset cover, eared handles, cobalt blue slip-quilled large ribbed leaf cluster w/small blossom below the impressed mark "F. Stetzenmeyer - Goetzman - Rochester, NY," long chip above left handle, chips in cover, ca. 1857, 1 gal., 9" h. (ILLUS.) **908**

Rare Fish-decorated Preserve Jar

Preserve jar, tapering cylindrical form w/molded rim & eared handles, slip-quilled cobalt blue swimming fish, impressed mark of H.M. Whitman, Havana, New York, trimmed in blue, w/original hand-wrought iron lid, ca. 1860, 1 gal., 9" h. (ILLUS.) **7,425**

Very Rare Cowden & Wilcox Preserve Jar with Moon Decoration

Cortland Preserve Jar with Flowers

Preserve jar, cov., cylindrical body tapering to a flaring flat neck & inset cover w/disk finial, two large cobalt blue slip-quilled two-petal flowers on curly stems below impressed mark "Cortland," Cortland, New York, cover probably not original, interior rim chip at back, ca. 1860, 2 gal., 9" h. (ILLUS.) **330**

Preserve jar, cov., slightly swelled cylindrical body tapering to a short wide cylindrical neck w/inset cover w/knob finial, eared handles, cobalt blue brushed Man in the Moon decoration below the impressed mark of Cowden & Wilcox, Har-

risburg, Pennsylvania, original cover, surface chip above left handle, ca. 1870, 1 gal., 9 1/4" h. (ILLUS., top of page) **11,550**

Preserve Jar with Drooping Flower Design

Preserve jar, cylindrical tapering slightly to a flared flat mouth, cobalt blue brushed design of drooping large flower & leaves, impressed mark of Cowden & Wilcox, Harrisburg, Pennsylvania, rim chip at back, use staining, ca. 1870, 1 gal., 9 1/2" h. (ILLUS.) **523**

Preserve Jar with Fancy Stenciled Mark

Preserve jar, slightly swelled cylindrical body w/thick molded rim, cobalt blue brushed bands flanking the blue stenciled mark of Hamilton & Jones, Greensboro, Pennsylvania, excellent condition, ca. 1870, 1 gal., 10" h. (ILLUS.).......................... **385**

Preserve Jar with Drooping Flowers

Preserve jar, slightly swelled cylindrical form w/short flared neck, cobalt blue brushed drooping flower design repeated three times around the shoulder, impressed size designation, unsigned, small dotted circle also on shoulder, minor surface chip at rim, some minor staining, ca. 1870, 1 gal., 10" h. (ILLUS.) **198**

Preserve Jar with Horse Head Decoration

Preserve jar, cylindrical body tapering to a short molded cylindrical neck flanked by eared handles, large cobalt blue slip-quilled picture of a horse head below the impressed mark "W. Hart - Ogdensburg - 2," New York, chips, surface wear & use staining, cinnamon clay color & dry glaze, hairline at back rim, ca. 1860, 2 gal., 10" h. (ILLUS., bottom previous page)...... **3,300**

Squatty Decorated Preserve Jar

Preserve jar, wide flat bottom w/tapering sides to a flared mouth, eared shoulder handles, cobalt blue large brushed flower design beside a "2" below the impressed mark "A.O. Whittemore - Havana, N.Y.," minor surface chips at interior rim, short hairlines down from rim, ca. 1870, 2 gal., 10" h. (ILLUS.) **303**

Unsigned Early Stoneware Preserve Jar

Preserve jar, cylindrical w/angled shoulder & low flaring flat wide mouth, brushed co-

balt blue stylized flower & leaf sprig around the center, leaf band around the shoulder, attributed to the N. Clark Factory, Mt. Morris, New York, ca. 1835, some surface wear on rim & base, tight hairlines down each side, early wire repair still in place, 10 1/2" h. (ILLUS.).................. **330**

Preserve Jar with Plume Design

Preserve jar, cylindrical body tapering to a short flared neck flanked by eared handles, cobalt blue slip-quilled plume design below the impressed mark "C. Hart & Son - Sherburne - 2," Sherburne, New York, kiln burn at base front, very minor rim chipping, ca. 1860, 2 gal., 10 1/2" h. (ILLUS.).. **187**

Preserve Jar with Large Leaf Design

Preserve jar, cylindrical sides curving in to a low molded neck, cobalt blue slip-quilled large three-leaf sprig below the impressed mark "Belmont Ave. Pottery - 6," probably Fort Edward, New York, stack mark & kiln burns at base, professional restoration to rim chip & hairline on front & short hairline on back, ca. 1870, 6 qt., 10 1/2" h. (ILLUS.) **176**

Bennington Preserve Jar with Flower

Preserve jar, cylindrical body tapering to a molded mouth & eared handles, dark cobalt blue slip-quilled very large flowers w/leaves below the impressed mark of J. Norton & Co., Bennington, Vermont, ca. 1861, 1 1/2 gal., 11" h. (ILLUS.)................ **2,420**

Preserve Jar with Nice Incised Flowers

Preserve jar, cylindrical tapering slightly to an upright rim & eared handles, finely incised design of large double pod-like flowers on leafy stems washed w/cobalt blue, impressed mark of J.M. Mott & Co., Ithaca, New York, washed w/blue, minor staining, ca. 1855, 2 gal., 11" h. (ILLUS.) . **3,630**

Preserve Jar with Large Wreath Design

Preserve jar, cylindrical tapering to a flaring flat rim flanked by eared handles, large bold cobalt blue brushed bull's-eye wreath flanked by two "2" numerals below the blue-trimmed impressed mark "T. Harrington - Lyons," New York, professional restoration to surface chips around rim, full-length hairline down the back, ca. 1850, 2 gal., 11" h. (ILLUS.)......... **413**

Preserve Jar with Floral Vine Decoration

Preserve jar, slightly swelled body tapering to a flaring molded mouth, cobalt blue brushed large running vine of flowers & leaves around the middle, marked by J. Weaver, Beaver County, Pennsylvania, rim chip on back, overall use staining, ca. 1850, 2 gal., 11" h. (ILLUS.)........................ **440**

Stencil-decorated Preserve Jar

Preserve jar, cylindrical body tapering slightly to a wide molded rim, cobalt blue stenciled design of large rose blossoms & leaves enclosing the marking "Dillner & Eneix - New Geneva - PA" above a freehand "2," chip at the rim on back, minor surface wear, ca. 1890, 2 gal., 12" h. (ILLUS.) **825**

Preserve Jar with Large Bird Design

Preserve jar, cylindrical body tapering to a wide molded rim flanked by eared han-

dles, cobalt blue slip-quilled large bird on a plume stem design, probably New York State, very overgrazed in the firing, ca. 1870, 2 gal., 12" h. (ILLUS.) **248**

Preserve Jar with Singing Bird

Preserve jar, cylindrical sides curving in to a low flaring molded neck flanked by eared handles, cobalt blue slip-quilled singing bird on branch, glossy Bristol glaze, probably made in New Jersey, age crazing to glaze, interior surface chips at rim, very tight hairline at front bottom, ca. 1880, 2 gal., 12" h. (ILLUS.) **198**

Preserve Jar with Rare Long Horn Cow

Preserve jar, cov., tapering cylindrical form w/eared handles & short flared rim w/inset cover, slip-quilled cobalt blue scene of a Texas Long Horn steer, impressed mark of Cowden & Wilcox, Harrisburg, Pennsylvania, & a "3," overglazed in the making, ca. 1870, 3 gal., 12 1/2" h. (ILLUS.) **14,300**

Preserve Jar with Large Sunflower Design

Preserve jar, cylindrical body tapering to a flaring flat mouth flanked by eared handles, cobalt blue slip-quilled large sunflower on large leafy stem w/a numeral "3" to one side, impressed mark for John Burger, Rochester, New York, professional restoration to various hairlines overall, ca. 1865, 3 gal., 13" h. (ILLUS.) **165**

Large Preserve Jar with Flower Design

Preserve jar, cylindrical slightly tapering to a molded rim & eared handles, cobalt blue slip-quilled large petaled flower & leaf cluster below the impressed blue-tinted mark for John Burger, Rochester, New York, a script "3" near the rim, very tight full-length hairline in back, ca. 1865, 3 gal., 13" h. (ILLUS.) **330**

Preserve Jar with Spearpoint Leaves

Preserve jar, cylindrical body tapering to a short flared neck flanked by eared handles, cobalt blue slip-quilled & dotted spearpoint leaf design below the impressed mark "C. Hart - Sherburne - 3," Sherburne, New York, professional restoration to surface chip along rim, ca. 1858, 3 gal., 13" h. (ILLUS.)........................ **198**

Preserve Jar with Stenciled Mark & Flower

Preserve jar, slightly swelled cylindrical body w/a molded rim & eared handles, cobalt blue stenciled mark of Williams Reppert, Greensboro, Pennsylvania enclosing a stenciled flower above a brushed "3" near the bottom, overall dark clay color from firing, minor surface wear & a chip at the rim, ca. 1870, 3 gal., 13 1/2" h. (ILLUS.) **275**

Bennington Preserve Jar with Stag

Preserve jar, cylindrical tapering body w/a molded rim & eared handles, slip-quilled cobalt blue elaborate scene of a large reclining stag w/fences & fir trees, impressed mark of J. & E. Norton, Bennington, Vermont, washed in blue, surface wear at rim interior, few glaze flakes, ca. 1855, 4 gal., 14 1/2" h. (ILLUS.)............... **9,350**

Preserve Jar with Stenciled Markings

Preserve jar, slightly swelled cylindrical body w/a molded rim & eared handles, cobalt blue stenciled mark of T.F. Reppert, Greensboro, Pennsylvania, further trimmed w/stenciled sprigs & free-hand bands & a "4" near the base, excellent condition, ca. 1880, 4 gal., 15" h. (ILLUS.) **633**

Preserve jar, cov., tapering cylindrical body w/flared rim & inset cover w/knob finial, cobalt blue extremely rare slip-quilled decoration of a three-quarter length profile portrait of a military general w/a goat-

ee in full military regalia including a plumed helmet & detailed uniform, impressed mark of C. Haidle & Co., Union Pottery, Newark, New Jersey, ca. 1871, 1 1/2 gal., 11" h. (couple of very tight hairlines down from rim, very minor glaze wear) **18,700**

New Jersey Preserve Jar with Flower

Preserve jar, cylindrical sides curving in to a low flaring molded neck flanked by eared handles, cobalt blue slip-quilled & brushed large flower on leafy stem below "4. - G.," & the impressed mark of Haidle & Zipp Union Pottery, Newark, New Jersey, professional restoration to surface chips all around the rim, some use staining w/stack mark on front, ca. 1880, 4 gal., 16" h. (ILLUS.) **165**

Salesman's Sample Stoneware Bird Bath

Group of Four Small Stoneware Spittoons

Salesman's sample, model of a birdbath, two-piece, buff unglazed clay, attributed to The Star Stoneware Company, Crooksville, Ohio, excellent condition, ca. 1900, 8 1/2" h. (ILLUS., bottom previous page) **121**

Shard, fragment of a large stoneware jug, incised w/a fish design & a portion of the impressed mark of the Crolius Factory, Manhattan Wells, New York, ca. 1800 (ILLUS. center with stoneware vase, crock, flowerpot & jar, bottom page 36) **121**

Spice jar, miniature barrel-shape w/incised bands around the top & bottom decorated w/wide cobalt blue bands, unsigned, rare form, ca. 1860, 3" h. **1,320**

Spittoon, waisted low cylindrical form w/indented top centered by a hole, band of cobalt blue brushed leafy plume designs around the sides, minor surface chips, ca. 1850, 7" d., 4" h. (ILLUS. second from left with three other spittoons, above) **275**

Spittoon, waisted low cylindrical form w/indented top centered by a hole, band of cobalt blue brushed leafy plume & flower designs around the sides, unsigned, minor surface wear at drain hole, ca. 1840, 8 1/2" d., 4" h. (ILLUS. second from right with three other unsigned spittoons, above) **495**

Spittoon, waisted low cylindrical form w/indented top centered by a hole, band of cobalt blue brushed leafy plume designs around the sides, unsigned, couple of rim chips, interior hairline, another short separation hairline near drain hole, ca. 1850, 9" d., 4 1/4" h. (ILLUS. far left with three other unsigned spittoons, above) **121**

Spittoon, waisted low cylindrical form w/indented top centered by a hole, cobalt blue crude brushed plume designs around the sides, unsigned, chip at base, very tight full-length hairline on side, ca. 1850, 7" d., 4" h. (ILLUS. far right with three other unsigned spittoons, top of page) **110**

Small Stoneware Labeled Mustard Jar

Storage jar, cov., cylindrical tapering slightly to a wide flat mouth w/inset cover, brown above white Bristol glaze, original red & gold paper label advertising Dusseldorfer Style Mustard, ca. 1900, 4" h. (ILLUS.) **33**

Storage jar, cov., advertising-type, cylindrical body w/molded rim & inset flat cover w/button finial, the upper & lower sides decorated w/pairs of thin blue bands flanking a white band, a large printed square on the side w/advertising reading "Where Quality - and Economy Meet - Wm. J. Moxley's Special - Oleomargarine - The Taste is the Best," also on the back "Made in the USA for Blakeslee Thomas Co. Inc., Buffalo, NY - Patented 6-2-14," ca. 1914, 7 1/2" h. **121**

Albany-glazed Advertising Storage Jar

Storage jar, cylindrical w/tapering shoulder to a thick molded mouth, advertising-type, impressed name "T. Cunningham - Druggist & Grocer - Mohawk," dark brown Albany slip glaze, minor surface wear on rim, ca. 1870, 2 pt., 7 1/2" h. (ILLUS.) **176**

Storage jug, beehive-shaped body tapering to a small flared neck, fine overall mustard brown alkaline glaze, unsigned, a couple of rim chips, ca. 1880, 1 gal., 9" h. (ILLUS. far right with small jug, pitcher & syrup jug, bottom page 93) **22**

Strainer, wide, deep cylindrical basket-form w/high arched overhead handle, pierced overall w/rows of small holes, overall dark brown Albany slip glaze inside & out, impressed size number on shoulder, unsigned, excellent condition, ca. 1870, 6 qt., 17" h. (ILLUS. center with large jar & washboard, bottom page 83) **187**

Strainer-jug, cylindrical body tapering to a short wide molded mouth, no handle, pierced overall w/strips of small holes down the sides, possibly an oyster strainer, unmarked, stack marks at base, some minor use staining, ca. 1870, 2 gal., 13 1/2" h. (ILLUS., top next column) **358**

Sugar bowl, cov., footed squatty bulbous body w/a wide flat rim & eared handles, domed cover w/button finial, the cover & upper body molded w/bands of small raised dotted design trimmed in cobalt blue, brushed cobalt blue stylized flowers around the body, unsigned but possibly Pennsylvania or Shenandoah Valley origin, scarce form, ca. 1840, 5" h. (cover broken in half & tightly reglued, chip in base also reglued) **6,600**

Syrup jug, wide flat-bottomed cylindrical body tapering sharply to a small mouth & strap handle, overall dark brown alkaline glaze, impressed mark of S. Hart, Fulton, New York, very minor stone ping, ca. 1880, 1 gal., 10" h. (ILLUS. second from

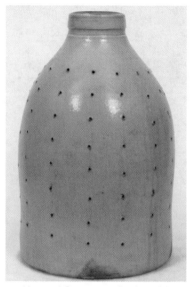

Unusual Stoneware Strainer-Jug

right with small jug, pitcher & storage jar, bottom page 93) **33**

Syrup jug, beehive-shaped tapering to a small cupped mouth w/pinched spout, strap handle, dark cobalt blue slip-quilled long parrot perched on a long feathery leafy branch, impressed & lightly blue-tinted mark of the Fort Edward Pottery Co., Fort Edward, New York, ca. 1860, 2 gal., 14" h. (professional restoration to a chip on the spout) **1,320**

Vase, sharply tapering ovoid body w/closed rim, overall diffused cobalt blue accents, probably New York state origin, minor interior flake at rim, short clay separation line from flake, ca. 1860, 5 3/4" h. (ILLUS. far left with crock, shard, flowerpot & jar, bottom page 36) **154**

Vase, bud-type, 6 1/2" h., footed bulbous ovoid body tapering sharply to a small trumpet neck, overall chocolate brown alkaline glaze, uncommon form, excellent condition, ca. 1900 .... **44**

Washboard, rectangular stoneware insert w/molded bumpy surface w/a light brown alkaline glaze w/sponged darker brown accents, fitted in a worn wooden frame w/good patina, unsigned, uncommon form, ca. 1880, 12 1/2" w., 23" h. (ILLUS. right with jar & strainer, bottom page 83) **550**

Water cooler, keg-shaped, thin incised blue-trimmed lines around the top & bottom, spigot hole in the center of the side, blue-tinted impressed mark "A.A. Co. Pat. Apld. For," intended to sit on its side in a wooden frame, X-shaped long line on the right side, three short clay separation lines on the bottom, ca. 1880, 1/2 gal., 8" l. (ILLUS. right with chicken feeder, bottom page 32) **99**

Two Molded Stoneware Water Coolers

Water cooler, barrel-shaped, Bristol-glazed w/a large relief-molded front panel w/a scene of polar bears framed w/floral scrolls above the spigot hole, all trimmed in cobalt blue, molded floral designs on the back, long tight hairline extending down from rim at back, ca. 1900, 2 gal., 12" h. (ILLUS. right with larger water cooler, above) **523**

Water cooler, barrel-shaped, Bristol-glazed body w/an incised overall cracked ice background design w/brick-work bands around the base, the center front w/a rectangular molded relief panel reading "Ice Water" & trimmed in cobalt blue, the sides molded overall w/relief-molded & blue-trimmed flower sprigs, a spigot hole w/original nickel-plate tap at the front bottom, ca. 1900, 3 gal., 13 1/2" h. (ILLUS. left with matching larger cooler, bottom of page)................... **275**

Two Matching Flower-embossed Ice Water Coolers

Water cooler, bulbous ovoid body tapering to a small mouth flanked by two arched loop handles to the shoulder, spigot hole at the front base, incised & cobalt blue-trimmed double flower design high on the shoulder just below the impressed mark of I. Seymour, Troy, New York, light blue accents at handles, stained overall but otherwise excellent condition, early, ca. 1830, 3 gal., 16" h. **3,190**

Water cooler, cylindrical tapering slightly to a wide flat mouth, eared handles, cobalt blue crudely brushed double plume flowers on front & back, blue band near top & around the spigot hole, impressed size number in a circle at front shoulder, unsigned, professional restoration to a T-shaped crack in the design in back & to a long clay separation line in front of right handle, minor surface chips, ca. 1850, 4 gal., 14 1/2" h. (ILLUS. right with very rare John Bell covered crock, bottom page 55).. **495**

Water cooler, cov., tall barrel shape w/a low domed cover w/a blue-washed button finial, molded spigot hole at front base, groups of four deeply incised bands trimmed in cobalt blue around the top & bottom w/a cobalt blue slip-quilled three-leaf sprig in the center front, impressed mark of the New York Stoneware Co., Fort Edward, New York, ca. 1880, 4 gal., 15 1/2" h. (minor surface chip, some minor overglazing on back).............................. **303**

Water cooler, large barrel shape w/12 thin incised lines decorated w/four wide brushed cobalt blue bands around the sides w/a large single brushed leaf in the center, script size number above the impressed mark of Charlestown, Charlestown, Massachusetts, brass spigot appears original, ca. 1850, 5 gal., 15" h. (dark clay coloring from firing, very minor surface chip on spout hole)........................ **495**

Water cooler, barrel-shaped, Bristol-glazed w/a bold relief-molded design of the Landing of Columbus on the front, the figures, ships & palm trees trimmed in brown, green & blue, the back w/a lovely molded vine design, uncommon design from Whites Pottery, Utica, New York, ca. 1900, 6 gal., 15" h. (ILLUS. left with smaller water cooler, top previous page).. **3,960**

Water cooler, wide ovoid body tapering to a wide molded rim flanked by eared handles, spigot hole at the bottom front, dark cobalt blue slip-quilled design of a large bird w/curved beak, comb & dotted tail perched on a curlicue plume below the impressed mark of O.L. & A.K. Ballard, Burlington, Vermont, couple of short,

tight hairlines down from rim, few glaze spider cracks & flakes, professional restoration to chip at spigot hole, ca. 1870, 6 gal., 15" h. (ILLUS. left with two rare deer-decorated Vermont pieces, bottom page 56).. **2,640**

Water cooler, barrel-shaped, Bristol-glazed body w/an incised overall cracked ice background design w/brickwork bands around the base, the center front w/a rectangular molded relief panel reading "Ice Water" & trimmed in cobalt blue, the sides molded overall w/relief-molded & blue-trimmed flower sprigs, a spigot hole w/original nickel-plate tap at the front bottom, ca. 1900, 6 gal., 16" h. (ILLUS. right with smaller matching water cooler, bottom previous page)............................. **275**

Water cooler, cov., wide cylindrical form relief-molded around the sides w/a scene of an elk in a forest setting, overall cobalt blue glaze, pine boughs & cones around the cover, metal spigot at the front base, minor chips under the cover, late 19th - early 20th c., 14 3/4" h. **345**

Large Blue-incised Water Cooler

Water cooler, cov., barrel-shaped w/original domed cover, narrow incised bands around the sides, wide panel at the top w/blue-tinted impressed name "The Kenton Cooler," spigot hole at bottom framed by a blue starburst, late 19th - early 20th c., 3 gal., 15" h. (ILLUS.)............................. **413**

Unusual Decorative Stoneware Water Cooler

Water cooler, wide disk foot supporting a wide tapering bulbous urn-form body w/loop shoulder handles, incised large addorsed perched birds trimmed in cobalt blue, brushed cobalt decoration of dots, lines & sprig bands around the neck & shoulder, the back w/a brushed cobalt blue double flower in a pot, mark of the Somerset Potters Works, Massachusetts, kiln burn on front, glued crack on front, in-the-making chip out of bung hole frame, ca. 1870, 3 gal., 15" h. (ILLUS.)..... **3,960**

Water Cooler with a Plump Bird

Water cooler, wide ovoid body w/bung hole at bottom front, eared handles, short cylindrical neck w/molded rim, slip-quilled cobalt blue large plump bird perched on a scrolled branch, fine detail, impressed mark of O.L. & A.K. Ballard, Burlington, Vermont, couple of very tight hairlines

from rim, few glaze spiders & flakes, professional restoration to chip at bung hole, ca. 1870, 6 gal., 15" h. (ILLUS.)....... **2,640**

Decorative Bennington Water Cooler

Water cooler, barrel-shaped w/bung hole at front bottom, decorated w/incised bands trimmed in blue & a band of cobalt blue slip-quilled large flowers & leaves around the middle, impressed mark of J. & E. Norton, Bennington, Vermont, X-shaped spider line to left of design, ca. 1855, 6 gal., 15 1/2" h. (ILLUS.) **1,760**

Water Cooler with Wreath & Bird Design

Water cooler, tall ovoid body tapering to a small molded mouth flanked by large strap handles, a spigot hole at the bottom front, cobalt blue slip-quilled decoration of a tall wreath enclosing a bird perched on a trumpet flower, unsigned, probably from Ohio, excellent condition, ca. 1870, 5 gal., 19 1/2" h. (ILLUS.)............................ **3,960**

Water cooler, tall domed beehive form w/short neck, applied shoulder handles, w/cobalt decoration of chicken pecking at an ear of corn, unusual orange peel glaze, impressed "6" & "New York Stoneware Co. Fort Edward...," 19 1/2" h. (two daubs of translucent glaze & short hairlines at base, made into a lamp but not drilled) **2,750**

Water Cooler with Bird & Branch Decor

Water cooler, cylindrical body tapering to a small molded mouth flanked by arched strap handles, bung hole at bottom front, cobalt blue slip-quilled fat bird w/small head perched on a leafy stem, impressed mark of Satterlee & Mory, Fort Edward, New York, professional restoration to extensive handle chipping & short lines down from the mouth, ca. 1870, 6 gal., 20" h. (ILLUS.) **605**

Whimsey, model of a lady's high-heeled shoe, blue-trimmed white Bristol glaze, overall crazing, ca. 1880, 5" l. (ILLUS., bottom of page).. **248**

Whimsey, model of a standing rooster, overall dark brown mottled Albany slip glaze, apparently hand-crafted, excellent condition, ca. 1870, 4" h. **303**

Whistle, figural, model of a seated poodle on a round base, overall Rockingham glaze, fine detail, rare, excellent condition, ca. 1870, 3 3/4" h. **248**

Whistle, figural, model of an owl perched on a stump, overall Rockingham glaze, excellent condition, ca. 1870, 3 1/2" h. **220**

Whistle, figural, stylized model of a bird, dark Rockingham glaze, hand-formed, couple of glaze chips, ca. 1870, 1 1/2" h. **88**

Wine cooler, wide barrel shape w/flat top centered by a large hole, a molded spigot hole at the front base, three wide molded brown-glazed bands alternating w/red-glazed bands in the upper & lower half, the wide brown center band printed w/the label "PORTER," unsigned, 19th c. (ILLUS. bottom row, far right, with full page of various other stoneware pieces, page 27) **176**

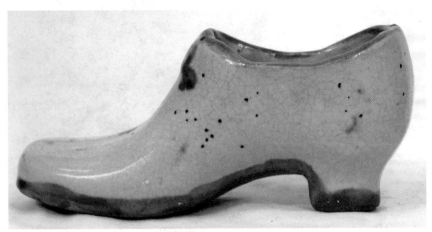

Blue & White Stoneware Victorian Shoe Whimsey

Red Wing Stoneware

by Gail Peck

History

The stoneware industry came to Red Wing, Minnesota, because the right conditions existed. Glaciers had deposited perfect clay in the area; there was capital and manpower in the town; and there was a functional need for the products at that time in history. It was only when the Red Wing Stoneware Company began producing stoneware on a large scale in 1878, however, that the product became known beyond the local area. The Red Wing Stoneware Company was later joined by two other stoneware manufacturers, the Minnesota Stoneware Company and the North Star Stoneware Company, and products of all three companies are collected by Red Wing enthusiasts.

From these three independent manufacturers, various mergers and unions developed in order to weather the economic difficulties and to form a united front in order to meet increasing competition from outside the Red Wing area. An understanding of these various Red Wing companies and the dates of their operation is important in putting their products in context:

1877-1906 — Red Wing Stoneware Company

1883-1906 — Minnesota Stoneware Company

1892-1896 — North Star Stoneware Company

1894-1906 — Union Stoneware Company (the joining of the three above stoneware companies for economic efficiency; each retaining its own identity, however)

1906-1936 — Red Wing Union Stoneware Company (the remaining two companies, Red Wing Stoneware and Minnesota Stoneware, united to form this new company)

1936-1967 — Red Wing Potteries

Five-gallon Red Wing crock with 6" wing and "Red Wing Union Stoneware Co." oval stamp, $175-200.

*Beehive-shaped
3-gallon Red Wing jug
with blue birch leaves
and Union Stoneware
Co. oval, $400-450.*

Buying, Dating and Valuing Red Wing Stoneware

The earliest products made by the Red Wing Stoneware companies were either hand-turned, hand-decorated salt-glazed pieces or small brown-glazed molded pieces. White ware was not introduced until the mid- to late-1890s. Stamped blue birch leaf designs were used as company markings on white ware until 1908 or 1909, when the familiar red "wing" logo was introduced as the Red Wing Union Stoneware Company trademark.

The importance of buying pieces signed with a company mark cannot be overstated. A company signature adds to the value of any piece, but other factors such as rarity, condition and desirability must also be considered. Eye appeal, decorating possibilities and personal taste very often determine the selling price of a particular piece.

It is important for collectors to buy only the pieces that have personal appeal to them. The uniqueness and variety of wares produced by the Red Wing clay industries over a 90-year history provides something for everyone, and is the main reason that collecting Red Wing wares is such a popular hobby today.

Editor's note: Gail Peck, a longtime collector of Red Wing stoneware, is a charter member of the Red Wing Collectors' Society and has written numerous articles on stoneware. She has co-authored two books on Red Wing: Red Wing Stoneware *and* Red Wing Collectibles, *both published by Collector Books, Paducah, Kentucky.*

Red Wing 2-gallon crock with black "elephant ear" leaves and "Union Stoneware Co." oval stamp, the bottom signed "Minnesota Stoneware Co.," $125-150.

A Guide to Trademarks on Red Wing Pottery

The Union Stoneware Company of Red Wing used a combination of markings between 1894 and 1906. Two variations are found on its pieces, each type being a combination of a pair of stamped leaves and an oval mark.

Before the turn of the 20th century, the firm marked pieces with a pair of large flaring leaves, referred to as "elephant ears," above the oval reserve printed "Union Stoneware Co. – Red Wing, Minn." (See Marks 1a & 1b on next page).

From about 1900 until around 1908-09, the larger leaves were replaced by a pair of smaller leaves, called "birch leaves," above the same oval mark. (See Mark 2).

The familiar red "wing" mark was introduced after 1908-09 and placed above the oval blue mark. This "wing" mark changed in size over the years and can help approximately date a piece. The rule of thumb: the larger the wing and oval marks, the older the piece.

— 6"-long wing – 1908-09 to the 1910s

— 4"-long wing – 1910s into the 1920s

— 2"-long wing – 1930s-40s

The oval mark used with the red wing mark also comes in two variations. The oval mark is so predominant in the 1910s and 1920s that collectors refer to it as the "standard" oval mark. (See Mark 3). The other oval mark, the first one used after the 1906 formation of the Red Wing Union Stoneware Company, is similar to the "standard"

"Wing" mark: This packing jar ($3,500-4,000) displays the 4" wing, which helps date this piece to the 1910s-1920s.

oval except that there is a slightly wavy line under the words "Red Wing" at the top of the oval. This is called the "ski" design because it resembles a ski. (See Mark 4.)

Editor's note: Our thanks to Red Wing experts Gary and Bonnie Tefft for sharing this information and the copies of the Red Wing marks. They are authors of the book Red Wing Potters and Their Wares.

Mark 1a:
The large "elephant ear" leaves mark used before 1900.

Mark 1b:
The oval mark of the Union Stoneware Company used before 1906 along with the "elephant ears" or "birch leaves" mark.

Mark 2:
The stamped blue "birch leaves" mark used with the Union Stoneware Company oval mark from around 1900 until 1908-09.

Mark 3:
The "standard" Red Wing Union Stoneware Company oval mark, widely used from the 1910s into the 1920s.

Mark 4:
The "ski" variation of the oval Red Wing Union Stoneware Company mark, the first oval mark used after 1906.

PART II: MIDWESTERN STONEWARE

Red Wing Stoneware

More Common Red Wing Ashtray

Ashtray, earthenware, model of a wing w/a deep red glaze, bottom marked earthenware, "Red Wing Potteries" (ILLUS.)....... **$50-60**

Rare "Pretty Red Wing" Wing Ashtray

Ashtray, earthenware, "Pretty Red Wing" style, model of a large red-glazed wing embossed w/a bust profile of an Indian maiden (ILLUS.) **400-450**

Two Views of a Maroon Baking Dish with Interior Advertising

Baking dish, advertising-type, wide flat bottom w/deep sides w/molded graduating bands, overall glossy maroon glaze, dark blue printed advertising on inside bottom (ILLUS. of two views) **375-425**

Sponged Advertising Baking Dish

Baking dish, advertising-type, wide flat bottom w/deep sides w/molded graduating bands, overall red & blue sponging on white, printed advertising on the inside bottom (ILLUS.)..................................... **375-425**

Brown & White Advertising Bean Pot

Bean pot, cov., advertising-type, wide bulbous flat-bottomed body tapering to a molded cylindrical wide neck flanked by loop handles, inset cover, dark brown glazed cover & upper body, white lower body printed w/blue Minnesota advertising (ILLUS.).. **100-125**

Beater jar, advertising-type, cylindrical w/molded flat rim, white-glazed w/blue bands & blue advertising reading "Red Wing Beater Jar - Eggs - Cream - Salad Dressing" (ILLUS. left with similar advertising beater jar, bottom of page) **125-150**

Beater jar, advertising-type, cylindrical w/molded flat rim, white-glazed w/blue bands & blue South Dakota advertising (ILLUS. right with similar Red Wing Beater Jar, bottom of page)......................... **275-325**

Two Cylindrical Red Wing Beater Jars

Two Banded Red Wing Beater Jars

Beater jar, Gray Line (Sponge Band) ware, narrow tapering base below the deep cylindrical ribbed sides & molded rim, white-glazed w/narrow orange sponged band flanked by thin blue bands near the rim (ILLUS. left with other beater jar, above) **325-375**
Beater jar, narrow tapering base below the deep cylindrical ribbed sides & molded rim, overall pale blue & red sponging on white (ILLUS., next column) **950-1,150**
Beater jar, narrow tapering base below the deep cylindrical ribbed sides & molded rim, white-glazed w/narrow blue bands near the rim (ILLUS. right with other Gray Line beater jar, top of page) **125-150**
Bowl, nappie or pudding pan-style, blue & white diffused decoration, molded picket fence design around top (ILLUS., bottom of page) **300-350**

Rare Blue & Red Sponged Beater Jar

Blue & White Picket Fence Design Bowl

Red Wing Saffron Ware Ribbed & Banded Bowl

Bowl, nappie-style, Saffron ware, ribbed sides below the wide flat rim decorated w/a white band flanked by thin brown bands (ILLUS.) **250-300**

Two Views of a Blue-glazed Red Wing Advertising 1/2-Pint Bowl

Bowl, mixing-type, advertising-type, rounded bottom w/thick flat rim band, blue-glazed exterior, white-glazed interior w/printed blue advertising, 1/2 pt. (ILLUS. of two views) **400-500**
Bowl, miniature, 3" d., 1 1/4" h., rounded base w/wide flat rim, overall black sponging on white (ILLUS. right with other miniature bowl, below) **600-700**

Two Miniature Red Wing Bowls

Bowl, miniature, 3" d., 1 1/4" h., rounded brown base w/wide flat white rim (ILLUS. left with other miniature bowl) **600-700**

Rare Small Paneled & Sponged Bowl

Bowl, 5" d., deep rounded paneled sides & a wide molded rim, overall red & blue sponging on white (ILLUS.).................. **550-650**

Rare Small Ribbed & Sponged Bowl

Bowl, 5" d., rounded bowl w/narrow ribs below the thick flat rim, overall red & blue sponging on a tan ground (ILLUS.)....... **375-425**

Small Blue-banded Saffron Ware Bowl

Bowl, 5" d., Saffron Ware, wide ribs around the lower base, wide flat rim w/two thin blue bands (ILLUS.)..**225-250**

Rare Small Ribbed & Sponged Bowl

Bowl, 5" d., wide ribs around the lower body, wide flat rim, overall red & blue sponging (ILLUS.)..**375-425**

Small Blue & White Greek Key Bowl

Bowl, 6" d., embossed Greek Key patt., pale blue on white glaze (ILLUS.) **125-145**

Rare Deep Cap-style Sponged Bowl

Bowl, 7" d., cap-style, footed deep cylindrical form w/narrow molded bands & molded rim, overall red & blue sponging on white (ILLUS.).. **1,000-1,200**

White-glazed Bowl with Pink & Blue Bands

Bowl, 7" d., deep rounded & ribbed sides, white-glazed & decorated w/pale pink & blue bands (ILLUS.)... **75-125**

Saffron Ware Sponged 7" Bowl

Bowl, 7" d., Saffron Ware, deep rounded bowl w/narrow ribbing below the thick flat rim, overall red & blue sponging (ILLUS.) **100-125**

Large Gray Line (Sponge Band) Bowl

Bowl, 9" d., Gray Line (Sponge Band) ware, deep rounded & ribbed sides w/a narrow sponged orange band flanked by thin blue bands (ILLUS.) **175-225**

Large Ribbed & Blue-banded Bowl

Bowl, 9" d., white-glazed, deep rounded bowl w/narrow molded ribs below the thick flat rim trimmed w/two blue bands (ILLUS.) **75-100**

Blue & Pink-Banded Saffron Bowl

Bowl, 10" d., Saffron ware, deep rounded & ribbed sides w/pink & blue bands below the thick flat rim w/matching bands (ILLUS.).. **75-125**

Large Paneled & Sponged Bowl

Bowl, 11" d., deep rounded paneled sides & a wide molded rim, overall red & blue sponging on white (ILLUS.).. **325-350**

Three All-Blue Red Wing Bowls

Bowls, mixing-type, deep fluted base & wide flat rim, overall dark blue glaze, bottom marked "Red Wing USA," 5", 6" & 7" d., each (ILLUS. of three)... **125-145**

Two Churns with Leaves Marks

Miniature Commemorative Butter Churn

Butter churn, cov., miniature, advertising-
and commemorative-type, swelled cylindrical body w/a flared rim, eared handles
& original cover w/wooden dasher, white-
glazed w/blue script number above a pair
of printed birch leaves above a printed
oval w/advertising, also marked "Iowa
Chapter Red Wing Collectors Society
2nd Annual Conf. 1994," 4" h. (ILLUS.) **127**

Butter churn, cov., tapering cylindrical body
w/molded rim, eared handles & inset cover, white-glazed w/a large blue printed
size number above a pair of birch leaves
over the oval Red Wing Union Stoneware
fancy "ski" mark, 2 gal. (ILLUS. left with 4-
gallon churn, top of page) **550-600**

Small 2-Gallon Red Wing Butter Churn

Butter churn, cov., tapering cylindrical
body w/molded rim & inset cover, white-
glazed w/a large blue printed size number above a 4" red wing mark & the blue
oval Red Wing Union Stoneware mark, 2
gal. (ILLUS.)... **475-525**

Rare 3-Gallon Advertising Butter Churn

Butter churn, advertising-type, tall slightly tapering cylindrical white-glazed body w/thick molded rim & eared handles, printed black "3" above two large birch leaves, printed rectangle w/Nebraska advertising, 3 gal. (ILLUS.).................. **3,000-3,500**

Churn with Fancy Red Wing "Ski" Mark

Butter churn, cov., tapering cylindrical body w/molded rim & inset cover, white-glazed w/a large blue printed size number above a 4" red wing mark & the blue oval Red Wing Union Stoneware fancy "ski" mark, 3 gal. (ILLUS.)..................... **450-500**

Butter churn, cov., tapering cylindrical body w/molded rim & inset cover, white-glazed w/a large blue printed size number above a pair of birch leaves over the oval Red Wing Union Stoneware fancy "ski" mark, 4 gal. (ILLUS. right with 2-gallon churn, top previous page) **450-500**

Very Rare Red Wing 4-Gallon Churn

Butter churn, tall slightly tapering cylindrical salt-glazed body w/thick molded rim & eared handles, cobalt blue slip-quilled "4" above a large leaf, impressed Red Wing Stoneware mark on the side, 4 gal. (ILLUS.) **3,000-3,500**

5-Gallon Red Wing Butter Churn

Butter churn, cov., tapering cylindrical body w/molded rim & inset cover, white-glazed w/a large blue printed size number above a large 6" red wing mark & the blue oval Red Wing Union Stoneware fancy "ski" mark, 5 gal. (ILLUS.) **550-600**

Large Rare Red Wing Butter Churn

Butter churn, tall slightly tapering cylindrical salt-glazed body w/thick molded rim & eared handles, cobalt blue slip-quilled "6" above a butterfly & flower design, unsigned, 6 gal. (ILLUS.) **2,500-3,000**

Banded Advertising Butter Crock

Butter crock, cov., advertising-type, cylindrical w/molded rim & inset cover, white glaze w/wide reddish pink bands at the rim & base, printed black rectangle enclosing advertising (ILLUS.) **350-400**

Butter crock, cov., Gray Line (Sponge Band) style, narrow flaring foot below the cylindrical ribbed body w/a narrow orange sponged band flanked by thin blue bands under the molded rim, inset matching cover, wire bail handle w/turned wooden grip, 3 lb. (ILLUS., top next column)... **550-600**

Gray Line (Sponge Band) Butter Crock

Rare 10-lb. Banded Advertising Butter Crock

Butter crock, cov., advertising-type, deep cylindrical form w/molded rim, decorated w/pairs of blue bands at the top & bottom, a large blue printed rectangle w/Chicago advertising in center, 10 lb. (ILLUS.)... **2,000-2,500**

Very Large Red Wing Butter Crock

Butter crock, wide cylindrical body w/molded rim, white-glazed, printed w/a large dark blue rectangle w/"20 lbs." above a 4" red wing mark, 20 lb. (ILLUS.) **1,000-1,200**

Three Sizes of Advertising Butter Crocks

Butter crocks, advertising-type, cylindrical w/molded rim, white-glazed, each w/a printed blue rectangle w/advertising, various sizes, each (ILLUS. of three) **150-300**

Rare Embossed & Sponged Casserole

Casserole, cov., wide rounded flat-bottomed bowl w/embossed leaves & flowers & a molded rim, low domed cover w/button finial, overall red & blue sponging on white (ILLUS.) **900-1,000**

Two Gray Line (Sponge Band) Red Wing Casseroles

Casserole, cov., Gray Line (Sponge Band) type, deep flat-bottomed bowl w/molded ribbing below a narrow orange sponged band flanked by thin blue bands, inset slightly domed cover w/button finial & matching decoration, 4 1/2" d. (ILLUS. left with larger casserole) **500-550**

Casserole, cov., Gray Line (Sponge Band) type, deep flat-bottomed bowl w/molded ribbing below a narrow orange sponged band flanked by thin blue bands, inset slightly domed cover w/button finial & matching decoration, 5 3/4" d. (ILLUS. right with smaller casserole, bottom previous page).. **500-550**

Cookie jar, cov., barrel-shaped w/molded rim & wide cover w/disk finial, molded in relief w/cattails & the word "Cookies" against a stippled ground, dark brown bands at the rim & base w/tan center (ILLUS., next column) **250-300**

Red Wing Pottery Cookie Jar

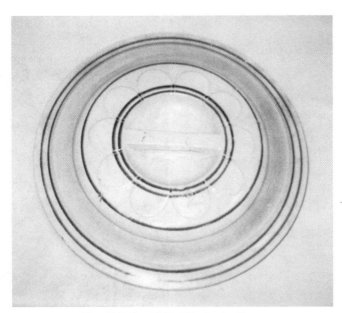

Rare 2-Gallon Molded Pantry Jar Cover

Cover, for pantry jar, slightly domed, white glazed decorated w/double blue stripes & a center ring of embossed petals, 2 gal. (ILLUS.)... **650-700**

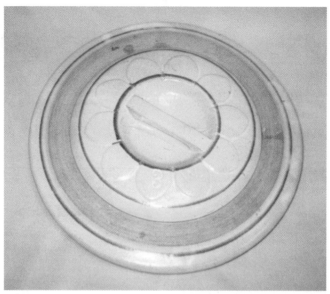

Red Wing 3-Gallon Water Cooler Cover

Cover, for water cooler, slightly domed, white glaze decorated w/double blue stripes & a center ring of embossed petals, 3 gal. (ILLUS.) **350-400**

Half-Gallon Advertising Honey Crock

Crock, advertising-type, cylindrical w/molded rim, white glaze printed in black w/an oval enclosing Wisconsin honey advertising, 1/2 gal. (ILLUS.)................ **200-250**

1-Gallon Red Wing Advertising Crock

Crock, advertising-type, cylindrical w/molded rim, white glaze printed in blue w/an oval enclosing Nebraska advertising, 1 gal. (ILLUS.).................................... **1,000-1,500**

1-Gallon Crock with Large Wing Mark

Crock, cylindrical w/molded rim, white glaze printed w/the large 4" red wing logo, 1 gal. (ILLUS.) **500-600**

2-Gallon Nebraska Advertising Crock

Crock, advertising-type, cylindrical w/molded rim, white glaze printed in black w/a script "2" above an oval enclosing Nebraska advertising, 2 gal. (ILLUS.)... **2,000-2,500**

Minnesota Stoneware 2-Gallon Crock

Crock, cylindrical w/molded rim, white glaze printed in black w/a script "2" above two elephant ear leaves & an oval Minnesota Stoneware Company mark, 2 gal. (ILLUS.) **125-150**
Crock, cylindrical w/molded rim, white glaze printed w/a large blue size number, large red wing logo & the oval mark of the Red Wing Union Stoneware Company, 2 gal. (ILLUS. right with 3-gallon crock, bottom of page).. **100-125**

2- & 3-Gallon Red Wing Double-marked Crocks

Red Wing 3- & 5-Gallon Crocks

Crock, cylindrical salt glazed body w/molded rim & eared handles, cobalt blue slip-quilled "3" above a lazy eight & target design, unsigned, 3 gal. (ILLUS. right with 5-gallon crock) **150-200**

Two Slip-decorated Red Wing Crocks

Crock, cylindrical salt-glazed body w/molded rim & eared handles, cobalt blue slip-quilled "3" above a lazy eight & target design, side stamped "Red Wing Stoneware," 3 gal. (ILLUS. left with 4-gallon crock) **900-1,000**

Crock, cylindrical w/molded rim, white glaze printed w/a large blue size number, large red wing logo & the oval mark of the Red Wing Union Stoneware Company, 3 gal. (ILLUS. left with 2-gallon crock, bottom previous page) **100-125**

Crock, cylindrical salt-glazed body w/molded rim & eared handles, cobalt blue slip-quilled "4" above a lazy eight & target design, side stamped "Red Wing Stoneware," 4 gal. (ILLUS. right with 3-gallon crock, above) **900-1,000**

Crock, cylindrical salt glazed body w/molded rim & eared handles, cobalt blue slip-quilled "5" above a red cage design, unsigned, 5 gal. (ILLUS. left with 3-gallon crock, top of page) **275-325**

Red Wing Crock with Wing & Oval Marks

Crock, cylindrical w/molded rim, white glaze printed w/a large blue size number, large red wing logo & the oval mark of the Red Wing Union Stoneware Company, 5 gal. (ILLUS.)... **175-200**

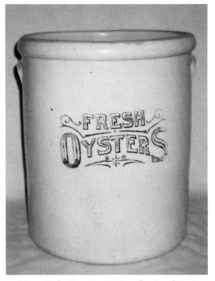

Rare 6-Gallon Red Wing Oyster Crock

Crock, cylindrical w/molded rim & eared handle, white glaze w/fancy printed blue marking "Fresh Oysters," 6 gal. (ILLUS.)... **2,000-2,500**

Rare Red Wing Decorated 6-Gallon Crock

Crock, cylindrical salt-glazed body w/molded rim & eared handles, cobalt blue slip-quilled "6" above a large leaf, side stamped "RWSCo.," 6 gal. (ILLUS.).. **1,000-1,200**

6-Gallon Handled Red Wing Crock

Crock, cylindrical w/molded rim flanked by small wire bail handles w/wooden grips, white-glazed w/large printed size number above a printed red wing & oval Red Wing Union Stoneware mark, 6 gal., 14 1/2" h. (ILLUS.) **92**

Very Rare Brown-glazed Red Wing Lion Doorstop

Rare 15-Gallon Red Wing Crock

Crock, cylindrical salt-glazed body w/molded rim & eared handles, cobalt blue slip-quilled "15" above a stylized butterfly & flower design, unsigned, 15 gal. (ILLUS.)... **1,200-1,500**

Doorstop, figural, model of a handsome seated lion on a thick rectangular base, overall dark brown glaze (ILLUS., top of page)... **3,000-4,000**

Rare Red Wing Pottery Bulldog Doorstop

Doorstop, figural, model of a standing bulldog, overall dark brown glaze (ILLUS.)... **800-1,000**

Fruit (or canning) jar, cylindrical body w/sloping shoulder to a small mouth w/original screw-on zinc lid, Bristol glaze w/blue printed square printed "Stone Mason Fruit Jar - Union Stoneware Co. - Red Wing, Minn.," also impressed on the bottom "Pat. Jan 24, 1899," ca. 1899, 1 gal., 10 1/2" h. (surface chip on very bottom front edge, overall light blue drip stain from use) **385**

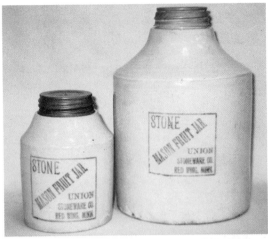

Two Union Stoneware Stone Mason Fruit Jars

Fruit (or canning) jar, cylindrical w/angled shoulder & twist-off metal lid, blue-printed Stone Mason Fruit Jar logo, 1 qt. (ILLUS. left with gallon jar, above) **275-300**

Fruit (or canning) jar, cylindrical w/angled shoulder & twist-off metal lid, blue-printed Stone Mason Fruit Jar logo, 1 gal. (ILLUS. right with quart jar, above).................. **900-1,100**

Fruit (or canning) jar, dome-top style, twist-on metal lid, printed blue shield logo of the Red Wing Union Stoneware Company, 1 gal. (ILLUS., next column) **4,500-5,500**

Fruit (or canning) jars, advertising-type, cylindrical w/angled shoulder & twist-off metal lids, Stone Mason-type, each w/panels of printed advertising on the front, each (ILLUS. of three, bottom of page) **2,800-3,200**

Very Rare Gallon Red Wing Fruit Jar

Group of Rare Red Wing Advertising Fruit Jars

Front & Back of Miniature Red Wing Advertising Jug

Jug, advertising-type, short cylindrical white body w/a tapering brown neck & handle, front w/blue-printed advertising, small red wing mark at the back (ILLUS. of front & back, above)... **550-650**

mark & an oval panel w/Kansas advertising (ILLUS.).................................... **2,500-3,000**

Miniature Red Wing Union Stoneware Jug

Jug, miniature, advertising-type, cylindrical w/rounded shoulder & small neck, white glaze printed w/oval mark for the Red Wing Union Stoneware Co. (ILLUS.) **600-700**

Advertising Beehive Jug with Birch Leaves

Jug, beehive-shaped, advertising-type, white glaze, printed blue birch leaves

Jug, miniature, advertising-type, fancy-type beehive-shaped w/brown top above a white bottom printed in blue w/advertising for the Merchant's Hotel, St. Paul, Minn., 1/8 pt. (ILLUS. left with two other miniature jugs, bottom of page) **550-650**

Three Miniature Brown & White Advertising Jugs

Two Views of Rare Labeled Minnesota Stoneware Miniature Jug

Jug, miniature, advertising-type, fancy-type beehive-shaped w/brown top above a white bottom printed in blue w/advertising for the Victoria Sanatorium, Colfax, Iowa, 1/8 pt. (ILLUS. center with two other miniature jugs, bottom previous page) **1,000-1,300**

Jug, miniature, advertising-type, fancy-type beehive-shaped w/brown top above a white bottom printed in blue w/advertising for J.D. Parker, Lincoln, Nebraska, 1/8 pt. (ILLUS. right with two other miniature jugs, bottom previous page) **1,000-1,300**

Jug, miniature, beehive-shaped, overall dark brown glaze, original yellow paper label for the Minnesota Stoneware Company on the base, 1/8 pt. (ILLUS. of side & bottom, top of page) **1,000-1,200**

Jug, miniature, fancy-style, white base & brown shoulder, printed in blue "Minnesota - Michigan," 1/8 pt. (ILLUS.) **275-325**

Very Rare Miniature Blue-sponged Jug

Jug, miniature, fancy-type, overall dark blue sponging, unsigned, 1/4 pt. (ILLUS.) **2,500-3,000**

Jug, miniature, souvenir-type, cone-top style, cylindrical white base & brown shoulder, printed in blue "Souvenir of Red Wing" (ILLUS. left with two other brown & white miniature jugs, bottom of page) **450-550**

Minnesota-Michigan Miniature Jug

Three Varied Brown & White Red Wing Miniature Souvenir Jugs

Two Fancy Style Miniature Souvenir Jugs

Rare Miniature Convention Souvenir Jug

Jug, miniature, souvenir-type, cylindrical white body w/rounded brown shoulder, printed on the base w/the emblem of the Minnesota State Federation of Labor w/dates of its 1909 convention (ILLUS.)... **700-800**

Jug, miniature, souvenir-type, fancy style, white base & brown shoulder, printed in blue "Souvenir of Red Wing" (ILLUS. right with two other brown & white miniature jugs, bottom previous page)........... **600-700**

Jug, miniature, souvenir-type, fancy style, white base & brown shoulder, printed in black "Excelsior Springs, MO - 1903" (ILLUS. left with other fancy style miniature jug, top of page)........................... **375-425**

Jug, miniature, souvenir-type, fancy style, white base & brown shoulder, printed in blue "Souvenir - Excelsior Springs, Missouri" (ILLUS. right with other fancy style miniature jug, top of page).................. **350-400**

Jug, miniature, souvenir-type, shoulder-type style, cylindrical white base & brown shoulder, printed in blue "Souvenir of Red Wing" (ILLUS. center with two other brown & white miniature jugs, bottom previous page)..................................... **800-900**

Jug, miniature, souvenir-type, white ovoid body tapering to a brown rim, printed in blue w/the Moose Lodge logo & the dates of its 1930 convention (ILLUS. left with two other miniature souvenir jugs, bottom of page).. **600-700**

Jug, miniature, souvenir-type, white ovoid body tapering to a brown rim, printed in blue w/"Souvenir of Red Wing" (ILLUS. center with two other ovoid souvenir jugs, bottom of page) **650-750**

Jug, miniature, souvenir-type, white ovoid body tapering to a brown rim, printed in blue w/Elks Lodge logo & dates of its 1929 convention (ILLUS. right with two other ovoid miniature souvenir jugs, bottom of page)... **600-700**

Three Miniature Ovoid Souvenir Jugs

Minnesota Stoneware Brown Jug

Jug, beehive-shaped, overall dark brown glaze, mark on bottom for the Minnesota Stoneware Company, 1/2 gal. (ILLUS.) **75-95**

3-Gallon Beehive Jug with Leaves

Jug, beehive-shaped, white w/printed blue size number, double birch leaves & oval Union Stoneware Co. mark, 3 gal. (ILLUS.)... **400-450**

Rare Minnesota Stoneware Sponged Jug

Jug, beehive-shaped w/small neck & wire bail handle w/wooden grip, white w/overall fine blue sponging, Minnesota Stoneware Company mark on the base, 1 gal. (ILLUS.)... **2,200-2,500**

3-Gallon Red Wing Pottery Jug

Jug, shoulder-style, cylindrical body w/rounded shoulder & small neck, white glaze, printed blue size number, oval Red Wing Union Stoneware mark & a 4" red wing, 3 gal. (ILLUS.) **100-150**

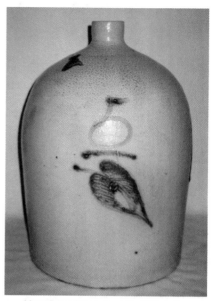

Red Wing Beehive-shaped Advertising Jug

Jug, beehive-shaped, advertising-type, white w/blue printed size number above a large printed blue shield w/Iowa advertising, 5 gal. (ILLUS.) **834**

Very Rare Decorated Red Wing Jug

Jug, beehive-shaped, salt-glazed & decorated w/a slip-quilled "5" above a large leaf, impressed mark of the Red Wing Stoneware Company on the side, 5 gal. (ILLUS.)... **7,000-9,000**

Brown-glazed Red Wing 5-Gallon Jug

Jug, beehive-shaped, overall dark brown glaze w/a large incised "5" on the shoulder, impressed "RWSCo" on the handle, 5 gal. (ILLUS.) **1,000-1,200**

Red Wing 5-Gallon Beehive Jug

Jug, beehive-shaped, white w/blue printed size number & oval mark of the Red Wing Union Stoneware Co. & the 4" red wing, 5 gal. (ILLUS.).. **400-450**

Red Wing 5-Gallon Marked Jug

Jug, shoulder-style, cylindrical body w/rounded shoulder & small neck, white glaze, printed blue size number, oval Red Wing Union Stoneware mark & a 4" red wing, 5 gal., 18" h. (ILLUS.) **173**

Extremely Rare Sample Master Waste Jar

Master waste jar, cov., miniature, embossed Lily patt., salesman's sample, w/original wire bail handle, 4" h. (ILLUS.) **6,000-7,000**

Model of a Miniature Baby Shoe

Model of a baby shoe, miniature, overall white glaze (ILLUS.) **450-550**

Rare Miniature Red Wing Doctor's Bag

Model of a doctor's bag, miniature, overall dark brown glaze (ILLUS.) **800-1,000**

Miniature Red Wing Spaniel Dog

Model of a dog, miniature, Staffordshire-style seated spaniel, white glaze w/blue eyes, 3" h. (ILLUS.) **250-300**

Rare Sleepy Eye Advertising Verse Mug

Mug, Sleepy eye verse-type, cylindrical white glazed form w/double blue bands flanking Sleepy Eye advertising, a bust of Chief Sleepy Eye & a verse (ILLUS.) **2,500-2,800**

Two Views of the Red Wing Transportation Mug

Mug, tall slightly tapering shape w/molded rings at top & base, angled handle, embossed around the sides w/various transportation scenes including a covered wagon, auto & airplane, overall dark brown glaze, ca. 1940 (ILLUS. of both sides).. **75-100**

Rare Wing-marked Packing Jar

Packing jar, beehive-shaped w/molded flaring mouth, white glaze, marked w/a 4" red wing, 4 gal. (ILLUS.) **3,500-4,000**

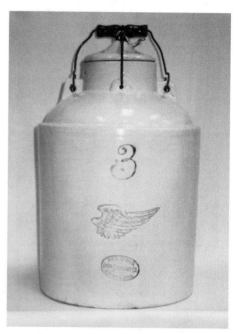

Red Wing Packing Jar with Cover & Seal

Packing jar, cov., cylindrical w/rounded shoulder & cylindrical neck w/original ball-lock sealing mechanism & wire bail handle w/wooden grip, white glaze, a script "3" above the 4" red wing & oval Red Wing Union Stoneware marks, 3 gal. (ILLUS.).. **275-325**

Front & Back of Red Wing Pantry Jar

Pantry jar, advertising-type, cylindrical w/molded rim, white glaze w/blue band trim, red wing mark on one side & printed blue rectangle w/South Dakota advertising on the other (ILLUS. of front & back) **1,200-1,500**

Blue-banded Red Wing Pantry Jar

Pantry jar, cov., advertising-type, cylindrical w/molded rim & ringed domed cover, white glaze w/double blue bands at the top & bottom, printed blue rectangle w/Nebraska advertising, red wing mark (ILLUS.)... **900-1,000**

Pantry jar, cov., cylindrical w/molded rim, decorated w/double blue bands & a large red wing mark, 1 lb. (ILLUS. far left with three other pantry jars, bottom of page)... **650-750**

Pantry jar, cov., cylindrical w/molded rim, decorated w/double blue bands & a large red wing mark, 3 lb. (ILLUS. second from right with three other pantry jars, bottom of page)... **750-850**

Pantry jar, cov., cylindrical w/molded rim, decorated w/double blue bands & a large red wing mark, 5 lb. (ILLUS. second from left with three other pantry jars, bottom of page)... **650-750**

Pantry jar, cov., cylindrical w/molded rim, decorated w/double blue bands & a large red wing mark, 1 gal. (ILLUS. far right with three other pantry jars, bottom of page)... **900-1,000**

Four Various Blue-banded Red Wing Pantry Jars

Two Rare Red Wing Embossed & Sponged Advertising Pitchers

Red Wing Brown & White Pipkin

Pipkin, cov., squatty bulbous pitcher-form body tapering to a wide flat mouth w/rim spout, C-form handle, white glaze on top half, brown glaze on lower half, marked "Minnesota Stoneware Co.," 3 pt. (ILLUS.)... **200-250**

Pitcher, advertising-type, embossed Cherry Band patt., cylindrical w/overall red & blue sponging, blue rectangle on front w/printed advertising (ILLUS. left with bulbous floral sponged pitcher, top of page).. **2,000-2,250**

Pitcher, advertising-type, embossed florals, bulbous body w/overall red & blue sponging, printed Iowa advertising inside the bottom (ILLUS. right with Cherry Band sponged pitcher, top of page) **2,000-2,250**

Pitcher, shorter cylindrical hall-boy style w/molded rings, overall blue sponging (ILLUS. right with tall blue-sponged pitcher, bottom page 212)............................ **700-800**

Pitcher, tapering cylindrical body w/ringed base, wide rim spout & angled handle, embossed scene of Dutch boy & girl, white glaze w/dark blue overglazing on lower half, Red Wing Union circle mark on base, largest size (ILLUS. at right with three smaller sizes, top page 213).. **2,000-2,500**

Pitcher, 6" h., embossed Cherry Band patt., advertising-type, white glaze w/blue bands around rim & base & a large blue rectangle w/Nebraska advertising below the spout (ILLUS. center with two other Cherry Band pitchers, top page 212).. **1,000-1,200**

Three Blue-trimmed Red Wing Cherry Band Pitchers

Two Red Wing Gray Line Pitchers

Pitcher, 6" h., embossed Cherry Band patt., white glaze w/light blue bands around rim & base (ILLUS. center with two other Cherry Band pitchers, bottom of previous page) **375-425**

Pitcher, 7 1/2" h., Gray Line ware, advertising-type, tapering cylindrical body w/molded ribbing below an orange sponged band & blue pinstripes, printed blue advertising dated 1929 at top, molded rim spout & angled handle (ILLUS. right with other Gray Line pitcher, top of page) **750-850**

Pitcher, 7 1/2" h., Gray Line ware, tapering cylindrical body w/molded ribbing below an orange sponged band & blue pinstripes, molded rim spout & angled handle (ILLUS. left with advertising pitcher, top of page) **300-350**

large cluster of irises & leaves, overall dark brown glaze, Red Wing Potteries, ca. 1940 (ILLUS.).................. **300-400**

Pitcher, 8 1/4" h., embossed Cherry Band patt., advertising-type, white glaze w/blue bands around rim & base & a large blue oval w/Nebraska advertising below the spout (ILLUS. right with two other Cherry Band pitchers, top next page)........... **800-1,000**

Pitcher, 8 1/4" h., embossed Cherry Band patt., white glaze w/light blue bands around rim & base (ILLUS. left with two other Cherry Band pitchers, bottom previous page)... **250-350**

Unique Cherry Band Advertising Pitcher

Pitcher, 9 1/4" h., embossed Cherry Band patt., advertising-type, white glaze w/large blue rectangle w/unique printed image of a two-story store above advertising dated 1914 (ILLUS.) **3,000-3,500**

Red Wing Potteries Pitcher with Irises

Pitcher, 7 3/4" h., tapering cylindrical body w/wide spout & angled handle, molded

Three Various Cherry Band Advertising Pitchers

Pitcher, 9 1/4" h., embossed Cherry Band patt., advertising-type, white glaze w/blue bands around rim & base & a large blue oval w/Nebraska advertising below the spout (ILLUS. left with two other Cherry Band pitchers, top of page) **1,000-1,500**

Pitcher, 9 1/4" h., embossed Cherry Band patt., white glaze w/light blue bands around rim & base (ILLUS. right with two other Cherry Band pitchers, bottom of page 210) **350-400**

Pitcher, 9 1/4" h., tall cylindrical hall-boy style w/molded rings, overall red & blue sponging (ILLUS., next column) **3,500-4,000**

Pitcher, 9 1/4" h., tall cylindrical hall-boy style w/molded rings, overall blue sponging (ILLUS. left with shorter blue-sponged pitcher, bottom of page) **600-800**

Very Rare Red Wing Sponged Hall Boy

Two Red Wing Blue-sponged Pitchers

Four Red Wing Dutch Boy & Girl Pitchers

Pitchers, tapering cylindrical body w/ringed base, wide rim spout & angled handle, embossed scene of Dutch boy & girl, white glaze w/dark blue overglazing on lower half, Red Wing Union circle mark on bases, each of three smaller sizes (ILLUS. at left with largest size)......................... **1,000-1,200**

Two Red Wing Saffron Ware Advertising Pitchers

Pitchers, 6 1/2" h., advertising-type, Saffron Ware, yellowware, tapering cylindrical body w/molded ribbing below thin white & brown bands below blue-printed advertising, pointed rim spout & angled handle, each (ILLUS. of two).. **300-350**

Two Red Wing Poultry Drinking Founts

Poultry drinking fount, bell-style, advertising-type, cylindrical w/domed shoulder & small mouth, white-glazed w/blue rectangular w/advertising "Oak Leaf - Simmons Hardware Co. - Made in U.S.A.," w/original wide underplate, 1 gal. (ILLUS. left with quart fount top) **200-250**

Two Red Wing Eureka-style Poultry Drinking Founts

Red Wing Advertising Poultry Fount

Poultry drinking fount, bell-style, advertising-type, cylindrical w/domed shoulder & small mouth, white-glazed w/printed blue circle w/Iowa advertising, complete w/underplate, 1 gal., 9" h. (ILLUS.)...................... **196**

Poultry drinking fount, Eureka-style, cylindrical, oval Red Wing Union Stoneware mark, 1 gal. (ILLUS. right with 2-gallon fount, top of page).................................. **175-225**

Poultry drinking fount, Eureka-style, cylindrical, oval Union Stoneware Co. blue mark & Minnesota Stoneware Co. mark on the bottom, 2 gal. (ILLUS. left with 1-gallon fount, top of page) **350-400**

Poultry drinking fount top, bell-style, advertising-type, cylindrical w/domed shoulder & small mouth, white-glazed w/blue rectangular w/wording "Red Wing - Poultry Drinking Fount - and - Buttermilk Feeder," 1 qt., top only (ILLUS. right with complete fount, bottom previous page)... **200-250**

Red Wing Advertising Refrigerator Jar

Refrigerator jar, advertising-type, short cylindrical stacking-type w/molded rim, white glaze decorated w/blue band & printed w/advertising for a Nebraska merchant, early 20th c. (ILLUS.) **500-600**

Short Red Wing Refrigerator Jar

Refrigerator jar, stacking-type, short wide cylindrical form w/molded rim, white glaze printed w/blue bands & "Red Wing Refrigerator Jar," early 20th c. (ILLUS.).. **250-350**

Very Rare Red Wing Stoneware Spittoon

Spittoon, deep cylindrical salt-glazed form w/top opening & oval side drain opening, double-stamped on the side "Red Wing Stoneware Company" (ILLUS.) **3,000-3,500**

Red Wing German-style Spittoon

Spittoon, German-style, ring-molded short cylindrical body w/top opening & side drain opening, white glaze w/thin blue bands (ILLUS.) **1,000-1,200**

Brown & White Miniature Spittoon

Spittoon, miniature, squatty bulbous base tapering to a widely flaring trumpet neck, brown neck above white base (ILLUS.) **400-500**

Red Wing Blue-sponged Spittoon

Spittoon, squatty bulbous base tapering to a widely flaring trumpet rim, white w/overall blue sponging, center mold seam, early 20th c., 10" d. (ILLUS.) **800-900**

Rare Sponged Red Wing Umbrella Stand

Umbrella stand, cylindrical w/flaring molded base & banded rim, overall red & blue sponging, 18" h. (ILLUS.) **2,000-2,500**

Rare Red Wing Florist-style Vase

Vase, advertising florist-type, cylindrical w/flared base & molded flat rim, white glaze trimmed w/blue bands & blue rectangle enclosing "Alpha Floral Co.," early 20th c. (ILLUS.) **1,000-1,200**

Red Wing Stoneware 3- and 5-Gallon Water Coolers

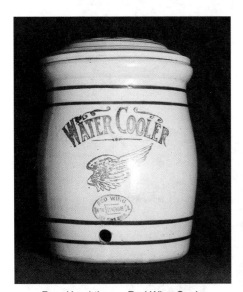

Rare Hand-thrown Red Wing Cooler

Water cooler, cov., hand-thrown ovoid wide body w/molded rim, white glazed w/blue bands, large 4" red wing mark & oval Red Wing Union Stoneware mark, "Water Cooler" in blue, "2" on inside bottom, 2 gal., no spigot, rare (ILLUS.) **5,000-6,000**

Water cooler, bulbous barrel-shaped body w/wide cylindrical neck & molded rim, cylindrical base band w/metal spigot, Red Wing Union Stoneware oval mark & red wing below "3 - Water Cooler" in blue, trimmed w/blue bands, wire bail handles w/wooden grips, no cover, 3 gal. (ILLUS. left with 5-gallon water cooler, top of page) **500-600**

Water cooler, bulbous barrel-shaped body w/wide cylindrical neck & molded rim, cylindrical base band w/metal spigot, Red Wing Union Stoneware oval mark & red wing below "5 - Water Cooler" in blue, trimmed w/blue bands, wire bail handles w/wooden grips, no cover, 5 gal. (ILLUS. right with 3-gallon water cooler, top of page) **350-450**

Very Rare Red Wing Stoneware Cooler

Water cooler, slightly tapering cylindrical salt-glazed body w/molded rim & eared handle, molded hexagonal spigot hole at bottom front, blue slip-quilled "8" above a stylized daisy, side stamped "Red Wing Stoneware Co.," 8 gal. (ILLUS.) **8,000-10,000**

Monmouth-Western Stoneware & Others

MONMOUTH-WESTERN STONEWARE COMPANY: *The Western Stoneware Company of Monmouth, Illinois, was formed in April 1906 by the merger of seven existing potteries located in three different states — five in Illinois, one in Missouri and one in Iowa. The fact that the Red Wing Union Stoneware Company was organized just one month earlier is no coincidence. Correspondence between the companies shows that the two remaining Red Wing companies contemplated an offer from the organizers of the new Western Stoneware Company to join them. As we know, the Red Wing companies themselves chose to merge and compete with the new company to the south, rather than join it. It is not surprising, then, that the Western Stoneware Company and the Red Wing Union Stoneware Company produced similar product lines (crocks, jugs, churns, water coolers and kitchenwares). The wares also featured similar glazes and decorations (white or "Bristol", blue and white, red and blue sponging) as well as somewhat similar marks and logos (a stenciled maple leaf for Western vs. a red wing for Red Wing; both also used a printed oval mark). Even the companies' advertising catalogs and pamphlets resembled each other. One of the enduring mysteries, however, is why the Red Wing company, apparently, never made rolling pins even though they were big sellers for Western. One of the most profitable (and prolific) sellers for Western was the "Sleepy Eye" product line. Red Wing may have experimented with a competing line, but it never duplicated the success of the Sleepy Eye pieces. The Western Stoneware Company continues to operate today in Monmouth, Illinois.*

BRUSH-MCCOY POTTERY (Zanesville Ohio) & BLUE RIBBON BRAND (Buckeye Pottery, Macomb, Illinois, 1882-1941): *The Brush-McCoy Pottery was a successor to the first Brush Pottery that operated in Roseville, Ohio, from 1907 to 1911. It operated a plant in Roseville from 1911 until 1925 and had another plant in nearby Zanesville that produced artwares until it burned in 1918. This company was succeeded by a second Brush Pottery in Roseville in 1925 that was unrelated to the first Brush firm. It is this pottery, which operated until 1982, that is famous for cookie jars as well as various other useful wares.*

Pottery pieces with the trademark "Blue Ribbon Band" were produced by the Buckeye Pottery (NOT related to Buckeye Stoneware) between 1882 and 1941. Not much historical information is available on this firm. Thanks to Gary and

Bonnie Tefft, authors of Red Wing Potters and Their Wares, *for this information.*

Blue Ribbon Pottery Painted Bean Pot

Bean pot, cov., wide bulbous flat-bottomed shape tapering to a short cylindrical neck flanked by small loop handles, inset cover w/disk finial, white ground h.p. under the glaze w/a landscape of a lake, palm trees, birds & a snow-capped peak in the distance, in shades of blue, white & green, Blue Ribbon Brand mark of the Buckeye Pottery, Macomb, Illinois, early 20th c. (ILLUS.) **$150-200**

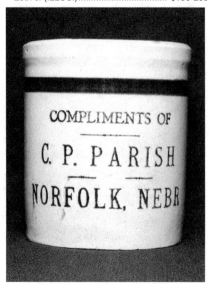

Fine Western Advertising Beater Jar

Beater jar, advertising-type, cylindrical w/molded rim, a dark blue band above printed blue Nebraska advertising, Monmouth-Western Stoneware (ILLUS.) **300-400**

Four Various Pieces in the Colonial Pattern

Beater jar, Colonial patt., ribbed cylindrical form printed around the top w/a printed band of blue swags, Monmouth-Western Stoneware, early 20th c. (ILLUS. second from left with various other Colonial pattern pieces) **325-375**

Beater jar, cylindrical w/flaring rim, white-glazed & decorated w/dark blue bands, Monmouth-Western Stoneware (ILLUS., next column) **175-225**

Bowl, advertising-type, wide cylindrical shape, the exterior lightly molded w/a drapery design glazed in dark blue, white-glazed interior w/printed blue Wisconsin advertising, Monmouth-Western Stoneware (ILLUS., bottom of page)..... **150-175**

Bowl, 5" d., Colonial patt., slightly flaring rounded shape w/molded ribs below a printed band of blue swags, Monmouth-Western Stoneware, early 20th c. (ILLUS. second from right with various other Colonial pattern pieces, top of page).. **350-400**

Western Blue-banded Beater Jar

Two Views of a Blue Drapery Bowl with Interior Advertising

Two Sizes of Western Stoneware Sponged Bowls

Western Sponged Rolled-rim Bowl

Bowl, 5" d., smooth rounded sides & rolled rim, overall orangish red & blue sponging, Monmouth-Western Stoneware (ILLUS.).. **100-125**

Bowl, 5" d., smooth sides & wide flat molded rim, overall orangish red & blue sponging, Monmouth-Western Stoneware (ILLUS. right with large sponged bowl, top of page)................................... **150-175**

Bowl, 7" d., advertising-type, wide short cylindrical shape w/molded rim, white-glazed exterior w/blue bands, interior w/printed blue advertising on the bottom, Monmouth-Western Stoneware (ILLUS., of two views, bottom of page).............. **125-175**

Large Bowl with Blue Blossoms & Scrolls

Bowl, 8" d., deep slightly flaring rounded sides w/molded panels & a smooth upper band printed w/a repeating blue design of a stylized blossom & scrolls, Monmouth-Western Stoneware (ILLUS.)................ **175-225**

Two Views of a Blue-banded Western Stoneware Advertising Bowl

Two Sizes of Bowls (Nappies or Pudding Pans)

Deep Blue-banded Western Bowl

Bowl, 9" d., deep rounded sides w/a rolled rim, white-glazed & decorated w/blue bands around the middle, Monmouth-Western Stoneware (ILLUS.) **75-95**

Bowl, 9" d., smooth sides & wide flat molded rim, overall orangish red & blue sponging, Monmouth-Western Stoneware (ILLUS. left with small sponged bowl, top previous page) **100-125**

Bowls (nappies or pudding pans), each w/a wide flat bottom & shallow bisque-finished sides molded in low-relief w/geometric design, wide flat blue-glazed sawtooth rim band, Monmouth-Western Stoneware, 8" & 10" d., each (ILLUS. with 8" atop the inverted 10", top of page) **125-150**

Butter crock, cov., Colonial patt., deep ribbed cylindrical base w/ribs below a printed band of blue swags, inset cover w/disk finial, Monmouth-Western Stoneware, early 20th c., 2 lb. (ILLUS. far right with various other Colonial pattern pieces, top of page 218) **450-500**

Western Stoneware 10-lb. Butter Crock

Butter crock, cylindrical w/molded rim, white-glazed & printed w/the blue Western Stoneware maple leaf logo, 10 lb. (ILLUS.) **100-125**

Western 1-lb. Advertising Butter Crock

Butter crock, advertising-type, cylindrical w/molded rim, glazed white & printed overall w/blue advertising for Lambrecht Butter, 1 lb. (ILLUS.) **75-100**

Blue-trimmed Cookie Jar & Salt Crock

Western Blue 2-lb. Butter Crock

Butter crock, cov., cylindrical w/molded rim, overall shaded blue decorated on the front w/a printed fancy scroll rectangle enclosing the word "Butter," Monmouth-Western Stoneware, 2 lb. (ILLUS.) **175-225**

Western Tall 5-lb. Butter Crock

Butter crock, cov., tall cylindrical form w/molded rim & wire bail handle w/wooden grip, pale blue shaded to white, printed on the front w/a blue rectangle enclosing the word "Butter," signed on the bottom "Western Stoneware Co.," 5 lb. (ILLUS.) **225-275**

Cookie jar, cov., wide cylindrical form w/inset cover, pale blue bands at rim & base, printed in large dark blue Gothic letters "Cookies" flanked by small maple leaves, part of a canister set, Monmouth-Western Stoneware (ILLUS. left with hanging salt crock, top of page) **350-400**

Creamer (pitcher), #1 size, Sleepy Eye design, embossed Indian Chief blue & landscape in blue on white, Monmouth-Western Stoneware (ILLUS. right with sugar bowl, top of page 227) **200-250**

Brown & White Western Stoneware Crock

Crock, cylindrical w/deep molded rim, top half glazed in dark brown, white-glazed bottom half printed w/the blue Western Stoneware maple leaf logo, 1 gal. (ILLUS.) **100-125**

Crocks with Stenciled Flowers or Leaves

Crock, cylindrical w/molded rim, white glazed & stenciled in dark blue w/a bouquet of stylized flowers, Monmouth-Western Stoneware, 1 gal. (ILLUS. right with crock decorated with leaves, above) **50-75**

Crock, cylindrical w/molded rim, white glazed & stenciled in dark blue w/a cluster of long stylized leaves, Monmouth-Western Stoneware, 2 gal. (ILLUS. left with floral bouquet-decorated crock) **50-75**

Crock, cylindrical w/molded rim, white-glazed w/large blue-stenciled size number above the large Monmouth Pottery (early Western Stoneware) maple leaf logo, 2 gal. (ILLUS., next column) **50-75**

Crock, cylindrical w/molded rim, salt-glazed & stenciled near the rim w/a large "3" in a dotted circle above a cobalt-blue slip-quilled winged design, Monmouth Pottery (early Western), 3 gal. (ILLUS. left with 20-lb. crock, bottom of page) **175-225**

2-Gallon Monmouth Pottery Crock

Two Early Monmouth Pottery Salt-glazed Crocks

A Brush-McCoy Pottery Jardiniere & Pitcher

10-Gallon Western Stoneware Crock

Crock, cylindrical w/molded rim flanked by small wire bail handles w/wooden grips, white-glazed w/the blue-printed Western Stoneware maple leaf logo above a blue-printed cluster of tall leaves, Monmouth-Western Stoneware, 10 gal., 17" h. (ILLUS.) **81**

Crock, short wide cylindrical form w/molded rim, salt-glazed & stenciled in cobalt blue w/a large "3" in a dotted circle, Monmouth Pottery (early Western), rare 20 lb. size (ILLUS. right with 3-gallon crock, bottom previous page) **300-350**

Custard cup, Colonial patt., deep cylindrical shape w/rounded bottom molded w/ribs below a printed blue band of

swags, Monmouth-Western Stoneware, early 20th c. (ILLUS. far left with other various Colonial pattern pieces, top page 218) **750-850**

Jardiniere, cylindrical w/sharply tapering base, molded around the upper body w/a continuous woodland scene, the lower band w/molded overlapping spearpoints, overall glossy green glaze, Brush-McCoy Pottery, Zanesville, Ohio, ca. 1917, 5" h. (ILLUS. right with Brush-McCoy corn pitcher, top of page) **85-100**

Scarce Sleepy Eye Mug

Mug, Sleepy Eye design, embossed Indian Chief blue & landscape in blue on white, Monmouth-Western Stoneware (ILLUS.)... **300-400**

Group of Four Various Mugs

Two Blue & White Advertising Mugs

Mug, barrel-shaped, dark blue rim shading to white, Monmouth-Western Stoneware, 4 1/2" h. (ILLUS. far right with three other mugs, bottom previous page).................. **50-75**

Mug, advertising-type, embossed Bands & Rivets patt., blue & white w/printed blue advertising on the side, Monmouth-Western Stoneware, 4 3/4" h. (ILLUS. left with other advertising mug, top of page) **100-125**

Mug, embossed Bands & Rivets patt., blue & white, Monmouth-Western Stoneware, 4 3/4" h. (ILLUS. second from right with three other mugs, botom previous page) .. **50-75**

Embossed Cattails Blue & White Mug

Mug, embossed Cattails patt., blue & white, Monmouth-Western Stoneware, 4 3/4" h. (ILLUS.)... **150-200**

Mug, advertising-type, blue & white w/embossed panels & a raised oval on the side w/printed blue advertising, Monmouth-Western Stoneware, 5 1/2" h. (ILLUS. right with other advertising mug, top of page)... **125-150**

Mug, tankard-style w/angled handle, blue & white, Monmouth-Western Stoneware, 5 1/2" h. (ILLUS. far left with three other mugs, bottom previous page) **75-100**

Mug, tankard-style w/angled handle, white w/dark blue bands near the rim & base, Monmouth-Western Stoneware, 5 1/2" h. (ILLUS. second from left with three other mugs, bottom previous page) **50-75**

Pitcher, Colonial patt., ovoid ribbed body w/plain neck printed w/a repeating dark blue swag design, D-form handle w/thumbrest, Monmouth-Western Stoneware, early 20th c. (ILLUS. right with other Colonial pattern pieces, bottom of page)... **1,000-1,200**

Pitcher, cylindrical molded yellow ear of corn w/green leaves & squared branch handle, Brush-McCoy Pottery, Zanesville, Ohio, ca. 1917 (ILLUS. left with Brush-McCoy jardiniere, top previous page)... **150-200**

Three Rare Colonial Pattern Pieces

Sleepy Eye #4 & #5 Pitchers

Pitcher, Sleepy Eye design, embossed Indian Chief blue & landscape in blue on white, blue rim band, Monmouth-Western Stoneware, #4 size (ILLUS. left with #5 pitcher, above) **500-600**

Pitcher, Sleepy Eye design, embossed Indian Chief blue & landscape in blue on white, pale blue rim band, Monmouth-Western Stoneware, #5 size (ILLUS. right with #4 pitcher)............................. **500-600**

Pitcher, 6" h., embossed Bands & Rivets patt., blue & white, Monmouth-Western Stoneware (ILLUS. far left with three other Bands & Rivets pitchers, bottom of page) **300-350**

Pitcher, 6" h., embossed Cattails patt., bulbous shape, blue & white, Monmouth-Western Stoneware (ILLUS. second from left with four other Cattails pitchers, top next page) **600-700**

Pitcher, 7" h., embossed Bands & Rivets patt., blue & white, printed blue Nebraska advertising on the side, Monmouth-Western Stoneware (ILLUS. second from right with three other Bands & Rivets pitchers, bottom of page) **700-800**

Pitcher, 7" h., embossed Cattails patt., bulbous shape, blue & white, Monmouth-Western Stoneware (ILLUS. second from right with four other Cattails pitchers, top next page) **175-225**

Pitcher, 8" h., embossed Bands & Rivets patt., blue & white, Monmouth-Western Stoneware (ILLUS. second from left with three other Bands & Rivets pitchers, bottom of page)... **250-275**

Pitcher, 8" h., embossed Cattails patt., bulbous shape, blue & white, Monmouth-Western Stoneware (ILLUS. far left with four other Cattails pitchers, top next page)... **250-300**

Pitcher, 9 1/4" h., embossed Bands & Rivets patt., blue & white, Monmouth-Western Stoneware (ILLUS. far right with three other Bands & Rivets pitchers, below) **500-600**

Pitcher, 9" h., embossed Cattails patt., straight-sided shape, blue & white, Monmouth-Western Stoneware (ILLUS. center back with four other Cattails pitchers, top next page) **225-250**

Pitcher, 9 1/4" h., embossed Cattails patt., bulbous shape, blue & white, Monmouth-Western Stoneware (ILLUS. far right with four other Cattails pitchers, top next page)... **600-700**

Four Various Sizes of Bands & Rivets Pitchers

Group of Five Cattails Pitchers by Monmouth-Western Stoneware

Two Bands & Rivets Blue & White Advertising Pitchers

Pitchers, advertising-type, embossed Bands & Rivets patt., side-handle, blue & white w/printed blue advertising, Monmouth-Western Stoneware, each (ILLUS. of two) **800-900**

Rare Rust-decorated Advertising Rolling Pin

Rolling pin, advertising-type, white-glazed body decorated w/rust red bands & printed flour advertising, turned wood handles, Monmouth-Western Stoneware (ILLUS.)................................... **700-800**

Rare Monmouth-Western Colonial Pattern Rolling Pin

Sleepy Eye Sugar Bowl & Creamer

Rolling pin, Colonial patt., cylindrical w/printed blue swag bands at each end, no handles, Monmouth-Western Stoneware, early 20th c. (ILLUS. bottom previous page) **1,000-1,200**

Salt crock, cov., hanging-type, Colonial patt., deep rounded & ribbed body w/tall arched back tab w/hanging hole, inset cover, decorated around the top w/a printed repeating band of dark blue swags, Monmouth-Western Stoneware, early 20th c. (ILLUS. left with other Colonial pattern pieces, page 224) **450-500**

Salt crock, hanging-type, cylindrical w/curved & peaked back tab w/hanging holes, dark blue bands around the top & base, printed on the front w/"Salt" in large Gothic letters flanked by small maple leaves, part of a canister set, Monmouth-Western Stoneware (ILLUS. right with matching cookie jar, top page 221) **225-250**

Sugar bowl, open, Sleepy Eye design, embossed Indian Chief blue & landscape in blue on white, Monmouth-Western Stoneware (ILLUS. left with #1 pitcher-creamer, top of page) **800-900**

Trivet (hot plate), Sleepy Eye Flour advertising piece, molded design of Chief Sleepy Eye in the center surrounded by a band of teepees & trees in blue on white, Monmouth-Western Stoneware (ILLUS.) **4,000-4,500**

Tumbler, Colonial patt., ribbed slightly swelled cylindrical form w/the top decorated w/a printed repeating back of blue swags, Monmouth-Western Stoneware, early 20th c. (ILLUS. center with other Colonial pattern pieces, page 224) **1,000-1,200**

Early Grey & Blue Sleepy Eye Vase

Vase, Sleepy Eye design, salt-glazed stoneware w/cobalt blue trim, cylindrical w/molded bands at top & base & relief-molded profile bust of Chief Sleepy Eye on the side, early 20th c., Monmouth-Western Stoneware, 9 1/2" h. (ILLUS.) **460**

Very Rare Sleepy Eye Trivet

A Sampling of Blue & White Patterns Available to Collectors

by Steve and Karen Stone

Apple Blossom

Pieces with the embossed Apple Blossom design are extremely popular with collectors of Blue & White Stoneware. The Apple Blossom line was manufactured by Burley-Winter Pottery Company, Crooksville, Ohio. Although none of the Burley-Winter catalogs we have seen are dated, the line was probably produced in the teens to about the mid-1930s. Burley-Winter did not name these pieces as Apple Blossom. It referred to the various pieces only as "Blue Tint," "Blue Tint-Stone Covered," "Mottled (Sponged)," or "Brown Tint." As far as we can determine, the first colloquial application of the name "Apple Blossom" to this design was by Joseph and Harbin (1973). The basic common design on these pieces is a spray of flowers that does, indeed, resemble apple blossoms on a background of diagonal lattice.

The Apple Blossom line offered a variety of pieces with varied uses. Although most pieces were toilet articles, some were intended for the kitchen and a few for their intrinsic aesthetic value. The No. 36 10-piece Blue Tint toilet set is illustrated in the 1917 Burley-Winter product catalog. It consists of large ewer and basin, mouth ewer, mug, brush vase, covered soap dish with drainer, and standard size covered combinet with bail. A 9s chamber pot (open or covered) was also available but it was not included in the packaged toilet set. Kitchen pieces included the No. 4 sanitary water cooler with lid and spigot in 3-, 4-, 6- and 8-gallon sizes and the No. 2 salt box with stone lid. Also available was a covered bailed butter tub in various sizes.

Other Apple Blossom pieces include a No. 2 Blue Tint or Brown Glazed cuspidor and a No. 25 Blue Tint or brown 7 1/2-inch jardiniere (no mention of a pedestal and we do not know whether one was produced). The No. 25 Blue Tint

Embossed Apple Blossom pattern 8"-high ewer by Burley-Winter Pottery Co., $395.

Burley-Winter jardiniere is illustrated in Harbin (1977:24, r. 3, #1).

Apple Blossom bowls are also frequently seen. In the early Burley-Winter catalogs bowls are listed as the "Blue Flemish Bake Pan" and were available in 7-, 9-, and 11-inch diameters with no bail. Other Burley-Winter bowls in this line were the 11-inch "Blue Flemish Cord Roaster" with lid and the "Blue Flemish Stew Pan" with bail but no lid, in 2-, 3-, and 5-quart sizes.

The pattern of flowers and lattice on the Blue & White Cosmos jardiniere and pedestal illustrated in Harbin (1977:62, r. 1, #3) bears a striking resemblance to the Blue Flemish or Apple Blossom bowls. Although we have yet to positively identify the manufacturer of the Cosmos jardiniere, it seems reasonable to assume that Burley-Winter Pottery Company could have produced it by virtue of the striking similarities of the flowers and lattice on the Cosmos jardiniere and the Burley-Winter Blue Flemish bowls and stewers.

Apple Blossom prices (taken from the 1917 Burley-Winter Pottery Company catalog)

Water Cooler (No. 4, Blue Flemish Water Coolers, Covers Included, 25¢ gal.)
Blue Flemish Bake Pans
    7 inch . . . .$1.20/doz.
    9 inch . . . .$1.80/doz.
    11 inch . . . .$2.40/doz.
Blue Flemish Stew Pans
    2 qt. . . . .$2.00/doz.
    3 qt. . . . .$2.50/doz.
    5 qt. . . . .$3.20/doz.
Covered Blue Flemish Cord
    Roaster. . . . .$6.50/doz.
Cuspidor, No. 2 Blue
    Tint. $25.92/gross
No. 2 Salt Box, Blue
    Tint-Stone Covered $26.40/gross
Chamber Pot, Blue Tint or Mottled
    (Sponged)
    9s Open . . . .$2.00/doz.
    9s Covered . . . .$3.00/doz.
Jardiniere, No. 25, Blue Tint or
    Brown, 7 1/2 Inch . . . . . . -$2.00/doz.
Toilet Set. . . . .$20.00/doz.
Basin & Ewer (Standard
    Size) . . . .$13.33/doz.
Mouth Ewer (Small Size), Mug, Brush
    Vase, Covered 3-piece Soap, Covered
    Combinet Jar. . . . . $8/doz.
    (Combinet cover counts as 1/3 of the
    price complete)
    Covers only . . . .$1.80/doz.

Peacock

The peacock line is well known to collectors of Blue & White Stoneware and Brush-McCoy and Brush pottery.

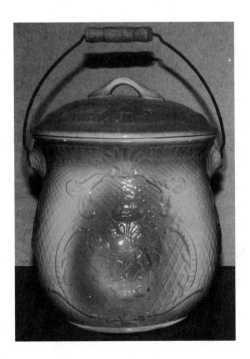

Burley-Winter Pottery Co. 10"-high embossed Apple Blossom pattern slop jar, $350.

The peacock design was manufactured from about 1915 to 1925 by the Brush-McCoy Pottery Company and later by the Brush Pottery Company (both in Zanesville, Ohio) from 1925 to 1928. The Peacock line is variously illustrated in many of the Brush-McCoy and Brush catalogs from that period.

This line has been alternatively called "Peacock at the Fountain," "Peacock at the Well," "Peacock on the Fence," or simply "Peacock." The first two names reflect the embossed scene that, on some pieces, includes a gushing well or fountain. Such pieces are the chamber pot, jardiniere, salt crock, butter tub, baking dish, cooking or preserving kettle, and the spittoon. Pieces without a well or fountain are the pitcher, custard cup, nesting bowl set (three bowls), the ramekin or nappy, and the coffeepot. On all pieces, the scene clearly shows the peacock standing or strutting on what appears to be a brick wall or fence, hence the popular name "Peacock on the Fence." The Brush-McCoy Pottery Company catalogs rarely applied a name to these pieces, but when named, they were simply listed as "Peacock" or "Blue Tint."

With the exception of the jardiniere, this entire line was offered in Blue & White and several pieces were also available in "Nurock" (various shades of mottled brown ranging from very pale to a deep, rich, dark brown). Yellowware examples of all the Peacock pieces are also known and are extremely uncommon.

The salt crock and butter tub always had a flat rectangle on the bottom of the front of the piece for the stenciled name SALT or BUTTER, as appropriate. However, the name was not always applied, which resulted in a blank, flat rectangle.

Not much is known about the Peacock jardiniere, and references to it throughout the literature are scarce. The Peacock jardiniere is illustrated on sheet 113 of the 1915 Brush-McCoy catalog. Known colors include brown, green, and blended brown and green. It would not be surprising to see a Blue & White Peacock jardiniere pop up.

Peacock Prices (taken from 1916 Brush-McCoy Product Catalog)

Embossed Peacock pattern pitcher, left, and coffeepot by Brush-McCoy Pottery Co., $1,250 and $4,000 respectively.

Butter . . . . .Gross, $30.00
Spittoon . . . . $30.00, gross
Salt . . . . $20.50, gross
Custard cup . . . . 72¢ doz.
Coffee Pot . . . .$24.50 doz.

Tulip Jardiniere and Pedestal

From about 1905 to 1930 the Tulip jardiniere was manufactured by at least three pottery companies: Nelson McCoy Sanitary Stoneware Co., Roseville, Ohio (7-, 8-, 9-, and 10-inch diameter); Burley-Winter Pottery Co., South Crooksville, Ohio (7-, 8-, 9-, 10-, and 12-inch diameter); and A.E. Hull Pottery Co., Crooksville, Ohio (7 1/2-inch diameter jardiniere and 7 1/2-inch tall pedestal). In the original pottery company product catalogs we have seen, pedestals are listed only by A.E. Hull and they are all 7 1/2 inches tall.

Blue & White Tulip jardinieres, or pedestals in any color, are not illustrated in any pottery company catalog we have seen. Nelson McCoy catalogs list the

Tulip jardiniere as "Tulip Jars, Fine Mahogany Finish" and Burley-Winter catalogs simply illustrate the piece and state "Brown Glazed Jardiniere." A.E. Hull identifies its pieces as "Jardiniere – 7 1/2-in. Brown Tulip, Gross $21.60; 7 1/2-in. Ped. to Match, Gross $21.60."

Since the only references we have seen to Tulip pedestals are from the A.E. Hull catalogs, it seems possible that most brown and Blue & White Tulip pedestals are attributable to that pottery company and they could very well have been available in just the one size – 7 1/2 inches tall. So it is likely the Blue & White Tulip jardiniere and pedestal sets are products of A.E. Hull Pottery Company.

Plum (Apricot) Line

This is a line that can be positively traced through company catalogs and brochures to at least two pottery companies, Burley-Winter and A.E. Hull, both of Crooksville, Ohio. The Burley-Winter catalogs we have seen illustrate only the pitcher and do not give it a name. The A.E. Hull catalogs identify only the pitcher as "Dairy Jug" or "Plum Dairy Pitcher." The Plum line includes the pitcher, a covered butter crock, hanging salt crock, bailed and covered milk crock, at least two sizes of bowls, and a jardiniere.

The pitcher has a capacity of 5 pints; known colors include Blue Tinted (Blue & White), solid blue, brown, and yellow. In a 1910 A.E. Hull product catalog the yellow jugs were $30.00 a gross and Blue Tinted jugs were $24 a gross. The 3-pound

Embossed Tulip pattern jardiniere and pedestal base, made by Nelson McCoy Sanitary Stoneware Co., Burley-Winter Pottery Co., and A.E. Hull Pottery Co., $1,500 for the set.

Embossed Apricot pattern 5-pint pitcher by A.E. Hull Pottery Co., $235.

butter came with a bail and lid and sold for $3.50 a dozen. Known colors of the butter include Blue & White and green and cream. Most all Apricot butters have the word "BUTTER" embossed on the front (the word is not painted). On some Apricot salts the embossed "SALT" on the front is painted blue, while on others it is unpainted.

The bailed 10-by-5-inch shouldered milk crock is seldom seen with a lid. Lids with the embossed scroll and Apricot design that fit the milk crocks quite well have been found, so the shouldered milk crocks were probably produced with lids, or lids could be purchased separately for them.

At least two sizes of smaller, unbailed, lidless Apricot bowls are known; one is 2 3/4 inches tall and 7 1/2 inches in diameter and the other is 3 3/4 inches tall and 9 1/2 inches in diameter. The milk crock and both bowls are shouldered and have swirled bottoms. Known colors of the Apricot milk crock and bowls include Blue & White, a really lovely green and cream, and solid yellow with a blue band around the shoulder.

The Apricot jardiniere is 10 inches tall and 9 inches across the top; there could have been a pedestal, but if they exist, they are extremely uncommon. Known colors of the jardiniere are brown, pale green, and blended brown and green.

'Wildflower'

The Wildflower line was manufactured by Brush-McCoy Pottery Company, Zanesville, Ohio, from 1899 to 1923. Brush-McCoy did not place the specific name "Wildflower" on this line but simply used the name of the piece (i.e., Hall Boy, Salt Box, etc.), and usually some mention of blue decoration; a product number was used to identify the piece. The name "Wildflower" was applied to this design by authors of earlier Blue & White stoneware books.

The Wildflower name is applied to two basic designs. One is a rectangular stencil composed of flowing vines, leaves with serrated edges, and tiny flowers. The second Wildflower design resembles

Covered soap dish with drainer, stenciled Wildflower pattern on embossed Arches & Columns shape, by Brush-McCoy Pottery Co., $600.

Our Lucille (Bowtie) ewer with Wildflower stencil, $625 with matching basin.

Wildflower pieces than any other series or line of Blue & White Stoneware.

There are over a hundred canisters in three shapes (barrel, straight-sided, and straight-sided with flared top rim) in several sizes ranging from 5 1/2 inches tall to 12 inches tall. There are at least nine spice jars in two shapes (barrel-shaped and straight-sided) in two sizes from 2 3/4 inches tall to 3 1/4 inches tall.

There are at least five distinguishable sets of nesting bowls, each set with between eight and 13 bowls.

There are dozens of pitchers in various shapes, styles, sizes and decorations. In various sizes and capacities there are butter crocks, milk pipkins, batter pails, mugs, tumblers, roasters, double boilers, stewers, milk crocks, bakers, pudding dishes, chamber pots, slop jars, salt boxes, rolling pins (the baker's size stoneware roller all by itself is 14 1/2

a six-pointed snowflake. Some pieces are decorated only with the rectangle of vines, leaves and flowers. Some pieces are blessed with both designs, and some pieces, although rare, are decorated only with the six-pointed stencil.

The Wildflower pattern apparently was quite popular, and literally hundreds of pieces are known, mostly toilet and kitchen pieces but a few others as well. Unquestionably there are more

Stenciled 15"-diameter basin and 11"-tall ewer in the Wildflower pattern by Brush-McCoy Pottery Co., $650 for the pair.

inches long), a meat tenderizer, 3-piece covered soap dish, 1-piece soap slab, three sizes of ewers and basins, spittoons, water coolers, brush vases, coffeepots, and teapots.

Advertising can be found on many Wildflower pieces. Rolling pins were enormously popular for this purpose as were bowls, pitchers, salt and butter crocks and other pieces.

Mostly, the Wildflower stencil was applied to pieces that were not embellished with any other decoration or embossed design. However, the Wildflower stencil can be found on the Bowtie (Our Lucille) toilet set (embossed ribbon and bowtie) and on bowls with the embossed sawtooth decoration encircling the top rim.

There are so many Wildflower pieces one could specialize just in Wildflower and amass an impressive and sizeable collection. Of course, some pieces are very scarce, and it would take quite a while to find them, but that's the thrill of the hunt!

Butterfly

The Butterfly line was manufactured by the Nelson McCoy Sanitary and Stone

Ware Company, Roseville, Ohio, and the Crooksville Pottery Co., Crooksville, Ohio, from about the mid-1920s to perhaps the mid- or late 1930s. There are at least five Butterfly pieces known: a large pitcher, a smaller creamer, a butter crock (two styles and four sizes), a salt crock, and a spittoon.

The large pitcher was available in at least Blue & White, brown, and white; the butter crocks and creamer are known in Blue & White and brown (a 10-pound butter is known with the top half brown and the bottom half white). The salt and spittoon are most frequently seen in Blue & White, but other colors are definitely possible. With the exception of the spittoon and the large 10-pound butter, all pieces were usually finished as "orange peel." The orange peel surface is not from salt glazing; rather the molds of the pieces were designed to carry the orange peel surface.

The large pitcher is 9 inches tall with a capacity of 5 pints. In the 1929 Nelson McCoy catalog it is listed as "No. 6 Tankard, Capacity 5 Pints." In other Nelson McCoy catalogs it is identified simply as "Butterfly Tankard." The Butterfly Cream Pitcher is 5 inches high and holds 1 1/2 pints. It is found in Blue & White, solid blue, and brown. In the Nelson McCoy catalogs it is listed simply as "Butterfly Creamer."

The Butterfly Butter Crock was produced in 2-, 3-, 5-, and 10-pound capacities; all sizes were available with or without a bail and with or without a lid. The surface was usually orange peel and sometimes the word "BUTTER" would be stenciled on the crock and sometimes not. This piece, in brown, is also known in a smooth finished style

Small pitcher with embossed Butterfly pattern by Nelson McCoy Sanitary Stoneware Co., $600.

with butterflies on two sides and a cluster of grapes, complete with leaves and vines, on the opposing two sides.

The Butterfly salt was designed for hanging from the wall and has the orange peel surface texture. Wooden or stoneware lids were offered; stoneware lids have embossed butterflies. The word "SALT" is embossed on the piece and sometimes painted blue and sometimes left unpainted. We have seen Butterfly salt crocks where the butterflies on the crock and the lid are painted blue as well as the word "SALT."

The Butterfly spittoon is a fairly uncommon piece. The only illustration we could find of this 7 1/2-inch diameter piece is in Nelson McCoy catalogs from the late 1920s. The Nelson McCoy Butterfly spittoon bears a striking similarity to the Blue & White "Rose" spittoon of A.E. Hull Pottery Company, Crooksville, Ohio, of about this same time. The two spittoons are almost identical, the only significant difference being roses on the Hull piece instead of butterflies on the Nelson McCoy piece.

Stag and Pine Trees (Raglaze Stag) Pitcher

A standing stag is on one side and a pine forest scene, complete with stream and clouds, is on the other. This pitcher is illustrated in a 1930 product catalog from Robinson-Ransbottom Pottery Co., Roseville, Ohio. It is listed as a "Raglaze Stag Pitcher, Ivory Colored, Blue Tint Effect, 5 Pints." Known colors include Blue & White (white inside), Blue & Yellow (yellow inside), Brown (white inside), and YellowWare.

The Stag pitcher design is very similar – particularly the design on the back of the pieces – to the (Stag) Luxor sand jar and hotel cuspidor and (Stag) Raglaze water jars (water coolers), also produced by Robinson-Ransbottom and the Red Wing Pottery Co., which also produced a covered bread crock with the same pine forest but without the standing stag.

Basketweave And Morning Glory (Willow Ware)

Willow Ware was manufactured by the J.W. McCoy Pottery Co., Roseville, Ohio, from 1899 to 1910, the Brush-McCoy Pottery Co, Roseville, Ohio, from 1911 to 1923, and later by the Nelson McCoy Sanitary Stoneware Company, Roseville, Ohio, until the mid-1930s.

Willow Ware was called "Rose and Basketweave" and "Basketweave and Morning Glory" in early books on Blue & White Stoneware. Indeed, the embossed background of these pieces is rather like a woven basket of willow canes upon which is a stem, leaves, and flower closely resembling the Morning Glory.

Embossed Willow (Basketweave & Morning Glory) pattern brush vase, 4 3/4" high, by Brush-McCoy Pottery Co., $325.

Willow Ware was an apparent hit with the public, and many different pieces of widely varied uses were offered. Most pieces were for kitchen use and there was also a 13-piece wash set.

Kitchen pieces include the 13-piece canister set, which includes canisters for cereal, salt, tobacco, crackers (two sizes), beans, coffee, raisins, tea, rice, barley, sugar, and "Put Your Fist In" cookie jar; the 6-piece spice set, which includes cinnamon, allspice, ginger, cloves, nutmeg, and pepper; two sizes of-bailed stewer, a kitchen pitcher or tankard, a mug, and two sizes of butter (with lid, with or without bail).

The 13-piece wash set consists of a large ewer and basin; mouth ewer; 3-piece covered soap dish (bowl, lid, and drainer); two styles of brush vase; another mug; combinet (offered with or without lid); chamber pot (with lid); and cuspidor.

On the canisters, spices, and butter tub the floral design was on the back of the piece. On the front of the canisters and spices was an unrolled scroll upon which was stenciled in blue the name of the contents, such as CRACKERS, RAISINS, CINNAMON, NUTMEG, etc. On the butter tub, the word "BUTTER" was embossed directly on the Willow design without benefit of an unrolled scroll.

WillowWare was produced in Blue & White although at least the kitchen pitcher was also produced in Yellowware. Additionally, all the wash set pieces, the kitchen pitcher and mug were also decorated with what Brush-McCoy called "Colorcraft" (blue shading along the top rim, brown shading along the bottom, with brown stems, green leaves and cobalt blue flowers all over a cream colored background). The wash set is-also known to be decorated with the flower, stem, and leaves traced or outlined with silver paint.

Willow Prices (taken from the 1911 Brush-McCoy Pottery Co. catalog)

The Willow Ewer and Basin set is illustrated on sheet 16 of the catalog. Both ewer and basin are identified as "No. 24, Willow Ewer and Basin, 9s Blue

Slop jar, left, and chamber pot in embossed Willow (Basketweave & Morning Glory) pattern by Brush-McCoy Pottery Co., $350 and $325 respectively.

Tinted (rolled edge basin)." A dozen sets sold for $10.

The Blue & White Willow tankard is listed on sheet 14 of the 1911 Brush-McCoy Pottery Co. catalog. It is identified as "No. 133, Willow Tankard, 4-pint, Blue Tinted Top and Bottom." A gross sold for $24. The Willow tankard reappears on sheet 12 of the 1911 Brush-McCoy Pottery Co. catalog. It is "No. 29, Willow Tankard, 4 pint, Blue Tint top and bottom." A gross sold for $24. On this same sheet is stated a Willow tankard and six mugs make a water set; a dozen sets sold for $10.80.

The Willow mug is illustrated as "No. 28, Willow Mug, 10-oz. Blue Tinted Top and Bottom" on sheet 12 of the 1911 Brush-McCoy Pottery Co. catalog. A gross sold for $15.

The Blue & White Willow stewer is listed on sheet 14 of the 1911 Brush-McCoy Pottery Co. catalog. Both 2- and 4-quart stewers were identified as "No. 152 Willow Stewer." The 2-quart stewer sold for $21 a gross and the 4-quart stewer sold for $27 a gross. The Willow stewer reappears on sheet 112 of the 1915 Brush-McCoy Company catalog No. 52. It is catalog "No. 152 – Willow Stewer" and was still available in 2-quart ($27 per gross) and 4-quart ($32.50 per gross) sizes.

The Blue & White Willow covered combinet is listed on sheet 16 of the 1911 Brush-McCoy Pottery Co. catalog. The piece is "No. 18, Willow Combinet, 9s Blue Tinted." The price was $9 per dozen. The piece is also illustrated on sheet 16L of the 1916 Brush-McCoy Pottery Co. catalog No. 16, and sheet 111 of the 1915 Brush-McCoy catalog No. 52.

It is catalog number 18 – Blue Willow, 9a size and sold for $10.80 per dozen.

The Willow cuspidor is illustrated on sheet 12 of the 1911 Brush-McCoy Pottery Co. catalog. It is listed as "No. 14, Willow Cuspidor, Blue Tinted." A gross sold for $20.

The Blue & White Willow canister set is listed on sheet 14 of the 1911 Brush-McCoy Pottery Co., catalog. The entire set is identified with the product number "150" and the various canisters are identified only with the staple's name, such as "Tea," "Sugar," etc. A gross of any one style (or name) of individual canister sold for $22.50. The Willow canister set is further listed on sheet 112 of the 1915 Brush-McCoy Co. catalog No. 52 and sheet 16L of the 1916 Brush-McCoy Pottery Co. catalog No. 16. In both catalogs this set is catalog "No. 150-Willow Cereal Jars – Six Names Assorted Gross $30.00." Large size canister sets include cereal, salt, tobacco, crackers, beans, coffee, raisins, tea, sugar, and "Put Your Fist In" cookie jar. More than six names were available.

The Blue & White Willow spice set is listed on sheet 14 of the 1911 Brush-

Embossed Willow (Basketweave & Morning Glory) pattern 9"-high yellowware pitcher, $300.

McCoy Pottery Co. catalog. All pieces of the entire spice set are identified with the same product number, "151." Like the Willow canister set, a gross of any one style (or name) of individual spice sold for $13.50. The spice set is further illustrated on sheet 112 of the 1915 Brush-McCoy Co. catalog No. 52 and sheet 16L of the 1916 Brush-McCoy Pottery Co. catalog No. 16. In both catalogs this set is catalog number "151 Willow Spice Jars – Any names or asst. Gross $18.00."

The 3-pound Willow butter pot is illustrated on sheet 13 of the 1911 Brush-McCoy Pottery Co. catalog. It is listed as "No. 154, 3-lb Butter Pot, Blue Tinted, Blue Letters." A gross sold for $24.

The Willow chamber is shown on sheet 16 of the 1911 Brush-McCoy Pottery Co. catalog. It is "No. 22, Willow Chamber, 9s Open, Blue Tinted, $27.00 and 9s Covered, Blue Tinted, $40.50" (price per quantity was not given but it was probably per dozen).

Leaping Deer, Swan, and Pine Cone Pitchers

The Pine Cone, Leaping Deer, and Swan pitchers were manufactured by the Burley-Winter Pottery Company, Crooksville, Ohio, from around 1910 to about the mid-1930s. They are among the most collectible and sought-after Blue & White stoneware pitchers.

We do not know what Burley-Winter named the Pine Cone pitcher or if it had a catalog number. The catalog we have illustrating the Pine Cone pitcher is missing the part of the page that carried the name of the piece. The Pine Cone pitcher is known in Blue & White, blue sponge, and solid brown; it is 9 inches tall with a capacity of 5 pints.

The Leaping Deer pitcher was identified only as "Blue Tint and Mahogany Deer Tankard, 5 Pint." It is known in Blue & White, blue sponge, and solid brown.

The Swan pitcher was identified as "Blue Tint Swan Tankard, 5 pint." Again, known colors include Blue & White, brown, and blue sponge.

The Leaping Deer and Swan pitchers are both about 8 1/2 to 9 inches tall. An examination of these pieces reveals they are identical in every way with the exception of the principal features — the Swan and the Leaping Deer.

Interestingly, a few very uncommon "hybrid" pitchers are known that have

Left: Pine Cone pattern embossed pitcher by Burley-Winter Pottery Co., $1,500.

Right: Swan pattern embossed pitcher by Burley-Winter Pottery Co., $235.

Leaping Deer pattern embossed pitcher by Burley-Winter Pottery Co., $400.

the Swan on one side and the Leaping Deer on the other; such a marriage of features is easy to do if one company owns both molds as did Burley-Winter. The Swan/Leaping Deer hybrid pitchers are known in solid brown and Blue & White.

One is tempted to believe the Swan/Leaping Deer pitcher was an accident resultant from the inadvertent combination of two mismatched mold halves, or perhaps a lunch hour piece produced by a potter intending it as a unique gift. But a large number of these hybrid pitchers are known, and in both Blue & White and solid brown, which suggests this hybrid pitcher could have been an intentional run and produced in large numbers.

Indian Good Luck Pitcher, Salt, and Butter

The Indian Good Luck pitcher was produced by at least three independent Ohio potteries of the early 1900s, The Crooksville Pottery Company, the Robinson-Ransbottom Pottery Company, and the Nelson McCoy Sanitary Stoneware and Sewer Pipe Company. In his 1977 book *Clay Giants*, which is a history of the various Red Wing potteries, Lyndon Viel includes a photograph of the Indian Good Luck pitcher, which he calls "Indian Pitcher" and attributes its manufacture to Red Wing, stating it is "in the [Red Wing] catalog."

Known colors of the Indian Good Luck pieces include Blue & White, blue sponge, brown, and green.

The Indian Good Luck pitcher was also offered for sale in early catalogs of the American Clay Products Pottery

Company, Crooksville, Ohio. The American Clay Products Company did not manufacture pottery but was an early 1900s association of potteries distributing the products of, among others, A.E. Hull, Star Stoneware, Ransbottom Brothers, Crooksville Pottery, Logan, Muskingum, Nelson McCoy Sanitary Stoneware Company, Burley, and Burley-Winter pottery companies.

Illustrations in the original Crooksville Pottery, Nelson McCoy, and American Clay Products catalogs identify the Indian Good Luck pitcher as only "No. 1 Tankard, Blue Tint or Mahogany Glaze, Full 5 Pints." The Indian Good Luck salt crock is illustrated in a Robinson-Ransbottom Pottery Company catalog (undated but probably circa early 1920s) as "SALT BOX, With Stone Cover, Green Glaze, $3.30 per dozen." In a second undated Robinson-Ransbottom catalog of that same era, it is listed as "RAGLAZE STONE COVERED SALT BOX, Ivory Colored Tint."

Many people have incorrectly identified these Good Luck pieces as "Nazi,", "Hitler," or "Swastika" and believe they were produced in Germany. The symbol of the Nazi movement was the swastika, which is the reverse of the Indian Good Luck design. The North American potteries produced these Good

Embossed Indian Good Luck (Swastika) pattern pitcher, made by Nelson McCoy Sanitary Stoneware Co., Robinson-Ransbottom Pottery Co., and The Crooksville Pottery Co., $225.

Luck pieces decades prior to the Nazi movement and any identification or association with the Nazi movement or Germany is incorrect.

Columns and Arches Pitcher and Mug (Colonial Jug and Mug)

This pitcher and mug has been identified as "Columns and Arches Pitcher" in earlier publications on Blue & White Stoneware. This pitcher and mug was manufactured by the Brush-McCoy Pottery Company, Zanesville, Ohio, from about 1911 to 1923; Brush-McCoy called it "Colonial Jug and Mug." Known colors are Blue & White and mostly all blue. The Colonial Jug measures

9 inches tall and has a capacity of 4 pints. Sheet 12 of the 1911 Brush-McCoy catalog lists individual jugs as "No. 27 – Colonial Jug, Blue Tint, 4 Pint, Per Gross $24.00." Interestingly, on this same sheet the jug and set of six mugs are listed together as "No. 29 – Colonial Lemonade Set, Consists of Colonial Jug and 6 Colonial Mugs." A dozen sets sold for $10.80.

Pitcher and extremely rare mug in embossed Columns and Arches pattern by Brush-McCoy Pottery Co., $600 for the pitcher, $650+ for the mug.

PART III: BLUE & WHITE DECORATIVE & UTILITARIAN POTTERY

Blue & White Pottery

Apple cider cooler, cov., w/spigot, 13" d., 15" h. **$425**

Embossed Peacock Baking Dish

Baking dish, embossed Peacock patt., round w/heavy egg-and-dart-molded rim over gently curved sides, Brush-McCoy Pottery Co., 9" d. (ILLUS.) **800**

Miniature Blue & White Bank

Bank, miniature, jug-form, stenciled rectangle w/"Money Bank" (ILLUS.) **650**

Miniature Uhl Pottery Barrel

Barrel, cov., miniature, Uhl Pottery Co., 2" d., 4 1/4" h. (ILLUS.) **80**

Basin, embossed Apple Blossom patt., Burley-Winter Pottery Co., 7" d. **165**

Basin, embossed Bow Tie patt. w/rose decal, Brush-McCoy Pottery Co., basin 15" d. **150**

Basin, embossed Apple Blossom patt., Burley-Winter Pottery Co., 9" d. **185**

Basin, embossed Apple Blossom patt., Burley-Winter Pottery Co., 14 d. **295**

Batter jar, cov., stenciled Wildflower patt., Brush-McCoy Pottery Co., small, 6" d., 5 3/4" h. (ILLUS. right with Wildflower batter pail, bottom of page) **350**

Wildflower Batter Jar & Pail

Miniature Bean Pot and Coffeepot

Batter jar, cov., stenciled Wildflower patt., Brush-McCoy Pottery Co., large, 7" d., 8" h. 400

Batter pail, bail handle, stenciled Wildflower patt., Brush-McCoy Pottery Co., 4 7/8" h. (ILLUS. left with batter jar, bottom previous page) 375

Bean pot, cov., marked "Boston Bean Pot," 10" d., 9" h.. 450

Advertising Beater Jar

Bean pot, miniature, cov., wide blue band, souvenir-type (ILLUS. left with miniature coffeepot, top of page)................................. 225

Beater jar, advertising-type, "Stop And Shop at Wagner's Cash Grocery, Kingsley, Iowa," 4 3/4" h. (ILLUS., to the left) 325

Beer cooler, cov., embossed Elves patt., includes spigot, 14" d., 18" h. 725

Bird bath, miniature, embossed birds around base, Western Stoneware Co., 10" h.. 2,500

Bowl, 3 1/2" d., miniature, w/bail handle, heavy dark blue rim band.............................. 50

Bowl, 4" d., 2" h., berry, embossed Flying Bird patt., w/advertising, A.E. Hull Pottery Co. 450

Bowl, 4" d., 2" h., berry or cereal, embossed Flying Bird patt., A.E. Hull Pottery Co. (ILLUS. right with Flying Bird grease jar, bottom of page)..................................... 250

Bowl, 4" d., 2" h., berry/cereal, plain w/pale blue rim band 55

Bowl, 4" d., 2" h., miniature, heavy blue rim band... 50+

Flying Bird Berry Bowl & Grease Jar

Peacock Berry Bowl & Custard Cup

Bowl, 4 1/2" d., 2 1/4" h., berry, embossed Peacock patt., Brush-McCoy Pottery Co., (ILLUS. left, top of page) **325**

Bowl, 4 1/2" d., 2 1/2" h., berry, plain w/pale blue rim band **55**

Bowl, 4 1/2" d., 2 1/2" h., embossed Reverse Pyramids patt., Ruckles Pottery **65-75**

Bowl, 4 1/2" to 14" d., embossed Pineapple patt., ten sizes, Brush-McCoy Pottery Co., price ranges .... **174+**

Bowl, 6" d., stenciled Wildflower patt., Brush-McCoy Pottery (ILLUS. top row, left, with other Wildflower pieces, bottom of page) .... **135+**

Bowl, 7" d., embossed Beaded Rose patt., A.E. Hull Pottery Co. **150**

Bowl, 7 1/2" d., 2 3/4" h., embossed Apricot with Honeycomb patt., A.E. Hull Pottery Co. **135**

A Variety of Stenciled Wildflower Pieces

Reverse Pyramids-Picket Fence Bowl

GrapeWare Pattern Bowls

Bowl, 7 1/2" d., 5" h., embossed Reverse Pyramids w/Reverse Picket Fence patt., Ruckles Pottery (ILLUS., top of page)..... **90-100**

Bowl, 8" d., embossed GrapeWare patt., Brush-McCoy Pottery Co. (ILLUS. left, above) **225**

Bowl, 9" d., nesting-type, embossed Pyramid patt. **130**

Bowl, 9 1/2" d., 3 3/4" h., embossed Apricot with Honeycomb patt., A.E. Hull Pottery Co. **150**

Bowl, 9 1/2" d., 4 1/2" h., embossed Gadroon Arches or Petal Panels patt. **175**

Bowl, 9 1/2" d., 5" h., embossed Currants and Diamonds patt. **230**

Bowl, 10" d., embossed GrapeWare patt. (ILLUS. right with other GrapeWare bowl, above) **275**

Bowl, 10" d., 5" h., embossed Heart Banded patt. **135**

Bowl, 10 1/2" d., 5 1/2" h., embossed Diamond Point patt. **170**

Bowl, stenciled Nautilus patt., rim handles, A.E. Hull Pottery Co. **325**

Bowl, 7" d., 2 1/2" h., embossed Venetian patt., same as Reverse Pyramids w/Reverse Picket Fence but w/honeycomb at bottom, Roseville Pottery (ILLUS., bottom of page)... **50**

Embossed Venetian Pattern Bowl

Embossed Beaded Rose Brush Vase, Small Ewer & Slag Soap Dish

Bowls, nesting-type, embossed Zig-Zag patt., depending on size **100-150**

Bowls, embossed Ringsaround (Wedding Ring) patt., A.E. Hull Pottery Co., six sizes, ranges **85-225**

Bowls, nesting-type, embossed Cosmos patt., A.E. Hull Pottery Co., depending on size, each **65-275**

Bowls, nesting-type, embossed Scallop patt., 6" d., 3 1/2" h., 8" d., 3 1/2" h., 9 1/2" d., 5" h., depending on size, each **85-125**

Bow Tie Blue-banded Brush Vase

Stenciled Wildflower Bowl

Bowls, nesting-type, stenciled Wildflower patt., Brush-McCoy Pottery Co., 4" to 14" d., depending on size (ILLUS. of 10" d. size) **150-450**

Brush vase, embossed Apple Blossom patt., Burley-Winter Pottery Co., 5 3/4" h. **500**

Brush vase, embossed Beaded Rose patt., A.E. Hull Pottery Co. (ILLUS. left with Beaded Rose small ewer & slab soap dish, top of page) **175-200**

Brush vase, embossed Bow Tie (Our Lucile) patt., w/narrow blue bands, Brush-McCoy Pottery Co., 5 1/2" h. (ILLUS., next column) **225**

Brush vase, embossed Bow Tie (Our Lucile) patt., w/rose decal, Brush-McCoy Pottery Co., 5 1/2" h. **115**

Brush vase, embossed Willow (Basketweave & Morning Glory) patt., Brush-McCoy Pottery Co., small, 4 3/4" h. (ILLUS., bottom next column) **325**

Willow Pattern Brush Vase

Advertising & Daisy Pattern Butter Crocks

Butter crock, cov., advertising "Compliments of J. Mueller," Western Stoneware Co., 4 1/4" h. (ILLUS. left w/Daisy patt. crock, above).. 295

Butter crock, cov., embossed Apple Blossom patt., Burley-Winter Pottery Co., 7" d., 5" h.. 500

Butter crock, cov., embossed Apricot patt., A.E. Hull Pottery Co., 7" d., 4" h.................. 250

Butter crock, cov., embossed Butterfly patt., Nelson McCoy Sanitary Stoneware Co., 10 lb. size, 9 1/2" d., 6" h...................... 275

Butter crock, cov., embossed Cow and Fence patt., 7 1/4" d., 5" h............................ 525

Butter crock, cov., embossed Cows and Columns patt., found in five sizes from 2 lbs. to 10 lbs., Brush-McCoy Pottery Co., ranges (ILLUS., top next column) ...... **425-650+**

Butter crock, cov., embossed Daisy and Basketweave patt., 7" d., 6 3/4" h. 350

Butter crock, cov., embossed Daisy and Trellis patt., 6 1/2" d., 4 1/2" h. 225

Butter crock, cov., embossed Daisy and Trellis patt., 6" d., 4" h. 175

Butter crock, cov., embossed Daisy and Waffle patt., 7" d., 6 3/4" h. 235

Cows & Columns Butter Crock

Butter crock, cov., embossed Daisy patt., Red Wing Pottery Co., 3 1/2" h. (ILLUS. right with advertising butter crock, top of page)... 395

Butter crock, cov., embossed Diffused Blue with Block Bands patt., 7 1/2" d., 5 1/2" h.. 225

Butter crock, cov., embossed Diffused Blues with Inverted Pyramid Bands patt., 6" d., 4" h. 150

Butter crock, cov., embossed Dragonfly and Flower patt., found in at least three sizes, Logan Pottery Co., large, 8" d.,

Dragonfly & Flower Butter Crocks

Eagle Butter and Salt Crocks

5" h. (ILLUS. right, bottom of previous page) 345

Butter crock, cov., embossed Dragonfly and Flower patt., smallest size, Logan Pottery Co., rare (ILLUS. left, bottom of previous page) 500

Butter crock, cov., embossed Eagle patt., A.E. Hull Pottery Co., 6" d., 6" h. (ILLUS. right, top of page) 700

Butter crock, cov., embossed Grape and Leaves Low patt., Robinson Clay Products, 6 1/2" d., 3" h. 250

Butter crock, cov., embossed Greek Column (Draped Windows) patt., Red Wing Pottery Co. & Nelson McCoy Sanitary Stoneware Co., found in 2, 3, 4 & 5 lb. sizes, ranges **225-295**

Butter crock, cov., embossed Indian & Deer patt., Brush-McCoy Pottery Co., 2 lb. 800

Butter crock, cov., embossed Indian & Deer patt., Brush-McCoy Pottery Co., 3 lb. 900

Butter crock, cov., embossed Indian Good Luck Sign (Swastika) patt., produced by Nelson McCoy Sanitary Stoneware Co., Robinson-Ransbottom Pottery Co. & The Crooksville Pottery Co., 6 1/4" d., 5 1/4" h. 175

Butter crock, cov., embossed Jersey Cow patt., 4" h. **1,000**

Butter crock, cov., embossed Leaf Flemish patt., 8" d., 7" h. 200

Lovebird Butter Crock & Flying Bird Salt Box

Peacock Butter Crock & Salt Box

Butter crock, cov., embossed Lovebird patt., A.E. Hull Pottery Co., 6" d., 5" h. (ILLUS. right with Flying Bird salt box, bottom previous page) 750

Butter crock, cov., embossed Peacock patt., w/bail handle, Brush-McCoy Pottery Co., 3 lb., 5" h. (ILLUS. right with Peacock salt box, top of page)..................... 800

Butter crock, cov., embossed Rose & Waffle patt., 5" d., 4 1/2" h................................. 300

Willow Pattern Butter Crock

Butter crock, cov., embossed Willow (Basketweave & Morning Glory) patt., bail handle, Brush-McCoy Pottery Co., 3 lb. (ILLUS.).. 285

Butter crock, cov., stenciled Cows patt., 6 1/2" d., 5" h.. 150

Butter crock, cov., stenciled Dutch Scene patt., Brush-McCoy Pottery Co., 6 3/4" d., 5" h.. 325

Butter crock, cov., stenciled Wildflower patt., Brush-McCoy Pottery Co., four sizes available, each 150

Three Diffused Blue Canisters

Canister, cov., Diffused Blue patt., "Raisins," "Salt" or "Tea," A.E. Hull Pottery Co., 5 3/4" d., 6 1/2" h. each (ILLUS.).......... 175

Canister, cov., embossed GrapeWare patt., various contents, Brush-McCoy Pottery Co., 6" h., each 400-800

Canister, cov., embossed Robinson Barrel patt., Robinson Clay Products Co............... 275

Canister, cov., embossed Willow (Basketweave & Morning Glory) patt., "Barley," Brush-McCoy Pottery Co., average 6 1/2 to 7" h., each.................................. 1,000

Embossed Willow Canisters

Canister, cov., embossed Willow (Basketweave & Morning Glory) patt., "Cereal," Brush-McCoy Pottery Co., average 5 1/2" to 6 1/2" h. (ILLUS. bottom row, far left, above) 550

Canister, cov., embossed Willow (Basketweave & Morning Glory) patt., "Coffee," Brush-McCoy Pottery Co., average 5 1/2 to 6 1/2" h. (ILLUS. bottom row, second from left, above).............................. 275

Canister, cov., embossed Willow (Basketweave & Morning Glory) patt., "Crackers" (short), Brush-McCoy Pottery Co., average 5 1/2 to 6 1/2" h., each. (ILLUS. top row, third from right, above) 550

Canister, cov., embossed Willow (Basketweave & Morning Glory) patt., "Crackers" (tall), Brush-McCoy Pottery Co., average 6 1/2 to 7" h., each (ILLUS. top row, third from left, above) 1,000

Canister, cov., embossed Willow (Basketweave & Morning Glory) patt., "Raisins," Brush-McCoy Pottery Co., average 5 1/2" to 6 1/2" h. (ILLUS. top row, second from right, above)................................. 625

Canister, cov., embossed Willow (Basketweave & Morning Glory) patt., "Rice," Brush-McCoy Pottery Co., average 6 1/2 to 7" h., each. 1,250

Canister, cov., embossed Willow (Basketweave & Morning Glory) patt., "Salt," "Beans," or blank, Brush-McCoy Pottery Co., average 5 1/2 to 6 1/2" h., each (ILLUS. of Salt, bottom row, center; Beans, top row, far right, above)................. 375

Canister, cov., embossed Willow (Basketweave & Morning Glory) patt., "Sugar," Brush-McCoy Pottery Co., average 5 1/2 to 6 1/2" h. (ILLUS. bottom row, second from right, above) 275

Canister, cov., embossed Willow (Basketweave & Morning Glory) patt., "Tea," Brush-McCoy Pottery Co., average 5 1/2 to 6 1/2" h. (ILLUS. bottom row, far right, above)... 275

Canister, cov., embossed Willow (Basketweave & Morning Glory) patt., "Tobacco," Brush-McCoy Pottery Co., average 6 1/2 to 7" h., each (ILLUS. top row, far left, above) 1,000

Printed Dutch Scene Sugar Canister

Canister, cov., stenciled Dutch Scene patt., "Sugar," Brush-McCoy Pottery Co., 5 1/2 to 6" h. (ILLUS.) 450-650

Row of Stenciled Vines Canisters

Stenciled Floral Pattern Canister

Canister, cov., stenciled Floral patt., "Coffee," probably A.E. Hull Pottery Co., 5 7/8" h. (ILLUS. at left) **275**

Canister, cov., stenciled Snowflake patt., various contents, A.E. Hull Pottery Co., 5 3/4" d., 6 1/2" h., each....................... **235-300**

Canister, cov., stenciled Vines patt., "Coffee," "Rice" & "Sugar," A.E. Hull Pottery Co., 5 1/2 to 6" h., each (ILLUS. center, top of page)... **250**

Canister, cov., stenciled Vines patt., "Prunes" & "Oat Meal," A.E. Hull Pottery Co., 7 1/4" h., each (ILLUS. far left & right, top of page).. **400**

Canister, cov., stenciled Wildflower patt., "Barley," "Cornstarch" or "Grape Nuts," Brush-McCoy Pottery Co., 5 3/4" h., each (ILLUS. second row from bottom with other canisters & spice jars, below)...... **550**

Canister, cov., stenciled Wildflower patt., "Beans," or "Peas," Brush-McCoy Pottery Co., 5 1/2 to 6 1/2", each (ILLUS. of Beans, second row from bottom, bottom of page)... **325**

Wildflower Canisters & Spice Jars

Canister, cov., stenciled Wildflower patt., blank title, Brush-McCoy Pottery Co. (ILLUS. bottom row with other canisters & spice jars, bottom previous page) **475**

Canister, cov., stenciled Wildflower patt., "Butter," tall w/flared rim, Brush-McCoy Pottery Co., 5 3/5" h. (ILLUS. top row with other canisters & spice jars, bottom previous page) **350**

Canister, cov., stenciled Wildflower patt., "Cereal (Sago)," Brush-McCoy Pottery Co., 5 1/2 to 6 1/2" h. (ILLUS. bottom row with canisters & spice jars, bottom previous page) **400**

Canister, cov., stenciled Wildflower patt., "Choice Sour Pickles," Brush-McCoy Pottery Co., 12" h. **850**

Canister, cov., stenciled Wildflower patt., "Cloves," Brush-McCoy Pottery (ILLUS. center top row with other Wildflower pieces, bottom page 243) **250**

Canister, cov., stenciled Wildflower patt., "Coffee," "Rice" or "Tea," 5 1/2 to 6 1/2", each (ILLUS. second, third & bottom rows with canisters & spice jars, bottom previous page) **225**

Canister, cov., stenciled Wildflower patt., "Corn Meal" (tall), Brush-McCoy Pottery Co., 10" h. (ILLUS. top row, right, with canisters & spice jars, previous page) **750**

Canister, cov., stenciled Wildflower patt., "Crackers" (tall), Brush-McCoy Pottery Co., 5 1/2 to 6 1/2" h. (ILLUS. top row with canisters & spice jars, previous page) **700**

Canister, cov., stenciled Wildflower patt., "Currants," Brush-McCoy Pottery Co., 5 1/2 to 6 1/2" (ILLUS. bottom row with canisters & spice jars, previous page) **425**

Canister, cov., stenciled Wildflower patt., "Farina," "Prunes" or "Raisins," Brush-McCoy Pottery Co., 5 1/2 to 6 1/2", each (ILLUS. second row from bottom & bottom row with canisters & spice jars, previous page) **375**

Canister, cov., stenciled Wildflower patt., "Flour," Brush-McCoy Pottery Co., 5 1/2 to 6 1/2" h. (ILLUS. top row with canisters & spice jars, previous page) **800**

Canister, cov., stenciled Wildflower patt., "Genuine German Dills," Brush-McCoy Pottery Co., 12" h. (ILLUS. top row, far left with canisters & spice jars, previous page) **850**

Canister, cov., stenciled Wildflower patt., "Oatmeal," Brush-McCoy Pottery Co., 5 1/2 to 6 1/2", each (ILLUS. second row

from bottom with canisters & spice jars, previous page) **400**

Canister, cov., stenciled Wildflower patt., "Sugar," Brush-McCoy Pottery Co., 5 1/2 to 6 1/2" (ILLUS. bottom row, far right, with canisters & spice jars, previous page) **250**

Canister, cov., stenciled Wildflower patt., "Sugar" (tall), Brush-McCoy Pottery Co., 10" h. (ILLUS. top row, second from left with canisters & spice jars, previous page) **500**

Canister, cov., stenciled Wildflower patt., "Tapioca," Brush-McCoy Pottery Co., 5 1/2 to 6 1/2" h. (ILLUS. second row from bottom with canisters & spice jars, previous page) **450**

Canister, cov., stenciled Wildflower patt., "Tobacco," Brush-McCoy Pottery Co., 5 1/2 to 6 1/2" h., each **600**

Canister, cov., wooden cover, stenciled Snowflake patt., six various in set, 5 3/4" d., 6 1/2" h., each............................ **235+**

Embossed GrapeWare Canister

Canister, embossed GrapeWare patt., "Pepper," no cover, 3 3/8" h. (ILLUS.) **400**

Canister, cov., stenciled Wildflower patt., blank, Brush-McCoy Pottery Co., 2 gal........ **425**

Canister, cov., stenciled Wildflower patt., blank, Brush-McCoy Pottery Co., 3 gal........ **525**

Canister/cookie jar, cov., embossed Willow (Basketweave & Morning Glory) patt., "Put Your Fist In," Brush-McCoy Pottery Co., average 6 1/2 to 7" h., each. (ILLUS. top row, second from left w/other Willow canisters, top page 249). **1,000**

Embossed Flying Bird Casserole

Embossed GrapeWare Casserole

Casserole, cov., embossed Flying Bird patt., A.E. Hull Pottery Co., 9 1/2" d. (ILLUS., bottom previous page) **600**

Casserole, cov., embossed GrapeWare patt., Brush-McCoy Pottery Co. (ILLUS. with extra cover, top of page) **425**

Apple Blossom Chamber Pot

Chamber pot, cov., embossed Apple Blossom patt., Burley-Winter Pottery Co., 11" d., 6" h. (ILLUS.) **375**

Chamber pot, cov., embossed Beaded Rose patt., A.E. Hull Pottery Co., large 9 1/2" d., 6" h. **250**

Chamber pot, cov., embossed Beaded Rose patt., A.E. Hull Pottery Co., small **225**

Chamber pot, cov., embossed Bow Tie (Our Lucile) patt. w/rose decal, Brush-McCoy Pottery Co., 11" d., 6" h. **225**

Chamber pot, cov., embossed Open Rose and Spearpoint Panels patt., A.E. Hull Pottery Co., 9 1/2" d., 6" h. **300**

Chamber pot, cov., embossed Peacock patt., Brush-McCoy Pottery Co., 11" d., 6" h. **1,250**

Chamber pot, cov., embossed Willow (Basketweave & Morning Glory) patt., Brush-McCoy Pottery Co., 9 1/2" d., 8" h. (ILLUS. right with Willow slop jar, bottom of page).. **325**

Chamber pot, cov., stenciled Wildflower patt., Brush-McCoy Pottery Co., 11" d., 6" h... **250**

Willow Chamber Pot & Slop Jar

Bull's-Eye & Diffused Blue Coffeepot

Open Beaded Rose Chamber Pot

Chamber pot, open, embossed Beaded
Rose patt., A.E. Hull Pottery Co., large,
9 1/2" d., 6" h. (ILLUS.) **250**

Chamber pot, open, embossed Beaded
Rose patt., A.E. Hull Pottery Co., small **200**
Chamber pot, open, embossed Bow Tie
(Our Lucile) patt., 11" d., 6" h....................... **165**
Coffeepot, cov., Diffused Blue patt., oval
design, w/bottom plate, 11" h. (ILLUS.
left with embossed Bull's-Eye pot, no bot-
tom plate, top of page) **2,700**
Coffeepot, cov., embossed Bull's-Eye patt.,
w/bottom plate (ILLUS. right, no bottom
plate, top of page) **3,250**
Coffeepot, cov., embossed Peacock patt.,
Brush-McCoy Pottery Co., 6 1/2" d.,
overall 10 3/4" h. (ILLUS. right with Pea-
cock pitcher, bottom of page)................... **4,000**

Rare Peacock Coffeepot & Pitcher

Coffeepot, miniature, cov., wide blue band, souvenir-type (ILLUS. right w/bean pot, top page 242) **300**

Coffeepot, cov., Swirl patt., tapering ovoid body w/a pointed rim spout, heavy C-form handle w/thumb rest, inset lid w/acorn finial, tin base, w/bottom plate, 11" h. **1,225**

Cold fudge crock, w/tin lid & ladle, marked "Johnson Cold Fudge Crock," various sizes known, 12" d., 13" h. **300**

Cookie jar, cov., Brickers patt., 8" d., 8" h. **750**

Rare Flying Bird Cookie Jar

Cookie jar, cov., embossed Flying Bird patt., A.E. Hull Pottery Co., 6 3/4" d., 9" h. (ILLUS.) **1,250**

Cooking or preserving kettle, cov., bail handle, embossed Peacock patt., Brush-McCoy Pottery Co., 5 qt. **1,100**

Stenciled Dutch Boy Creamer

Creamer, ovoid form, stenciled Dutch Boy patt., 4 1/4" h. (ILLUS.) **225**

Rare Anchovies Storage Crock

Crock, anchovies storage-type, swelled cylindrical form, three blue bands around top & bottom, stenciled on the side "A. Rensch & Co. - Anchois (sic) Mustard [over a fish] - Toledo, O.," impressed on the bottom "Burley, Winter & Co. - Crooksville, O.," 10 1/2" h. (ILLUS.) **575**

Cup, embossed Paneled Fir Tree patt., Brush-McCoy Pottery Co., 3" d., 3 1/2" h. **175**

Butterflies Cuspidor

Cuspidor, embossed Butterflies patt., 6" h. (ILLUS.)... **210**

Cuspidor, embossed Peacock patt., Brush-McCoy Pottery Co., 10" d., 9" h. **425**

Cuspidor, embossed Poinsettia and Basketweave patt., 9 3/4" d., 9" h. **180**

Cuspidor, embossed Sunflowers patt., 9 3/4" d., 9" h. **200**

Cuspidor, embossed Willow (Basketweave & Morning Glory) patt., Brush-McCoy Pottery Co., 7 1/2" d., 5 1/2" h. **185**

Blue & White Ewer & Pitcher

Miniature Blue Swirl Cuspidor

Cuspidor, miniature, souvenir-type, dark blue & white swirl design (ILLUS.) **224**

Miniature Diffused Blue Cuspidor

Cuspidor, miniature, souvenir-type, Diffused Blue patt., 2" h. (ILLUS.) **325**
Custard cup, embossed Fishscale patt., A.E. Hull Pottery Co., 2 1/2" d., 5" h. **125**
Custard cup, embossed Peacock patt., Brush-McCoy Pottery Co., 2 7/8" h. (ILLUS. right w/berry bowl, top page 243) **545**
Ewer, embossed Apple Blossom patt., large, Burley-Winter Pottery Co., 12" h. (ILLUS. right with embossed Feathers & Plume pitcher, top of page)......................... **450**

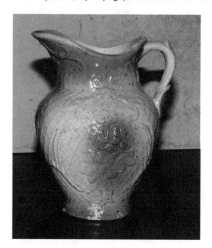

Small-mouthed Apple Blossom Ewer

Ewer, embossed Apple Blossom patt., small mouth, Burley-Winter Pottery Co., 8" h. (ILLUS.).. **395**
Ewer, embossed Beaded Rose patt., small, A.E. Hull Pottery Co., 7" h. (ILLUS. center with Beaded Rose brush vase & soap dish, top page 245) **300**

Stenciled Wildflower Ewers

Bow Tie/Bluebird Mouth Ewer

Ewer, embossed Bow Tie (Our Lucile) patt., mouth ewer, Bluebird decal, Brush-Mc-Coy Pottery Co., 8" h. (ILLUS.) **275**
Ewer, embossed Bow Tie (Our Lucile) patt., w/rose decal, Brush-McCoy Pottery Co., 11" h... **175**

Small Willow Pattern Ewer

Ewer, embossed Willow (Basketweave & Morning Glory) patt., Brush-McCoy Pottery Co., small, 7 1/2" h. (ILLUS.) **365**
Ewer, Floral Decal (Memphis patt.), Western Stoneware Co., small, 7" h. **175**
Ewer, stenciled Wildflower patt., pear-shaped, Brush-McCoy Pottery Co., 6 1/2" h. (ILLUS. left, top of page) **225**
Ewer, stenciled Wildflower patt., pear-shaped, Brush-McCoy Pottery Co., 8 1/2" h. (ILLUS. center, top of page) **295**
Ewer, stenciled Wildflower patt., pear-shaped, Brush-McCoy Pottery Co., 10 1/2" h. (ILLUS. right, top of page) **325**

Small Wildflower Ewer

Ewer, stenciled Wildflower patt., small w/angled handle, Brush-McCoy Pottery Co., 7 1/4" h. (ILLUS.) **295**
Ewer & basin set, embossed Apple Blossom patt., Burley-Winter Pottery Co., pr. **700**

Decorated Bow Tie Ewer & Basin Set

Ewer & basin set, embossed Bow Tie patt.
w/Flying Bird decal, Brush-McCoy Pottery Co., basin 15" d., ewer 11" h., pr.
(ILLUS.)... **625**

Bow Tie Ewer from Set

Ewer & basin set, embossed Bow Tie patt.
w/stenciled Wildflower decoration,
Brush-McCoy Pottery Co., basin 15" d.,
ewer 11" h., pr. (ILLUS. of ewer only) **625**
Ewer & basin set, embossed Feather and
Swirl patt., ewer 8 1/2" d., 12" h., basin
14" d., 5" h., pr. **550**

Embossed Lily Ewer & Basin Set

Ewer & basin set, embossed Lily patt., Red
Wing Pottery Co., pr. (ILLUS.) **1,750**
Ewer & basin set, embossed Willow (Basketweave & Morning Glory) patt., Brush-
McCoy Pottery Co., basin 15" d.,
4 1/2" h., ewer, 9" d., 13" h., pr. **675**
Ewer & basin set, Floral Decal (Memphis
patt.), Western Stoneware Co., basin
15" d., ewer 11 1/4" h., pr. **365**
Ewer & basin set, stenciled Wildflower
patt., stenciled designs inside the ewer &
the basin, basin 15" d., ewer 11" h.,
Brush-McCoy Pottery Co., pr. (ILLUS.,
bottom page).. **650**

Wildflower Ewer & Basin Set

Foot warmer, signed by Logan Pottery Co. **250**
Grease jar, cov., embossed Flying Bird patt., A.E. Hull Pottery Co., 4" h. (ILLUS. left with Flying Bird berry bowl, page 242).. **1,100**
Iced tea cooler, cov., plain barrel shape, printed "3 - Iced Tea Cooler," 3 gal., 11" d., 13" h.. **310**
Iced tea cooler, cov., w/spigot, Maxwell House, 13" d., 15" h. **325**

Apple Blossom Jardiniere

Jardiniere, embossed Apple Blossom patt., Burley-Winter Pottery Co., 6" h. (ILLUS.)..... **425**

Cosmos Jardiniere & Pedestal

Jardiniere & pedestal, embossed Cosmos patt., possibly Weller or Burley-Winter Pottery Co., jardiniere 6" h., pedestal 5 1/2" h. (ILLUS.) **2,000**

Tulip Pattern Jardiniere & Pedestal

Jardiniere & pedestal base, embossed Tulip patt., made by Nelson McCoy Sanitary Stoneware Co., Burley-Winter Pottery Co. & A.E. Hull Pottery Co., jardiniere 6" h., pedestal 7" h., the set (ILLUS.).. **1,500**
Jug, miniature, Diffused Blue w/advertising in gold letters, each (ILLUS. of three, bottom page)... **325**
Match holder, model of a duck, 5 1/2" d., 5" h... **250**

Three Miniature Advertising Jugs

Spear Point & Flower Panels Measuring Cup & Two Pitchers

Figural Rooster Match Holder

Match holder, model of a rooster (ILLUS.) **435**

Measuring cup, embossed Spearpoint and Flower Panels patt., A.E. Hull Pottery Co., 6 3/4" d., 6" h. (ILLUS. center, top of page) **450**

Meat tenderizer, stenciled Wildflower patt., turned wood handle, Brush-McCoy Pottery (ILLUS. right bottom row with other Wildflower pieces, page 243) .... **370+**

Milk bowl, embossed Daisy & Lattice patt., Burley-Winter Pottery Co., three sizes, depending on size **200-275**

Milk crock, embossed Apricot patt., A.E. Hull Pottery Co., 10" d., 5" h. **225**

Milk crock, embossed Lovebird patt., w/bail handle, A.E. Hull Pottery Co., 9" d., 5 1/2" h. (ILLUS., bottom of page) **500**

Mixing bowl, embossed Flying Bird. patt., A.E. Hull Pottery Co., 8" d. **340**

Lovebird Pattern Milk Crock

Graduated Peacock Mixing Bowls

Mixing bowl, nesting-type, flaring sides, molded rim, embossed Peacock patt., Brush-McCoy Pottery Co., 6" d. (ILLUS. right, top of page) **300**

Mixing bowl, nesting-type, flaring sides, molded rim, embossed Peacock patt., Brush-McCoy Pottery Co., 7" d. (ILLUS. center, top of page) **325**

Mixing bowl, nesting-type, flaring sides, molded rim, embossed Peacock patt., Brush-McCoy Pottery Co., 8" d. (ILLUS. left, top of page) **375**

Mixing bowl, embossed Flying Bird. patt., A.E. Hull Pottery Co., 6" d. **225**

Mixing bowl, embossed Flying Bird. patt., A.E. Hull Pottery Co., 7" d. **295**

Mug, Diffused Blue patt., banded design, w/advertising .... **300+**

Mug, embossed Apple Blossom patt., Burley-Winter Pottery Co., 5" h. **700**

Mug, embossed Beaded Rose patt., A.E. Hull Pottery Co., 7" d. **500**

Mug, embossed Bow Tie patt. w/Rose decal, Brush-McCoy Pottery Co., 3 3/4" h. **100**

Mug, embossed Cattail patt., w/advertising, Western Stoneware Co., 3" d., 4" h. (ILLUS., next column) **275**

Mug, embossed Cattail patt., Western Stoneware Co., 3" d., 4" h. **130**

Mug, embossed Columns and Arches patt., extremely rare, Brush-McCoy Pottery Co., 4 1/2" h. (ILLUS. left with Columns & Arches pitcher, bottom of page) .... **650+**

Embossed Cattail Advertising Mug

Mug, embossed Flying Bird patt., A.E. Hull Pottery Co., 3" d., 5" h. **200**

Mug, embossed Grape Cluster in Shield patt., 12 oz. **195**

Mug, embossed Rose & Fishscale patt., A. E. Hull Pottery Co., 5" h. **750**

Mug, embossed Willow (Basketweave & Morning Glory) patt., Brush-McCoy Pottery Co., 3" d., 5" h. (ILLUS. left with pitcher, bottom page 271) **175**

Mug, stenciled Cattail patt., Western Stoneware Co., 3" d., 4" h. **130**

Columns & Arches Mug & Pitcher

Embossed Loop Pie Baker

Printed Dutch Scene Mug

Stenciled Wildflower Mug

Mug, stenciled Dutch Scene mug, boy on one side, girl on the other, J.W. McCoy Pottery & Brush-McCoy Pottery Co., 4 1/4" h. (ILLUS.) **275**

Mug, stenciled Wildflower patt., Brush-McCoy Pottery, 4 1/2" h. (ILLUS. bottom row left with other Wildflower pieces, page 243) .... **200+**

Mug, stenciled Wildflower patt., Brush-McCoy Pottery Co., 4 1/2" h. (ILLUS., top next column) **250**

Mustard jar, cov., Diffused Blue, stenciled "Mustard," 3" d., 4" h. **200**

Pie baker, embossed Loop patt., light blue, unglazed rim & under collar, 8" d. (ILLUS., top of page) **40**

Pitcher, 9" h., 7" d., Bluebird decal, hall boy-style, Brush-McCoy Pottery Co. (ILLUS., next column) **425**

Bluebird Decal Hall Boy Pitcher

Miniature Advertising Pitchers

Pitcher, Diffused Blues, miniature w/souvenir markings in gold lettering, each (ILLUS., above) **325**

Pitcher, 7" h., 3 1/2" d., Diffused Blue w/rose decal, A.E. Hull Pottery Co. **125**

Pitcher, Diffused Blue, plain smooth shape, found in 1/4, 1/2, 5/8 & 1 gallon size, smallest is rarest, depending on the size.. **150-225**

Pitcher, 10" h., 7" d., embossed American Beauty Rose patt., Burley-Winter Pottery Co. (ILLUS. right, bottom of page).............. **475**

American Beauty Rose & Cosmos Pitchers

Apricot & Swan & Deer Pitchers

Pitcher, 8" h., embossed Apricot patt., A.E. Hull Pottery Co., 5 pt. (ILLUS. right, above) **235**

Avenue of Trees Pitcher

Pitcher, 8" h., embossed Avenue of Trees patt. (ILLUS.)... **325**
Pitcher, embossed Bands and Rivets patt., 1 gal. **275**
Pitcher, embossed Bands and Rivets patt., 1 pt. **285**
Pitcher, embossed Bands and Rivets patt., 1/2 gal. **285**
Pitcher, embossed Bands and Rivets patt., 1/4 gal. **285**
Pitcher, embossed Bands and Rivets patt., 5/8 gal. **225**
Pitcher, embossed Bands & Rivets patt., side-pour, molded bands, no advertising, Western Stoneware, several sizes, each **400**
Pitcher, embossed Bands & Rivets patt., side-pour, molded bands, w/advertising, Western Stoneware, depending on size, each (ILLUS. of two, bottom of page)... **400-1,200**
Pitcher, 10" h., embossed Beaded Rose patt., large, A.E. Hull Pottery Co. **425**

Western Side-Pour Pitchers

Beaded Swirl Pattern Pitcher

Pitcher, 6 1/2" h., embossed Beaded Swirl patt., A.E. Hull Pottery Co. (ILLUS.)............. **950**

Small Embossed Butterfly Pitcher

Pitcher, 4 3/4" h., embossed Butterfly patt., Nelson McCoy Sanitary Stoneware Co. (ILLUS.).. **600**

Embossed Butterfly Large Pitcher

Pitcher, 9" h., embossed Butterfly patt., Nelson McCoy Sanitary Stoneware Co. (ILLUS.).. **450**

Pitcher, 6 1/4" h., 6 3/4" d., embossed Capt. John Smith and Pocahontas patt., A.E. Hull Pottery Co. (ILLUS. bottom right, bottom of page)................................. **325**

Pitcher, 4 1/2" h., embossed Castle patt., A.E. Hull Pottery Co. **225**

Pitcher, 6" h., embossed Castle patt., A.E. Hull Pottery Co. **275**

Pitcher, 8" h., embossed Castle patt., A.E. Hull Pottery Co. (ILLUS. bottom left w/Capt. John Smith pitcher, bottom of page)... **325**

Capt. John Smith, Castle and Shield Pitchers

Cherry Cluster & Grape Pattern Pitchers

Embossed Cattails Pitcher

Pitcher, 5 3/4" h., embossed Cattails patt. (ILLUS.).. **400**

Pitcher, 9 1/2" h., embossed Cherry Band patt., Red Wing Pottery Co., 8 pt., available in numerous sizes, the smallest being the most valuable, often seen w/printed advertising, which adds $300 minimum to the value, without advertising (ILLUS., next column) **225-400**

Embossed Cherry Band Pitcher

Pitcher, 10" h., 8 1/2" d., embossed Cherry Cluster with Basketweave patt., A.E. Hull Pottery Co. (ILLUS. bottom row, left w/various grape pattern pitchers, top of page).. **325**

Chrysanthemum Pitchers & Salt Box

Pitcher, 8" h., embossed Chrysanthemum patt., White Hall Sewer Pipe & Stoneware Co. (ILLUS. right, top of page) **225**

Pitcher, 9 1/2" h., embossed Chrysanthemum patt., White Hall Sewer Pipe & Stoneware Co. (ILLUS. left, top of page) **275**

Pitcher, 9" h., embossed Columns and Arches patt., Brush-McCoy Pottery Co. (ILLUS. right with Columns & Arches mug, bottom page 260) **600**

Pitcher, 9" h., 6 1/2" d., embossed Cosmos patt., w/advertising, Nelson McCoy Sanitary Stoneware Co. **2,500**

Pitcher, 9" h., 6 1/2" d., embossed Cosmos (Wild Rose) patt., Nelson McCoy Sanitary Stoneware Co. (ILLUS. left with American Beauty Rose pitcher, bottom page 262) **415**

Pitcher, embossed Cow patt., A.E. Hull Pottery Co., five sizes, rarest 5 3/4" h. to 9" h. (ILLUS. of 9" size)........................ **250-600**

Pitcher, 7 1/2" h., 6 1/4" d., embossed Dainty Fruit patt., A.E. Hull Pottery Co......... **550**

Embossed Dandy Pitcher

Pitcher, 7" h., embossed Dandy patt., Brush-McCoy Pottery Co. (ILLUS.).............. **425**

Large Sized Cow Pitcher

Bulbous Daisy Cluster Pitcher

Pitcher, 8" h., 8" d., embossed Daisy Cluster patt., Burley-Winter Pottery Co. (ILLUS.).. **700**

Dutch Boy and Girl Kissing Pitcher

Pitcher, 9" h., embossed Dutch Boy and Girl Kissing patt., Brush-McCoy Pottery Co. or J.W. McCoy Pottery Co. (ILLUS.)..... **250**

Embossed Eagle Pattern Pitcher

Pitcher, 8" h., embossed Eagle patt., A.E. Hull Pottery Co. (ILLUS.) **650**
Pitcher, 8" h., embossed Feathers & Plume patt. (ILLUS. left with Apple Blossom ewer, top page 255).. **650**

Small Flying Bird Pattern Pitcher

Pitcher, 8" h., embossed Flying Bird patt., small edge flakes (ILLUS.).......................... **572**

Embossed Flying Bird Pitcher

Pitcher, 9" h., 6" d., embossed Flying Bird patt., A.E. Hull Pottery Co. (ILLUS.)............. **725**
Pitcher, 7 1/2" h., embossed Grape patt., Burley-Winter Pottery Co. **1,000**

Rare Girl with Dog Pitcher

Pitcher, 8 3/4" h., embossed Girl with Dog patt., Logan Pottery Co. (ILLUS.)............ **1,500**

Pitcher, embossed Grape Cluster in Shield patt., Nelson McCoy Sanitary Stoneware Co., 4 pt.. 450

Pitcher, embossed Grape Cluster in Shield patt., Nelson McCoy Sanitary Stoneware Co., 5 pt.. 475

Pitcher, 5 1/2" h., embossed Grape Cluster on Trellis patt., wide conical body w/a pointed rim spout & C-form handle 275

Pitcher, embossed Grape Cluster on Trellis patt., four sizes, 5" to 9 1/2" h., depending on size, each 165-245

Pitcher, embossed Grape Cluster on Trellis patt., squat body, 2 pt.................................. 400

Pitcher, embossed Grape Cluster on Trellis patt., squat body, 3 pt.................................. 425

Pitcher, embossed Grape Cluster on Trellis patt., squat body, 5 pt. 475

Pitcher, embossed Grape Cluster in Shield patt., Nelson McCoy Sanitary Stoneware Co., 2 pt. 400

Pitcher, embossed Grape Cluster in Shield patt., Nelson McCoy Sanitary Stoneware Co., 3 pt. 425

Pitcher, 7" h., embossed Grape Cluster on Trellis patt., squat body w/cover, Uhl Pottery Co. 350

Pitcher, 7" h., embossed Grape Cluster on Trellis patt., squat body w/no cover, Uhl Pottery Co. (ILLUS. top center with Cherry Cluster pitcher, top page 265)................. 200

Pitcher, 9 1/2" h., embossed Grape Leaf Band patt... 250

Pitcher, 7" h., embossed Grape Leaf Band patt... 165

Pitcher, embossed Grape with Rickrack patt., three sizes, smallest the most valuable, each (ILLUS. of smallest & largest, front center & right with the Cherry Cluster pitcher, top page 265)..................... **195-325**

Pitcher, 9" h., 7" d., embossed Indian Good Luck Sign (Swastika) patt., made by Nelson McCoy Sanitary Stoneware Co., Robinson-Ransbottom Pottery Co. & The Crooksville Pottery Co. (ILLUS. left, bottom of page).. 225

Pitcher, 9" h., 6 1/2" d., embossed Indian in War Bonnet patt., Nelson McCoy Sanitary Stoneware Co. (ILLUS. right with Indian Good Luck Sign pitcher, bottom of page)... 375

Pitcher, 9" h., 5 1/2" d., embossed Iris patt., J.W. McCoy Pottery Co. & Brush-McCoy Pottery Co. (ILLUS. bottom right w/Spear Point & Flower Panels measuring cup, top of page 259)... 400

Indian Good Luck Sign & Indian in War Bonnet Pitchers

Leaping Deer & Standing Deer Pitchers

Pitcher, 8 1/2" h., 6" d., embossed Leaping Deer patt., Burley-Winter Pottery Co. (ILLUS. left).... **400**

Graduated Lincoln Head with Log Cabin Pitchers

Pitcher, embossed Lincoln Head with Log Cabin patt., Uhl Pottery Co., five sizes, one gallon size largest & most valuable, depending on size (ILLUS.) **575-1,500**

Lovebird Pattern Pitcher

Pitcher, 8 1/2" h., 5 1/2" d., embossed Lovebird patt., A.E. Hull Pottery Co. (ILLUS.).. **500**

Pine Cone Pattern Pitcher

Pitcher, 9 1/2" h., 5 3/4" d., embossed Pine Cone patt., Burley-Winter Pottery Co. (ILLUS.).. **1,500**

Pitcher, 8 1/2" h., 7 3/4" d., embossed Poinsettia with Square Woven Cane patt., spherical shape.................................. **350**

Old Fashioned Garden Rose Pitcher

Pitcher, 7" h., 7" d., embossed Old Fashioned Garden Rose patt., Burley-Winter Pottery Co. (ILLUS.).................................... **500**

Pitcher, 7" h., 7" d., embossed Paul Revere patt., Whites Pottery Co. **450**

Pitcher, 8 1/2" h., embossed Peacock patt., Brush-McCoy Pottery Co. (ILLUS. left with Peacock coffeepot, bottom page 253).. **1,250**

Rare Remember Pitcher

Pitcher, embossed Remember patt., molded figure of Columbia standing beside an American shield, "Remember" on the interior rim (ILLUS.) **1,500**

Pitcher, 8 3/4" h., embossed Rose on Trellis patt., also comes in smaller size............. **375**

Scroll & Leaf Advertising Pitcher

Pitcher, 7" h., embossed Scroll & Leaf patt., printed Iowa advertising (ILLUS.)................. **750**
Pitcher, 8" h., embossed Scroll patt., Logan Pottery Co. **650**
Pitcher, 8 1/2" h., 6" d., embossed Shield patt. (ILLUS. top center w/Capt. John Smith pitcher, bottom page 264).................. **475**

Embossed Stag Pattern Pitcher

Pitcher, 9" h., 6 1/2" d., embossed Stag patt., Robinson-Ransbottom Pottery Co. (ILLUS.)... **1,000**
Pitcher, 8 1/2" h., 6" d., embossed Standing Deer with Fawn patt., Brush-McCoy Pottery Co. (ILLUS. right with Leaping Deer pitcher, top page 269) **275**

Embossed Strutting Stag Pitcher

Pitcher, 8 1/2" h., 6" d., embossed Strutting Stag patt., possibly Brush-McCoy Pottery Co. (ILLUS.)... **525**
Pitcher, 8 1/2" h., 6" d., embossed Swan patt., Burley-Winter Pottery Co. **450**
Pitcher, 8 1/2" h., 6" d., embossed Swan patt. on one side, Leaping Deer on reverse, Burley-Winter Pottery Co. (ILLUS. left with Apricot pitcher, top page 263)...... **1,500**
Pitcher, 8" h., 4" d., embossed Tulip patt., J.W. McCoy Pottery Co. & Brush-McCoy Pottery Co. (ILLUS. bottom left with Spear Point & Flower Panels measuring cup, top page 259)...................................... **350**
Pitcher, 9" h., 6 1/2" d., embossed Willow (Basketweave & Morning Glory) patt., tankard-type, Brush-McCoy Pottery Co. (ILLUS. right, bottom of page) **255**
Pitcher, 9" h., embossed Windmill and Bush patt., J.W. McCoy Pottery Co. & Brush-McCoy Pottery Co. .... **400+**

Willow Pitcher and Mug

Three Stenciled Blue & White Pitchers

Embossed Windy City Pitcher

Pitcher, 8 1/2" h., embossed Windy City patt., Robinson Clay Products Pottery Co. (ILLUS.) 325

Pitcher, 7" h., embossed Windmill & Bush patt., J.W. McCoy Pottery Co. & Brush-McCoy Pottery Co. 250

Pitcher, 8 1/2" h., Flying Bluebird decal, J.W. McCoy Pottery Co. 250

Pitcher, 8" h., stenciled Acorn patt., Brush-McCoy Pottery Co. (ILLUS. center, top of page) 300

Pitcher, 7 3/4" h., stenciled Bow Tie patt., possibly A.E. Hull Pottery Co. (ILLUS., next column) 175

Pitcher, stenciled Cattail patt., straight-sided, Western Stoneware Co. 195

Pitcher, stenciled Cattail patt., Western Stoneware Co., 1/4 gal. 195

Pitcher, stenciled Cattail patt., Western Stoneware Co., 1/2 gal. 250

Stenciled Bow Tie Pitcher

Pitcher, stenciled Cattail patt., Western Stoneware Co., 5/8 gal. 325

Pitcher, 5 3/4" h., stenciled Cattail patt., Brush-McCoy Pottery Co. (ILLUS. left with Acorn pitcher, top of page) 250

Pitcher, stenciled Cattail patt., Western Stoneware Co., 1 gal. 450

Pitcher, 5" h., stenciled Conifer Tree patt., Brush-McCoy Pottery Co. (ILLUS. right with Acorn pitcher, top of page) 250

Pitcher, 9" h., 8" d., stenciled Dutch Farm patt., J.W. McCoy Pottery Co. & Brush-McCoy Pottery Co. 250

Pitcher, 8 1/2" h., stenciled Dutch Scene (Dutch Landscape) patt. w/two Dutch children 275

Printed Nautilus Pattern Pitcher

Stenciled Snowflake Pattern Pitcher

Pitcher, 8 1/2" h., stenciled Nautilus patt., A.E. Hull Pottery Co. (ILLUS.) **300**

Pitcher, 8 3/4" h., stenciled Snowflake patt., A.E. Hull Pottery Co. (ILLUS., next column) **250**

Pitcher, 8 3/4" h., stenciled Stylized Floral patt., A.E. Hull Pottery Co. **225**

Pitcher, 6 3/4" h., stenciled Wildflower patt., hall boy-type w/cylindrical body & one stencil per side, Brush-McCoy Pottery Co. **375**

Pitcher, 8" h., 6" d., hot water-type, bulbous body w/stenciled Wildflower patt., Brush-McCoy Pottery (ILLUS. bottom row, center, with other Wildflower pieces, page 243) .... **225+**

Pitcher, 6" h., stenciled Wildflower patt., hall boy-type w/waisted body & five stencils per side, Brush-McCoy Pottery Co. (ILLUS. right with other Wildflower hall boy, bottom of page) **750**

Pitcher, 6 3/4" h., stenciled Wildflower patt., hall boy-type w/cylindrical body & five stencils per side, Brush-McCoy Pottery Co. (ILLUS. left with other Wildflower hall boy, bottom of page) **550**

Pitcher, 7 1/2" h., 4" d., stenciled Wildflower patt., hall boy-type, Brush-McCoy Pottery Co. **275**

Pitcher, 8" h., stenciled Wildflower patt., tall waisted body w/long spout, five stencils per side, Brush-McCoy Pottery Co., also found in 8 1/2" h. size **800**

Two Wildflower Hall Boy Pitchers

Small Wildflower Rolling Pin

Bulbous Wildflower Pitcher

Pitcher, 10 3/4" h., stenciled Wildflower patt., bulbous body, Brush-McCoy Pottery Co. (ILLUS.) **425**

Blue Stupid Pattern Pitcher

Pitcher, 8" h., 6" d., Stupid patt., Diffused Blue bands (ILLUS.)..................................... **450**

Pitcher, 9" h., 4" d., Swirl patt., Diffused Blue swirled bands up around sides **275**

Ramekin or nappy, embossed Peacock patt., Brush-McCoy Pottery Co., 4" d. **300**

Refrigerator jar, cov., Diffused Blue, stenciled "Refrigerator Jar," 3 lb., 7" d., 6 1/2" h... **325**

Roaster, cov., embossed Daisy, Burley-Winter Pottery Co., 9" d., 4" h. **250**

Roaster, cov., stenciled Wildflower patt., Brush-McCoy Pottery Co., 12" d., 8 1/2" h. **450**

Rolling pin, stenciled Wildflower patt., Brush-McCoy Pottery Co., small, 8" l. (ILLUS., top of page)................................... **300**

Rolling pin, stenciled Wildflower patt., w/advertising, large baker's type, Brush-McCoy Pottery Co., stoneware roller 14 1/2" l... **3,000**

Salt box, cov., Blue Band patt., 5" d., 6" h....... **130**

Salt box, cov., Diffused Blue patt., 6" d., 4" h.. **130**

Advertising Hanging Salt Box

Salt box, cov., Diffused Blue patt., Western Stoneware advertising-type, "You Need Salt, We Need You - The Hodgin Store, Whittier, Iowa," 4 1/4" h. (ILLUS.) **600**

Salt box, cov., embossed Apple Blossom patt., Burley-Winter Pottery Co., 6" d., 4" h... **400**

Salt box, cov., embossed Apricot patt., A.E. Hull Pottery Co., 5 3/4" d., 5" h. 250

Salt box, cov., embossed Basketweave & Grapes, patt., sponged blue decoration, 6" d., 4" h. 375

Salt box, cov., embossed Blocks patt., 6 1/2" d., 6 3/4" h. 175

Salt box, cov., embossed Butterfly patt., Nelson McCoy Sanitary Stoneware Co., 5 3/4" d., 5 3/4" h. 275

Salt box, cov., embossed Chrysanthemum patt., White Hall Sewer Pipe & Stoneware Co., 4 1/4" h. (ILLUS. front w/pitchers, top page 266) 210

Embossed Daisy on Snowflake Salt Box

Salt box, cov., embossed Daisy on Snowflake patt. (ILLUS.) **250-275**

Salt box, cov., embossed Daisy patt., 6" d., 6 1/2" h. 250

Salt box, cov., embossed Flying Bird patt., A.E. Hull Pottery Co., 6 1/2" d., 6" h. (ILLUS. left w/Lovebird butter crock, bottom page 247) 625

Salt box, cov., embossed Good Luck Sign (Swastika) patt., Nelson McCoy Sanitary Stoneware Co., Robinson-Ransbottom Pottery Co. & The Crooksville Pottery Co., 6" d., 4" h. 250

Salt box, cov., embossed Grape and Basketweave patt., 6" d., 4" h. 250

Salt box, cov., embossed Grape and Lattice patt., Brush-McCoy Pottery Co., 6 3/4" d., 6 1/2" h. 400

Salt box, cov., embossed Grape & Waffle patt. 350

Salt box, cov., embossed Raspberry patt., Brush-McCoy Pottery Co., 5 1/2" d., 5 1/2" h. 250

Salt box, cov., embossed Waffle patt. 220

Salt box, cov., embossed Waffleweave patt. 230

Salt box, cov., hanging-type, embossed Eagle patt., A.E. Hull Pottery Co., 6" d., 4" h. (ILLUS. left w/Eagle butter crock, top page 247) 600

Salt box, cov., hanging-type, embossed Peacock patt., Brush-McCoy Pottery Co., 5" d., 5" h. (ILLUS. left with Peacock butter crock, top page 248) 425

Salt box, cov., hanging-type, stenciled Nautilus patt., A.E. Hull Pottery Co.................... 275

Salt box, cov., hanging-type, stenciled Vines patt., hinged wooden lid, A.E. Hull Pottery Co., lid missing 200

Salt box, cov., hanging-type, stenciled Wildflower patt., hinged wooden cover, Brush-McCoy Pottery Co., 6" d., 4 1/2" h. 200-300

Salt box, cov., plain 100

Salt box, cov., hanging-type stenciled Wildflower patt., Brush-McCoy Pottery (ILLUS. top row right, without cover, with other Wildflower pieces, bottom page 243) .... 175+

Wildflower Salt with Compass Decor

Salt box, cov., stenciled Wildflower patt., hinged wooden cover, compass design around "Salt" on front, J.W. McCoy Pottery Co., 6" d., 4 1/2" h. (ILLUS. with no cover) 300

Wildflower Advertising Salt Crock

Salt box, open, hanging-type, stenciled Wildflower patt., printed advertising "Your Credit Is Good - Freed Furniture & Carpet Co.," Brush-McCoy Pottery Co., 6" d., 4 1/2" h. (ILLUS.) 550

Salt jar, embossed Polar patt., 11" d.,
13 1/2" h. .... **750+**
Sand jar, embossed Polar Bear patt., Uhl
Pottery Co., 11" d., 13 1/2" h. **750**
Sand jar, embossed Polar Bear patt., Uhl
Pottery Co., 12 1/4" d., 14 1/2" h. **1,250**
Sand jar, embossed Standing Stag patt.,
A.E. Hull Pottery Co., 14" h. **825**
Shaving mug, scuttle-form, 4" d., 6" h. **1,250**

Embossed Apple Blossom Slop Jar

Slop jar, cov., embossed Apple Blossom
patt., Burley-Winter Pottery Co., 10" h.
(ILLUS.).. **350**
Slop jar, cov., embossed Beaded Rose
patt., A.E. Hull Pottery Co., 8 1/2" h. **350**

Embossed Bow Tie Pattern Slop Jar

Slop jar, cov., embossed Bow Tie patt., bail
handle w/wooden grip, Brush-McCoy
Pottery Co., 9 1/2" h. (ILLUS.) **200**

Red Wing Lily Pattern Slop Jar

Slop jar, cov., embossed Lily patt., Red
Wing Pottery Co. (ILLUS.) **250-300**
Slop jar, cov., embossed Rose & Fishscale
patt., A.E. Hull Pottery Co., 10" h. **325**
Slop jar, cov., embossed Willow (Bas-
ketweave & Morning Glory) patt., Brush-
McCoy Pottery Co., 9 1/2" d., 12 1/2" h.
(ILLUS. left with chamber pot, bottom
page 252).. **350**

Miniature Inscribed Slop Jar

Slop jar, miniature, souvenir-type, one side
inscribed "Mar. 29.05," other side in-
scribed "J.A. Wells" (ILLUS.)........................ **425**
Soap dish, cov., embossed Beaded Rose
patt., A.E. Hull Pottery Co., 7" h.................. **500**
Soap dish, embossed Beaded Rose patt.,
slab-type, A.E. Hull Pottery Co., 4 3/4" d.
(ILLUS. right with Beaded Rose brush
vase & ewer, top page 245) **125**

Cat Head & Lion Head Soap Dishes

Soap dish, embossed Cat Head patt., small round style, 3 3/4" d. (ILLUS. right with Lion soap dish, above).................................. **155**

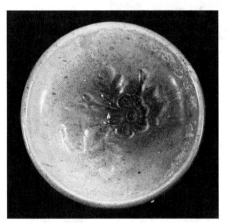

Embossed Flower Cluster Soap Dish

Soap dish, embossed Flower Cluster w/Fishscale patt., small round form, 4 1/2" d., 3/4" h. (ILLUS.) **135**
Soap dish, embossed Lion Head patt., small round style, 3 3/4" d. (ILLUS. left with Cat's Head soap dish, top of page) **155**
Soap dish, stenciled Wildflower patt., slab-type, Brush-McCoy Pottery Co., 3 5/8 x 5 1/4", 3/4" thick **275**

Soap dish, cover & drainer, embossed Bow Tie patt., Brush-McCoy Pottery Co., 5 1/4" d., 2 1/8" h., the set........................... **225**
Soap dish, cover & drainer, stenciled Wildflower patt., knob finial on cover, Brush-McCoy Pottery Co., 5 1/4" d., 2" h., the set... **600**

Wildflower/Arches & Columns Covered Soap Dish

Soap dish, cover & drainer, stenciled Wildflower patt. on embossed Arches & Columns shape, Brush-McCoy Pottery Co., 5 1/4" d., 2" h. (ILLUS.) **600**
Spice jar, cov., embossed GrapeWare patt., "Pepper," "Allspice," "Cinnamon," "Nutmeg," "Ginger" & "Cloves," Brush-McCoy Pottery Co., 3 3/8" h., each....... **400-800**
Spice jar, cov., embossed Willow (Basketweave & Morning Glory) patt., "Cinnamon," "Nutmeg," "Allspice," "Ginger," "Cloves" & "Pepper," each (ILLUS. of group, bottom of page)......................... **250-300**

Willow Pattern Spice Jars

White Hall "Lunch Hour" Stein

Spice jar, cov., stenciled Near Wildflower patt., uncommon design, found in "Allspice," "Pepper," "Cinnamon," "Nutmeg," "Ginger" & "Cloves," possibly by Brush-McCoy or A.E. Hull Pottery Co., 3 3/4" h., each **500**

Spice jar, cov., stenciled Near Wildflower patt., uncommon design, "Nutmegs" (plural) & "Mustard," possibly by Brush-McCoy or A.E. Hull Pottery Co., 3 3/4" h., each **700**

Spice jar, cov., stenciled Plume patt., "Nutmeg," A.E. Hull Pottery Co., 4 1/4" h. **150**

Spice jar, cov., stenciled Snowflake patt., various spices, A.E. Hull Pottery Co., each **150-225**

Spice jar, cov., stenciled Wildflower patt., "Allspice," "Pepper," "Cinnamon," "Nutmeg," "Cloves" & "Ginger," Brush-McCoy Pottery Co., 3 1/4" h., each (ILLUS. third row from bottom with canisters & spice jars, bottom page 250) **250**

Spice jar, cov., stenciled Wildflower patt., "Allspice," "Pepper," "Cinnamon," "Nutmeg," "Cloves" & "Ginger," Brush-McCoy Pottery Co., very rare size, 2 3/4" h., each (ILLUS. third row from bottom with canisters & spice jars, bottom page 250) **400**

Spice jar, cov., stenciled Wildflower patt., "Nutmegs" (plural) & "Mustard," extremely rare, Brush-McCoy Pottery Co., 3 1/4" h., each (ILLUS. third row from bottom with canisters & spice jars, bottom page 250) **500**

Spice jar, cov., stenciled Wildflower patt., "Nutmegs" (plural) & "Mustard," extremely rare & rare small size, Brush-McCoy Pottery Co., 2 3/4" h., each (ILLUS. third

row from bottom with canisters & spice jars, bottom page 250) **800**

Stein, embossed Grape with Leaf Band patt., 5" h. **125**

Stein, embossed grapevine design, "lunch hour" type, dated "1/31/41," White Hall Sewer Pipe & Stoneware Co., Illinois (ILLUS., top of page) **775**

Windy City Pattern Stein

Stein, embossed Windy City patt., 5 1/2" h. (ILLUS.) **165**

Stewer, cov., embossed Willow (Basketweave & Morning Glory) patt., Brush-McCoy Pottery Co., 2 qt. **325**

Stewer, cov., stenciled Wildflower patt., Brush-McCoy Pottery Co., 2 qt. **345**

Two Blue & White Daffodil Vases

Stewer, cov., embossed Willow (Basketweave & Morning Glory) patt., Brush-McCoy Pottery Co., 4 qt. 275

Stewer, cov., stenciled Wildflower patt., Brush-McCoy Pottery Co., 4 qt. 285

Tobacco jar, cov., embossed Berry Scrolls patt., Western Stoneware Co., 5" d., 6 1/2" h. 300

Tumbler, stenciled Wildflower patt., tapering cylindrical form, no printed designs inside, 5" h. 300

Stenciled Wildflower Tumbler

Tumbler, stenciled Wildflower patt., tapering cylindrical form, printed designs inside, 5" h. (ILLUS.)...................................... 350

Umbrella stand, embossed Two Stags patt., solid blue, Logan Pottery Co., 21" h. 1,500

Vase, 6" h., stenciled Nautilus patt., bulbous form, A.E. Hull Pottery Co. 325

Vase, 8" h., embossed Daffodil patt., incised on the bottom "WPC" (ILLUS. left with matching larger vase, top of page) 200

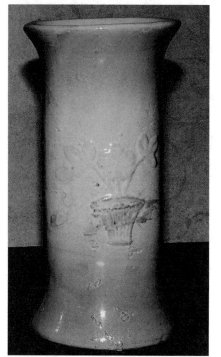

Wicker Basket and Bouquet Vase

Vase, 11" h., embossed Wicker Basket and Bouquet patt. (ILLUS.) 300

Apple Blossom Water Cooler

Vase, 12" h., embossed Daffodil patt., incised on the bottom "WPC" (ILLUS. right with smaller vase, top previous page).......... **275**

Diffused Blue Ovoid Vase

Vase, Diffused Blue, wide ovoid body w/short flared neck & pointed shoulder handles (ILLUS.) .... **300+**
Water cooler, cov., embossed Apple Blossom patt., w/spigot, 13" h. (ILLUS., top of page).. **1,000**
Water cooler, cov., embossed Cupid patt., w/spigot, Western Stoneware, 5 gal............. **725**
Water cooler, cov., embossed Elk and Polar Bear patt., w/spigot, A.E. Hull Pottery Co., 9 1/2" d., 14" h. **825**
Water cooler, cov., embossed Polar Bear patt., w/ spigot, Uhl Pottery Co., 10 gal..... **1,250**
Water cooler, cov., embossed Polar Bear patt., w/ spigot, Uhl Pottery Co., 2 gal......... **600**
Water cooler, cov., embossed Polar Bear patt., w/ spigot, Uhl Pottery Co., 4 gal......... **725**
Water cooler, cov., embossed Polar Bear patt., w/spigot, Uhl Pottery Co., 6 gal........... **850**

Water cooler, cov., embossed Polar Bear patt., w/spigot, Uhl Pottery Co., 8 gal........... **975**
Water cooler, cov., embossed Standing Stag patt., w/spigot, A.E. Hull Pottery Co., several sizes known **825**

Wildflower Water Cooler and Base

Water cooler, cov., stenciled Wildflower patt., w/spigot & base, 3 gal. (ILLUS.) **4,000**

Flying Bird Water Set

Blue & White Polar Jug

Water jug, Polar jug, footed flat-sided moon-shape w/short cylindrical top spout, Uhl Pottery Co., 9 3/4" d., 10" h. (ILLUS.)... **650**

Water set: pitcher & six mugs; embossed Flying Bird patt., A.E. Hull Pottery Co., the set (ILLUS., top of page).................... **2,400**

Other Colors

Jardiniere & pedestal, embossed Cosmos patt., green & cream spongeware, possibly Weller or Burley-Winter Pottery Co., jardiniere 6" h., pedestal 5 1/2" h. **2,500**

Pitcher, 10" h., embossed Grape patt., yellowware (ILLUS. left with other yellowware pitcher, bottom of page) **395**

Pitcher, 9" h., embossed Willow (Basketweave & Morning Glory) patt., yellowware (ILLUS. right with other yellowware pitcher, bottom of page) **300**

Yellowware Pitchers with Patterns Matching Blue & White Pottery Pieces

Spongeware

Spongeware's designs were spattered, sponged or daubed on in colors, sometimes with a piece of cloth. Blue on white was the most common type, but mottled tans, browns and greens on yellow-ware were also popular. Spongeware generally has an overall pattern with a coarser look than Spatterwares, to which it is loosely related. These wares were extensively produced in England and America well into the 20th century.

Blue Spongeware Covered Canister

White-banded Blue Spongeware Bowl

Bowl, 8 3/4" d., 3 1/2" h., three bands of blue on white sponging alternating w/two narrow white bands, minor surface wear, late 19th - early 20th c. (ILLUS.) **$88**

Canister, cov., cylindrical w/molded rim & inset flat cover, light blue fine overall sponging on cream, very tight hairline through bottom, stack mark on cover, late 19th - early 20th c., 7" h. (ILLUS.) **303**

Blue-sponged Butter Crock

Butter crock, wide flat-bottomed cylindrical form, overall dark blue sponging on white w/the printed word "Butter," excellent condition, 6 1/2" d., 4 1/4" h. (ILLUS.).......... **143**

Miniature Blue Sponged Chamber Pot

Chamber pot, miniature, cream w/overall light blue sponging, ca. 1900, 1 1/2" h. (ILLUS.)... **88**

Chamber Set in Cream with Blue Sponging

Chamber set: washbowl & pitcher, round soap dish, shaving mug & master waste jar w/cover; cream background w/overall coarse blue sponging, minor losses to pitcher, late 19th - early 20th c., pitcher 10" h., the set (ILLUS., above) **546**

Dark Blue Sponged Charger

Charger, round dished form w/overall dark blue sponging on white, minor wear, late 19th c., 10 1/8" d. (ILLUS.)........................... **173**

Spongeware Creamer with Molded Design

Creamer, bulbous wide body tapering to a wide cylindrical neck w/wide spout & loop handle w/pointed thumb rest, the lower body molded in relief w/a scene of a heron holding a snake in its beak in a garden setting, dark blue overall sponging on white, late 19th - early 20th c., 5 1/2" h. (ILLUS.).. **495**

Creamer, footed bulbous ovoid body w/a rim spout & C-form handle, overall light blue sponging on white, 3 3/4" h. (some very minor spout roughness) **220**

Rare Blue Spongeware Harvest Jug

Harvest jug, beehive-shaped w/high arched handle across the top above the short angled shoulder spout & round raised back shoulder opening, overall heavy blue sponging on white w/the incised & blue-tinted name "A. Noland," long U-shaped glued crack on the back, rare, ca. 1860, 13" h. (ILLUS.) **688**

Master potty (slop jar), wide baluster-form body tapering to a flat rim w/a stepped domed cover w/button finial, small vertical loop handles at upper sides, overall dense dark blue sponging on white w/two narrow white bands flanking a dark blue band near the base, excellent condition, late 19th - early 20th c., 13" h. **963**

Mug, bulbous ovoid body w/small C-form handle, bands of dark blue sponging on white around the rim & base, a relief-molded geometric design around the center of the body, 3" h. (one minor glaze flake on rim) **165**

Spongeware Pitcher with Pointed Handle

Pitcher, 6 1/2" h., cylindrical body w/mold-ed rim & pointed rim spout, pointed scroll loop handle, overall dark blue sponging on white, minor interior stains, late 19th - early 20th c. (ILLUS.) **201**

Pitcher, 8" h., paneled cylindrical form w/rim spout & C-form handle, all over scattered large blue dot sponging on white, professional restoration to a large chip at spout & a couple of interior glaze flakes at rim, overall glaze crazing, late 19th - early 20th c. (ILLUS. second from left with three larger sponged pitchers, second from top, next page) **143**

Pitcher, 8 3/4" h., cylindrical body w/a flat rim & small pointed spout, large C-form handle, overall dense dark blue spong-ing on white, surface chip at side of base (ILLUS. far right with three other sponged pitchers, center next page) **132**

Pitcher, 8 3/4" h., ovoid body w/a flat rim & small pinched spout, long molded C-form handle, a plain band around the rim & bottom, the wide center section & the handle decorated w/a finely textured dense dark blue sponging on white w/a thin accent line at the top & bottom of sponging, late 19th - early 20th c. (minor age crazing & staining).............................. **413**

Pitcher, 9" h., cylindrical body w/a flat rim & large pointed spout, small C-form handle, overall medium blue dense sponging on white w/a blue accent band at the rim, faint hairline from rim at left side of spout, couple of interior glaze flakes (ILLUS. far left with three other sponged pitchers, center next page) **176**

Pitcher, 9" h., cylindrical body w/a flat rim & large pointed spout, small C-form handle, overall coarse banded blue sponging on white, early 20th c. (ILLUS., top next col-umn)... **403**

Pitcher, 9" h., cylindrical body w/flat rim & large pointed spout, large C-form handle, overall medium blue repeating leaf-like sponged rows on white, very minor glaze flake on right side of spout (ILLUS. sec-

ond from right with three other sponged pitchers, center next page) **209**

Blue Sponge Banded Pitcher

Pitcher with Medium Blue Sponging

Pitcher, 9" h., cylindrical body w/flat rim & pointed spout, squared loop handle, overall fine medium blue sponging on white, flake on base, early 20th c. (ILLUS.)... **288**

Pitcher, 9" h., cylindrical body w/swelled band near the bottom, rim spout & angled handle, very dark blue overall sponging in an unusual triangular leaf-like design on white, one minor interior rim chip (ILLUS. second from right with three other 9" pitch-ers, top next page)...................................... **605**

Pitcher, 9" h., cylindrical w/a flat rim & pinched spout, C-form handle, dark blue overall coarse sponging on white, late 19th - early 20th c. (tight hairline down from rim, minor flake at end of spout, mi-nor use staining) **176**

Pitcher, 9" h., cylindrical w/a flat rim & pinched spout, C-form handle, medium blue finely mottled overall sponging on white, late 19th - early 20th c. (profes-sional restoration to spout chip).................. **132**

Four 9" Blue-sponged Pitchers

Group of Four Spongeware Pitchers

Pitcher, 9" h., cylindrical w/rim spout & C-form handle, dark blue large "chicken wire" design sponging on white, interior rim chip, small hairline left of spout, few glaze flakes (ILLUS. second from left with three other 9" pitchers, top of page)............. **220**

Pitcher, 9" h., cylindrical w/rim spout & C-form handle, medium blue repeating wavy vertical bands of sponging on white, interior rim flake near spout (ILLUS. far left with three other spongeware 9" pitchers, top of page) **275**

handle, overall blue on white "chicken wire" design, tight T-shaped hairline in bottom rim up into the sides, late 19th - early 20th c. (ILLUS.).................................... **165**

Wavy Navy Blue Spongeware Pitcher

Pitcher, 9" h., slightly tapering cylindrical body w/pointed rim spout & small C-form handle, dark overall navy blue on white wavy design, hairline from rim near handle, late 19th - early 20th c. (ILLUS.) **176**

Pitcher, 9" h., slightly tapering cylindrical body w/rim spout & C-form handle, medium blue vertical stripes of rounded sponging on white, three faint hairlines at

Spongeware Pitcher with Chicken Wire Design

Pitcher, 9" h., slightly tapering cylindrical body w/pointed rim spout & small C-form

rim, minor spout glaze flake (ILLUS. far right with three other 9" pitchers, top previous page)... **468**

Spongeware Pitcher with Angled Handle

Pitcher, 9" h., swelled bottom below the cylindrical body w/a pointed rim spout & angled loop handle, overall blue sponging on white, minor glaze flake at spout, late 19th - early 20th c. (ILLUS.)......................... **303**

Boldly Sponged Blue & White Pitcher

Pitcher, 9" h., tall slightly tapering cylindrical body w/a molded rim w/pointed spout, C-form long handle, overall bold blue sponging on white, minor crazing in glaze, late 19th - early 20th c. (ILLUS.)........ **303**

Nice Uhl Pottery Spongeware Pitcher

Pitcher, 9 1/2" h., bulbous ovoid body tapering to a cylindrical neck, pinched spout & long C-form handle, overall medium blue sponging on white, marked on the base by the Uhl Pottery Co., Huntingburg, Indiana, early 20th c., excellent condition (ILLUS.) **303**

Blue Sponged Oblong Platter

Platter, oblong shape, overall fine dark blue sponging on white, late 19th c., 10 1/4 x 13 3/4" (ILLUS.) **173**

Spongeware Combination Salt & Pepper

Spongeware Spittoon, Teapot & Washbowl

Salt & pepper shaker, one-piece, ovoid body divided into two halves w/two short spouts w/metal caps, overall blue & brown sponging on white, some small cap dents, excellent condition, early 20th c., 3" h. (ILLUS.).. **154**

Spittoon, footed bulbous rounded body tapering to a widely flaring rim, grey ground w/molded overall basketweave design decorated w/scattered bold dark blue sponging, few glaze flakes, small tight hairline at rim, 8" d., 5" h. (ILLUS. right with spongeware teapot & washbowl, top of page)... **66**

spout, late 19th - early 20th c., 5 1/4" h. (ILLUS.)... **495**

Teapot or pipkin, cov., wide bulbous slightly tapering cylindrical body w/a low flared rim w/spout, small C-form handle, white w/overall light blue "chicken wire" design sponging on white, minor glaze crazing, glaze flake at spout, unusual form, late 19th c., 5 3/4" h. (ILLUS. left with spongeware spittoon & washbowl, top of page)... **1,265**

Rare Blue Spongeware Toothbrush Vase

Toothbrush vase, footed baluster-form, wide dark blue on white sponged bands alternating w/two narrow white bands, excellent condition, late 19th - early 20th c., 5" h. (ILLUS.) **440**

Umbrella stand, tall cylindrical form, decorated w/four wide bands of fine banded blue sponging on white, sponged bands separated by three bands composed of two white bands flanking a narrow blue center band, late 19th - early 20th c., excellent condition, 20 1/2" h.......................... **770**

Vegetable or loaf dish, shallow oblong form w/arched ends & flaring sides, overall very dense dark blue sponging on white, late 19th c., 9 1/4" l., 2" h. (minor glaze fleck imperfection on exterior) **99**

Small Advertising Sponged Syrup Jug

Syrup jug, advertising-type, bulbous beehive-shaped w/short rim spout & wire bail handle w/black turned wood grip, overall blue sponging w/lower oval reserve stenciled "Grandmother's Maple Syrup of 50 Years Ago," relief-molded vine design around top half, bottom molded in relief "Mfg'd by N. Weeks - Style XXX Pat. Pending - Akron, O.," surface chips on

Washbowl, footed deep rounded flaring sides w/rolled rim, white ground decorated w/dark blue sponging around the top & base, the center w/two plain white bands flanking a dark blue band, full-length tight glued crack, late 19th - early 20th c., 14" d., 4 1/2" h. (ILLUS. center with spongeware teapot & spittoon, top previous page) **121**

Blue Sponged Washbowl & Pitcher Set

Washbowl & pitcher, bulbous ovoid pitcher tapering to a wide flaring neck, C-scroll handle, matching bowl w/rolled rim, the

pitcher w/overall coarse blue sponging on white w/a wide band in blue & white around the bottom, sponged rim & base bands on the bowl flank the wide blue & white bands, attributed to Red Wing, Minnesota, early 20th c., minor hairline & glaze flake on pitcher, pitcher 12" h. (ILLUS.)... **633**

Blue Spongeware Pig Whimsey Figure

Whimsey, model of a standing pig, white Bristol glaze w/scattered blue spots, some surface chipping, ca. 1990, 5" l. (ILLUS.)... **303**